AGAINST SORTITION?

THE PROBLEM WITH CITIZENS' ASSEMBLIES

Edited by
Geoffrey Grandjean

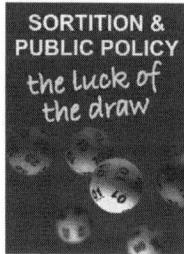

SORTITION &
PUBLIC POLICY
the luck of
the draw

ia

imprint-academic.com

Published in the UK by
Imprint Academic, PO Box 200, Exeter EX5 5YX, UK

Distributed in the USA by
Lightning Source,
La Vergne, TN 37086, USA

ISBN 9781788361163 Hardback

A CIP catalogue record for this book is available from the
British Library and US Library of Congress

Contents

Geoffrey Grandjean

Introduction

Sortition in Politics: Towards an Apolitical Model of Representation?

Abstract: *This chapter contextualises the editorial project by identifying the two lines of argument for understanding the limits of sortition in our political systems, namely the equality argument and the neutrality argument. This chapter shows the link between these two arguments, which is not sufficiently examined in the scientific literature.*

Sortition as a means of selecting political representatives dates back to antiquity. Far from being consigned to the Greek calendar, sortition has become surprisingly topical since the publication of David Van Reybrouck's book *Against Elections* (2013). This book aims to mark a break with Van Reybrouck's theses by providing a critical analysis of the use of sortition in our political systems. But let us be clear, this is not about sanctifying elections by opposing the sortition. By offering a critical look at sortition, we are giving citizens and representatives a wider range of arguments with which to make informed decisions should they wish to change the way representatives are selected, and above all, if they wish to share political power.

Citizens and political representatives thus seem to have rediscovered the great virtues of sortition, which can ensure a rotation of offices and, at the same time, resolve the major crisis of confidence between the governed and those who govern. Progressively, the revival of sortition as a method of selecting the latter is aimed at completing the electoral system by creating a whole series of 'citizens' panels'. For instance, in Belgium, we are witnessing a real institutionalisation of sortition through the creation of citizens' panels in the various community and regional parliaments.

This introduction questions sortition through the prism of equality. It invites the reader to consider the various criticisms of sortition based on the different stages of the deliberation process, as envisaged in the context of citizens' panels. We therefore propose a pathway for the reader through the implementation of citizens' panels by making a series of steps that will allow us to reintroduce a dose of equality into their reflections on the mode of selection of political representatives.

The first step is to question the representativeness sought by the random selection of citizens to sit in deliberative assemblies. Experts and political representatives seem to be firmly convinced that probabilistic selection is the best way to ensure descriptive representation in order to achieve, according to John Pitseys, "the ideal of similarity", understood as "the idea that the representation of political activity requires a visible, or at least apparent, community of experience between the representative and the represented" (Pitseys, 2017, p. 504). However, there are three problems with descriptive representation, as Annabelle Lever and Chiara Destri point out (in their chapter in this book). Firstly, they argue that it is necessary to take into account the small number of citizens who devote time to deliberative initiatives. We will come back to this when questioning the voluntary nature of participation. Secondly, they note that the descriptive representation sought by the proponents of citizens' panels does not take into account a certain type of inequality: that which sees a lack of self-confidence on the part of the citizen and a lack of belief that one deserves the same opportunities as others. Finally, they point to the intrinsic nature of citizens' panels, namely their very small size in relation to the population as a whole. They agree with Hélène Landemore who is convinced that randomly selected assemblies are too small for all the different characteristics of citizens to be represented proportionately (Landemore, 2020).

Behind the question of representativeness, there is a presupposition that needs to be questioned: does probabilistic selection on the basis of socio-economic criteria guarantee the representation of the diversity of political opinions? To answer this question, Jessy Bailly shows that representativeness can undermine deliberation (chapter in this book). Indeed, by analysing the Conference on the Future of Europe, this author shows that the co-presence of sociologically different individuals does not necessarily lead these individuals to debate and deliberate by expressing a plurality of points of view. On the contrary, his observations show the minority expression of highly critical opinions on the European Union.

Jessy Bailly concludes that the lack of diversity of opinions expressed leads to the fact that citizens were unable to deliberate in the sense of Bernard Manin (1985, pp. 84–5). An absence of interactivity was thus noted, with citizens not responding to each other and the discussions amongst citizens always being stimulated by the moderator.

In other words, the assumption that people are selected on the basis of socio-economic, professional, geographical and other categories that are supposed to reflect the diversity of ideas among citizens seems to be wrong. Indeed, this type of presupposition allows us to assert that belonging to one of these categories implies that citizens think in a certain way according to the category to which they belong. Didier Mineur addresses this very point when he notes that mirror-representation (on this concept, see Pitkin, 1967, pp. 71–5) stems from the ordered structure of society. He also draws the conclusion that "while society considered as a whole is represented, because it is reproduced in miniature, individuals as such are not" (see his chapter in this book). This is a major determinism of the process. Let us take an example. If we want statistical diversity to be guaranteed, in terms of professional status, as was the case for the citizens' panels set up in the various Belgian regional and community parliaments, we must ensure the presence of citizens from different socio-economic backgrounds: workers, the self-employed, the unemployed, employees and bosses, in particular. But who can guarantee that belonging to these socio-professional categories implies different political ideas? In fact, statistical sampling locks citizens into boxes. It is assumed that the worker should represent certain political attitudes and the boss other political attitudes. But is this the case? Do we know their ideas? The random selection method does not allow us to know these attitudes at all.

The Belgian *Conseil d'État*, the Belgian administrative court that advises the legislator (among others) has clearly stated in relation to a proposed decree to institutionalise sortition in the Walloon Parliament that the lottery procedure cannot be considered "as guaranteeing the political representativeness of the inhabitants selected randomly" (Parlement wallon, 2021, p. 9). Didier Mineur draws the same conclusion when he writes that "there is no guarantee that the representative sample of a social category would put forward the same reasons and arguments as would the members of that category if they were to deliberate directly" (see his chapter in this book). At the time of selection, before the exercise of a mandate which would allow the political attitudes of citizens to be known, sortition does not guarantee the debate of ideas. In this respect

Jérôme Hergueux underlines the importance of electoral campaigns as carefully institutionalised political moments (chapter in this book). From this perspective, sortition is an apolitical mode of selection that neither guarantees the equal presence—nor the equal importance—of political attitudes.

Looking back at the Conference on the Future of Europe, Yves Sintomer proposed during the discussions at that Conference to introduce an additional criterion (citizens' attitudes towards the European Union) to those usually used in the construction of the representative sample to address this criticism. Nevertheless, Jessy Bailly believes that it is difficult to obtain a representative sample on the criterion of citizens' attitudes towards the European Union. This view is supported by the research of Dorota Dakowska and Nicolas Hubé who have pointed out that many citizens have both positive and negative ambivalence towards European integration (Dakowska and Hubé, 2011). Pierre-Étienne Vandamme raises the same issue when he questions the consciousness of injustices by citizens selected randomly: "the selection process takes no account what-soever of whether or not people are interested in politics, are active in civil society organizations, or are conscious of the scale of existing injustices" (Vandamme, 2021, p. 114).

The second stage consists of questioning the voluntary participation of citizens in the framework of citizens' panels composed on the basis of sortition. Proposals to institutionalise sortition within deliberative assemblies are, for the moment, based on the principle of voluntary participation by citizens drawn by lot. Doesn't this lack of obligation to participate undermine the representativeness desired by the random selection method? In this respect, Jessy Bailly underlines in his chapter that the bias of sortition that could be detrimental to the plurality and quality of the deliberations stems from self-selection, as the citizens who took part in the Conference on the Future of Europe volunteered to participate in this experiment. In other words, does voluntary participa-tion by citizens fail to constitute a vector of demobilisation or, in any case, a vector of the constitution of a "participatory elite", as David Van Reybrouck (2015, p. 37) points out? In the context of the citizens' panels set up in the parliaments of the various Communities and Regions in Belgium, citizens and elected representatives have, in this respect, had the opportunity to stress the limits of the absence of any obligation to partici-pate. For example, following the citizens' panel on ageing issues, citizens insisted that the voluntary process almost automatically excluded certain minority, cultural and/or marginalised groups (Parlement wallon, 2017a, p. 9; 2017b, p. 7). Several elected representatives went in the same direction, fearing that the institutionalisation of the citizens' assembly and the citizens' council at Walloon level would only see one category of the population taking part in these institutions (Parlement wallon, 2020, p. 6) and noting that the people most motivated by participatory mechanisms "are those with a high socio-cultural gradient" (*ibid.*, p. 8).

In other words, doesn't the random mode of selection based on the principle of voluntary participation risk favouring the replacement of one elite by another elite? As Bernard Manin has shown, election is an aristo-cratic or oligarchic procedure, in so far as mandates are reserved for eminent individuals whom their fellow citizens judge to be superior to others. Historically, three types of elites succeeded one another in the nineteenth and twentieth centuries: the elites of notables, of parties and finally of communication (Manin, 2012). With the institutionalisation of sortition on a voluntary basis, are we not in the process of replacing this elite with another: the one that has the interest, the means and the time? In this respect, Alex Kovner and Keith Sutherland do not hesitate to point out the "self-selection bias" (see their chapter in this book) which means that members of citizen panels "are not really selected randomly from the general population, but from among the population *with an interest in climate change*" (*ibid.*). The equality of opportunity arising from the random selection method is thus undermined by the self-selection bias. Despite this argument, we should emphasise one of the positive dimensions of sortition for a political system in terms of office rotation. Indeed, Oliver Dowlen emphasises the possible value of building institutions that use the lottery specifically by stressing the possibility that this mode of selection offers to replace concentrated forms of personal or group power with more diffuse and collective forms of power (see his chapter in this book).

Despite their elitist dimension, both the election and sortition embody, in different ways, the ideal of equality. Let us therefore insist on this ideal of equality also promoted by sortition. Jason Brennan insists that random selection removes "pernicious biases". Indeed, right now, in every electoral democracy, the advantaged tend to have more de facto power than the disadvantaged. Sortition can therefore overcome this unequal situation (chapter in this book). When Peter Stone defines voting rights and access to public office as scarce goods that need to be allocated according to criteria of *allocative justice*, he gives us a better understanding of how sortition and elections refer to the criterion of democratic equality, while responding to it differently (Stone, 2016). According to him, these methods of selecting representatives would in fact respond to two different definitions of the principle of equality of opportunity defined by the political scientist Lesley Jacobs (2003, p. 14). On the one hand, sortition would correspond to the *prospect-regarding equality* approach, i.e. a situation in which each participant has an equal probability of obtaining a good. Elections, on the other hand, would correspond more to a *level playing field equality* approach, with candidates being on an equal footing at the start of the competition. The two procedures, although driven by the same democratic ideal of equality, therefore respond to different logics. Pierre-Étienne Vandamme has proposed a similar distinction, stating that sortition translates the ideal of political equality into an *equal probability of* holding political office, while the election translates it into an equal opportunity for all citizens to participate in political self-determination by allowing them to choose their representatives (Vandamme, 2018, p. 887).

The third step is to question the deliberative process that takes place within the citizens' panels. Once the random selection has taken place, we must turn our attention to the deliberation itself, which Stefan Rummens and Raf Geenens consider to be a veritable "black box" in the case of mini-publics (see their chapter in this book). In their view, the decision-making process remains invisible:

> [...] the sortition chamber lacks all visibility and appears to outsiders as a black box. The randomly selected citizens have no electoral incentive to face public scrutiny and the media have no interesting adversarial story to tell. The citizens might perhaps be interested to learn about what goes on inside the box but will find it very hard if not impossible to understand which decisions have been made, for what reasons and over which alternatives. They will, most certainly, feel frustrated by their inability to hold their randomly selected representatives to account. The lack of visibility implies that the allotted chamber is unable to make a real democratic connection with the wider audience of citizens on the outside and that it is incapable of supporting the collective opinion and will-formation processes that are essential in a genuinely democratic society. (chapter in this book)

The issue of equality thus arises again at the deliberation stage, in three different ways. First of all, the deliberation process can itself be a source of inequality because of the psychological discomfort that face-to-face interactions can entail, as Bernard Manin has pointed out. He favours debate over deliberation in this respect because, in his view, the "debate format—

in which speakers address an audience that merely listens to them—is a more promising set-up for exposure to conflicting positions than inter-active personal engagement amongst holders of opposing views, as people tend to avoid face-to-face disagreement" (Manin, 2005, p. 18). In other words, encountering disagreement in face-to-face interactions generates psychological discomfort (*ibid.*, p. 13). Not all citizens are equal when faced with this discomfort.

Secondly, the structuring of assemblies—particularly parliamentary ones—on the basis of the majority model raises obvious questions in terms of issue conflation, obstructive bias and lack of specificity of propo-sals, as illustrated by Keith Sutherland and Alex Kovner. The questions put forward by these two authors allow them to note a "basic fact": "consensus-based assemblies favour those who have the least concern for the public good, and the greatest willingness to inflict pain on political adversaries, regardless of the consequences to the general public" (see their chapter in this book). In other words, the consensus process favours unequal postures in discussions. Both authors argue that none of the concerns raised about issue conflation, the obstructive bias and the lack of specificity of proposals would disappear because they are not the direct result of elections. In other words, parliamentary assemblies seem to have difficulty accommodating sortition, unless they encourage unequal postures on the part of certain representatives.

Thirdly, it is important to consider the decisions that result from the deliberations, which can also be a source of inequality in terms of the inclusion of citizens. Alex Kovner and Keith Sutherland argue that "the work product of the assembly is a reflection of highly volatile and trans-formational social processes" (chapter in this book). Indeed, they argue that "not everyone participates in a citizen panel, and public debate is by no means a rational conversation. The result is that policy proposals from citizen panels can evoke strong opposition" (*ibid.*). Clarisse Van Belleghem agrees when she notes that "deliberative assemblies do not resolve the tension between the ideal of well-reasoned deliberation and the inclusion of the largest number of citizens in public deliberation, because a truly inclusive deliberation presupposes that all citizens have been able to develop their own views on the policy" (chapter in this book). Two avenues are favoured by the contributors to face the unequal inclusion of citizens in the decisions produced by the citizens' assemblies. On the one hand, Alex Kovner and Keith Sutherland believe that it is essential to focus our attention on the acceptability of the results produced by processes based on the random selection mode. To do so, they propose to use the criterion of centrism to assess this acceptability; centrism being understood in a statistical sense, "as being the policy that minimises some notion of a policy 'distance' between the views of citizens and the policy adopted" (chapter in this book). On the other hand, Pierre-Étienne Vandamme believes that the decisions resulting from the deliberations must be considered in the light of the long term, because this temporality is the only one that favours the consciousness and politicisation of citizens, thus enabling them to become conscious of injustices and to act on them (Vandamme, 2021, p. 119).

The fourth step consists of questioning the presence of facilitators or experts in the deliberations of the citizens' panels. For example, in the Belgian context, a scientific committee is systematically involved to facilitate the deliberations. However, this supervision is not questioned in any way. I would argue that it is essential to question this scientific framework from three points of view.

First of all, the political representatives supporting the citizens' panel projects seem, on many occasions, to be in favour of the idea that the scientific experts are impartial and therefore best placed to supervise the deliberations (see e.g. Parlement de la Région de Bruxelles-Capitale, 2018, p. 2; Chambre des représentants, 2019, p. 8). According to some political representatives, this impartiality should enable the scientific committee to compile a portfolio of documents or any other means of providing useful information to members of the joint committees. It should be noted, however, that some elected representatives are not convinced by this impartiality when they state that they do not believe in the impartiality of the experts and that they call for the latter to take a position (Parlement de la Région de Bruxelles-Capitale and Assemblée réunie de la Commission communautaire commune, 2019, pp. 6–7). Is it not a complete illusion to believe that experts are impartial, especially when it comes to compiling portfolios of documents impartially? If "axiological neutrality" (Weber, 1965) is to enable researchers to suspend any value judgement in the context of their scientific analysis, it is a means that is only at the service of the scientific process.

Secondly, should this not lead to a real debate on the place given to experts in political deliberations? Accompanying and framing a political deliberation is far from being a trivial action. Didier Mineur questions the role of the experts in investigative techniques and notes that sortition, despite the appearance of giving the power back to ordinary citizens, presupposes a kind of epistocracy. The experts of survey techniques are the only ones to know how the assembly of representatives chosen by lot might think (chapter in this book). Alex Kovner and Keith Sutherland argue that once citizens' assemblies start making binding decisions on public policy issues with multiple stakeholders, the position of facilitator will be the first to be politicised. As a result, they argue, "Well-resourced stakeholders will move heaven and earth to exert some influence on the facilitator selection process" (chapter in this book). From this perspective and to some extent, there is a transfer of sovereignty from citizens and representatives to these experts. However, this transfer of sovereignty is not discussed in the parliamentary debates, as if it were self-evident that this framework could only be neutral. More fundamentally, Jason Brennan questions the epistocratic political system—also known as the "enfranchisement lottery" (see López-Guerra, 2014, p. 4)—put in place through the sortition. In such a system, a greater knowledge is a legal prerequisite for holding power or constitutes the legal grounds for being granted greater power through law (chapter in this book).

Finally, it should be noted that the same experts are constantly called upon by political representatives, particularly during parliamentary hearings. No diversity is sought by these representatives, particularly in terms of opposition to participatory processes. However, the "entre-preneurs of sortition" have certain characteristics, including a high level of cultural capital, which differentiate them from the normality of citizens defended by the theorists of sortition. Why do we not use sortition to appoint the experts?

In other words, does the presence of scientific facilitators, which seems to go hand in hand with sortition, not lead to an unequal vision of the deliberation? Indeed, the latter could only take place through the presence of facilitators who are above the fight and whose posture of neutrality must, at the very least, be discussed.

The fifth step consists of questioning the consensus, or at least the method of consensual decision-making, which is the purpose of the deliberation processes of citizen panels. At this stage, we do not address the non-binding dimension of the decisions adopted by the citizens' panels. As Vincent Aerts shows, the "decentralisation of the State" is ultimately misleading when analysing the Citizens' Climate Convention (chapter in this book). The scientific literature has demonstrated the neutralising dimension of sortition. Some authors have argued that the main virtue of the lottery should not be located in its egalitarian aspect, but rather in its neutralising dimension (Dowlen, 2009; Stone, 2009; 2011). The authors highlighting the neutralising features of lottery do not deny the egalitarian effects of random selection. However, for them, the main advantage of this method of selection of representatives is not that it leads to an equal probability of being assigned a political office, but rather that sortition is a decision-making procedure whose results do not require any justification, thus neutralising illegitimate (but also legitimate) arguments that may motivate a decision, and consequently leading to an anaesthesia of political conflicts. It seems essential to us to discuss the neutralising dimension of deliberation. Is this the model of decision-making that we want in the twenty-first century? What if oppositions arise during deliberation and it is impossible to overcome them? We find it difficult to maintain that the political decision-making process can easily accommodate consensus. Let us therefore detail the neutralising effects of sortition.

In that way, Peter Stone refers to the *sanitising effects* of random selection as the immunity of this method of selection to the influence of reasons, whether good or bad (Stone, 2009). Oliver Dowlen says the same thing when he describes the random procedure as an arational procedure in which the human faculties of reason along with other human faculties such as passion, instinct or emotions would not intervene (Dowlen, 2008). Sortition would therefore be neither rational nor irrational, and would in fact aim to create a "blind break" in the decision-making process, during which no human factor would intervene. In this perspective, sortition would serve above all to prevent "bad" justifications (discriminatory justifications, for example, or justifications based on the private interest of the political decision-maker) from being used within the framework of the decision-making process in cases where the mobilisation of good reasons would prove impossible. This would be the case in particular when the good reasons had already been invoked or when a context of uncertainty characterises the decision-making and does not allow access to the information necessary to distinguish between those reasons deemed to be legitimate (Stone, 2011).

From this neutralising perspective, the use of the lottery would save resources, in that it would simplify and accelerate the selection procedure (Delannoi, 2010, p. 15). The reason for the mobilisation of the lottery in politics would therefore be explained, in this perspective, by a lack of time, information or resources. For example, a person might have to be appointed in a hurry, without having the time to organise an election preceded by some form of deliberation. In this perspective, the neutralising properties of sortition would therefore serve to save time or resources. By recognising this quality in sortition, are we not, however, falling into the trap of an illusion of political immediacy where everything always has to happen quickly?

The main advantage of the use of sortition in politics would therefore not be its achievement of greater political equality, but the possibility it offers of not having to justify the selection of representatives, neutralising, as Manuel Cervera-Marzal and Yohan Dubigeon point out (Cervera-Marzal, 2013, p. 174), two phenomena. On the one hand, the lottery neutralises the selection process, since people are designated independently of the reasons put forward to select them. On the other hand, the lottery would neutralise the results of the designation process, as no candidate could feel aggrieved by his or her non-selection, as the lottery is deemed impartial. Sortition would therefore have an effect of limiting competition between elites (Delannoi, Dowlen and Stone, 2013, pp. 15–16), in the sense that they cannot mutually attribute responsibility for their respective failures, which echoes perfectly the medieval use of lots in Italian cities such as Florence or Venice, where lots were mainly used to attenuate political competition between the different socio-political elites (Manin, 2012; Sintomer, 2011a). From this perspective, random selection can be thought of "as an impartial method for resolving a controversial issue" (Sintomer, 2011a, p. 194), namely the allocation of political offices within a political community.

Sortition would thus have an egalitarian dimension, reflected in an equal probability of access to a political office.[1] It would also include a neutralising dimension, as the random selection is not based on selection criteria, and therefore, unlike the election procedure, leaves no possibility for candidates for a position to reveal the distinctive politically advantageous traits they possess. In other words, the egalitarian and neutralising characteristics of sortition are intrinsically linked. Indeed, if the use of the lottery allows the notion of *prospect-regarding equality* to flourish within a political system, it is difficult to overlook the neutralising attributes of random selection, since these attributes of the lottery help to explain why this procedure is particularly egalitarian. This can be illustrated by the

---

[1] Some authors have pointed out that there are different conceptions of probability. Peter Stone, for example, distinguishes four of them: the frequentist conception, the objective conception, the subjective conception and the logical conception of probability, which is his preference (Stone, 2010).

possibility offered by sortition to neutralise the principle of distinction embodied in the election (Manin, 2012).

Another way of accounting for the simultaneous action of the egalitarian and neutralising dimensions of sortition is to focus on the distortions associated with the effects of economic inequalities on political competition. Some authors have argued that elected assemblies favour the interests and ideas of contributors who have provided financial support to the electoral campaign of the political parties in power (Gastil and Wright, 2018, p. 307). It would also be easier in an electoral competition to transmit political messages with large economic resources, which would favour the more affluent. On the other hand, money is not involved at all in a selection procedure by lottery (*ibid.*). Random selection of political assemblies would therefore have a clear advantage over election in neutralising economic inequalities in political competition, while ensuring the ineffectiveness of a principle of distinction resulting in financial disparities, making political competition more equal.

We can go even further in this criticism of a dichotomy between the neutralising use and egalitarian function of sortition (Bonin, 2017; Lopez-Rabatel, 2019; Delannoi, 2010, p. 10; Sintomer, 2011a, p. 193). Hugo Bonin, analysing a number of studies on the use of lottery and election in politics, notes that most of these studies aim to attribute intrinsic qualities to these decision-making mechanisms, with the aim of defining the "nature" of these procedures. On the one hand, the essence of elections would be to be both democratic and aristocratic, while on the other hand, sortition would be egalitarian and neutralising *by nature*. For Hugo Bonin, the effects of these appointment procedures can only be understood by considering the whole institutional system in which these appointment procedures are embedded. The random method could indeed lead to an unequal result, if it were not combined, for example, with very short terms of office, or with equal access to the deliberations. In other words, contradicting Montesquieu, sortition would not be "of the nature of democracy" (Montesquieu, 1973, p. 17), any more than suffrage by choice would be of the nature of aristocracy. It would indeed be necessary to reserve such a judgement by means of the study of the concrete institutional mechanisms in which these procedures evolve. Hugo Bonin therefore prefers to speak of the potentialities of appointment procedures, rather than the essence or nature of sortition, and stresses the need to carry out an empirical study of the different leadership selection mechanisms in order to highlight their advantages and disadvantages.

To conclude, a fundamental question remains: do we want our political system to be placed under the seal of neutrality?

If the answer is positive, this would mean that the exercise of political power would be limited to neutralising the multiple conflicts within a society. In our view, however, the political system is an "agonistic" public space of contestation, to use Chantal Mouffe's terms (2016, pp. 29–36), where different hegemonic projects can clash and where the political actors do not show any moderation before entering into negotiations. From this perspective, the neutralising attributes of sortition make it apolitical. The permanent neutralisation of conflicts would consequently favour the immutability of a political system.

If the answer is negative, this means that the exercise of political power, far from neutralising these conflicts, seeks to reveal them and, above all, to ensure that its foundation is the permanent questioning of the norms that a society sets for itself.

By defining the political system as an agonistic public space, we hope that constant questioning will foster the constant progress of humanity. From this point of view, sortition is not synonymous with progress for a political system.

Part I

The Terms of the Debate

Gil Delannoi

On Political Procedures
Pay Close Attention
to All the Details

Abstract: *The presentation broaches the title question of the book in its most general and detailed dimension: what are the constraints, possibilities and limits of political activity? What is a political procedure and in particular a democratic procedure? In its most specific passages, the text makes recommendations for a lucid use of two procedures: sortition and the direct vote.*

This title is true for procedures in general and with a special mention for democratic procedures, in which so many requirements and parameters are needed.

I will not repeat today what I have already developed in books and articles. As a prelude to our conference, I will limit myself to generalities on the procedures and to proposals on some of them. I would like to give a broader perspective, as a reminder for all of us, myself included, and as a way to avoid too much optimism and too much suspicion about procedures.

A broad perspective means I am not just talking about sortition; only note that the general perspective also applies to sortition. In such an approach, the specific operation of sortition does not affect the reasoning. This general reflection on procedures is based on comparative advantages and defects, comparable expectations and limitations.

I will mention two examples to highlight the fact that sortition is just a part of a larger ensemble. I add a second example to show that these remarks apply to all procedures. I include the referendum, and I do this not just because it is sometimes combined with sortition. I could have taken examples from the elections of a parliament or of a president, or even in the markets or in the bureaucratic procedures of administrations or courts of justice. Nine points will follow.

1. One Question, Several Points

"For or against sortition" is the question that brings us together today. To speak "against sortition" is a useful provocation in so far as it responds to a contrary and previous provocation which speaks totally against the election, namely against the vote as if its existence prevented the use of the draw.

Should all vote-based procedures be abandoned? Are we going to abandon all elections in favour of other procedures? As antithesis after thesis, it can be a good way to draw attention to issues, at least as long as we stand on the ideological battlefield. So which votes are worth keeping? Referendums instead of elections? No votes at all?

In terms of knowledge, this kind of duel is neither possible nor thinkable. What must be found are points favourable to voting procedures and other points favourable to sortition. This indispensable open-mindedness comes from the simple fact that no procedure can give everything. It also means that no procedure is without interest. Since Aristotle, a good method has been to move constantly from practice to theory and then from theory to practice. Each procedure has many advantages and disadvantages.

Hell is when we keep the worst of every procedure in bad and ineffective combinations—and there is no paradise. Democracy, political fairness and good decision-making only consist of combinations and hybridisations of procedures. One-dimensional paradises based solely on voting, or solely on the market, or solely on scientific testing, or on expertise, or solely on sortition, have never existed and never will.

2. Towards a Third Age or Third Type

My work on sortition over the last three decades has taken place in several periods that I have experienced and observed.

The 1990s are a decade of political philosophy, allusive mentions, philosophical narratives, historical studies, more or less scholarly, which constitute a capital discovery of a lost continent of political theory. Bernard Manin acted as a pedagogue not really favourable but precise in political science. Robert Dahl suggested supplementing representative democracy with a sortition-based assembly, Barbara Goodwin reflected on the use of random selection for social justice, partly utopian, perhaps as an amazing new form of socialism.

The 2000s are a decade that allows observers to study a few isolated experiences. Theoretical reflections were suggested by these experiments.

For example, I launched a collective discussion in 2008, an international research programme. The first conference is printed in the book that I edited with Oliver Dowlen in 2010.

The 2010s are a decade of relative success. You gradually ceased to be eccentric when you evoked the use of sortition in contemporary democracies. Political actors and the media became receptive.

We can say that sortition gained momentum in France in 2017 because it was seriously advocated by the main candidates in a national election for the first time. Several candidates proposed the use of lottery as a new political procedure. This novelty, though it may have been secondary to other campaign promises, was one of the many singularities in the election. During the campaign, the ambitions linked to the introduction of the lottery were very different in nature and degree. In each case, a lack of precision can be noticed in the way that the practices were described.

The immediate future of these proposals was dependent on the fate of the candidates who suggested them: the first candidate, Arnaud Montebourg, was dismissed in the primaries (there were two primaries which preceded the presidential elections); the second, Jean-Luc Mélenchon, after the first round; and the third, Emmanuel Macron, was elected President of the Republic. His promise favoured the convening of the first citizens' convention: the CCC, "Convention citoyenne pour le climat", from 2019 to 2020.

Such success is also a danger. How much of it is serious use? And is it as serious and democratic as it should be? We are gathered here today to discuss such issues. This is precisely why I call this decade *a crucial decade*. It is high time to know precisely the uses and limits of sortition, that is to say to dispel certain illusions, not to become dogmatic, and to be ready to combine procedures. First, we must resist procedural manipulators, whether in China or in a liberal democracy. Facilitation sometimes comes very close to manipulation.

We come out of these periods with the very beginnings of knowledge and experience. We must better prepare for these encounters of the third kind, a procedure which has almost become alien in our societies.

3. Democratic Means First and Foremost Political and Procedural

What is common to all political procedures? The realm of politics. The political dimension.

To believe in the epistemic superiority of a procedure is naïve and over-ambitious. Politics is anything but scientific. It doesn't tell the truth. It does not produce any rigorous knowledge. "An ideology cannot be refuted. One can only limit or increase its effects in a population" (Zinoviev).

And pure science is not the truth either. "Science is the asymptote of truth" (Victor Hugo). Science is a curve that is getting closer and closer to the straight line of a pure and complete knowledge and will never reach this line.

Yes, but what about collective intelligence? Is it a mirage? No, but it's just a mixture of reliable information, thoughtful argumentation, free discussion for better decision-making — along with the indispensable goodwill. Passions and interests are likely to derail the best-laid procedure if goodwill and some concern for the general interest are absent.

Uncertainties about the future mitigated by anticipation and preparation are the only possible horizon of politics. Physics tells you that the moon will be at its zenith at a specific time in a few years on a specific day. Political decision-making belongs to a totally other world, formerly called sub-lunar, in which no event will ever be predicted with such precision. The world of betting and bookmakers is closer to political decision-making than a scientific approach can be. The comparison makes sense: serious gamblers do not bet without information and a political decision must be informed. The probability of the outcome is generally greater in the world of betting than in the realm of democratic decisions.

This long development has only one purpose: to remind us that the main preference for democracy lies in the sole fact that the system is democratic rather than dictatorial. And it must be added that dictatorship sometimes disguises itself as democracy: better to repeat this than forget it before using procedures that are supposed to reinforce democracy.

If politics is not a science, and not just a confrontation of well-argued bets, what is it?

Politics is made up of acts of balance. It cannot be otherwise or, if it seems so in some cases, please suspect that we are beyond the realm of politics. Either politics then overstepped its boundaries, turning into false science or disguised morality, or it tried to dominate in a non-political sphere. All people who practise politics have had to devise balancing acts, voluntarily or not. Policies are better when they are smart enough to grasp this necessity. And balance what? It's an endless list…

Order/disorder
Values/results
Passions/impartiality
Bested interest/general interest
Short term/long term
Knowledge/freedom
Dogmatism/scepticism
Realism/idealism
Precaution/risk
Harmony/conflict
Equality of rights/unequal performance
Rest/effort
Tragedy/comedy
Self-avoidance of the effects of decisions/no personal or social
escape from the effects of the decision
(Make your own additions...)

4. Don't Confuse Outcomes and Procedures

In the spring of 399 (BC) a jury of 501 citizens drawn by lot condemned Socrates to death. During the summer of 1934 (19 August) the German people by referendum allowed the Chancellor of the Reich to combine the functions of President and Chancellor. The case is heard: sortition and the referendum are to be avoided at all costs.

Pay attention to context! Socrates provoked his judges by demanding supreme honours and, unusually, his accusers demanded death and not banishment. In 1934 Nazi terror, manoeuvres and propaganda had been going on for more than one year.

Objections are often not received. These facts are too serious, they say. Without popular jury, no death of Socrates. Without referendum, no Führer. But it turns out that the Nazi party also won parliamentary elections on 5 March 1933 (43% of the vote, 44% of the seats), so? This was after the Reichstag fire, but this incandescent clue was (rightly) not turned against the existence of parliaments.

The lack of method here consists in judging a procedure (or anything else) on the basis of an extreme example, or an exceptional fact. Judging the desirability of a procedure consists of evaluating all or the vast majority of its uses.

There is neither essence nor nature in matters of procedure. Any procedure has a margin of uncertainty, unpredictability and something blind to the consequences of its results. Judging it by reference to what a particular participant or ideology hopes for is equivalent to engaging in a sport only when certain of victory. We do not refuse a sport on the pretext that we will not win all the matches.

The Chileans, who had approved, by referendum at 78%, the need to replace the "Pinochet" constitution of 1980 have just, in September 2022, largely rejected by 62% the new constitution drafted by an elected constituent assembly. This example proves nothing in terms of the ratification of constitutions. Likewise the Brexit vote proves nothing in terms of the association or dissociation of states by referendum.

In the debate on the choice of procedures, the first wisdom is to give up seeking the best in all respects, because such a thing does not exist and never will.

No procedure is always guaranteed to be democratic, or populist, or meritocratic, or efficient, or able to satisfy this or that principle. It is preferable to take these risks into account in the detailed adjustment of the procedures.

Ironically, Trump's election spared the referendum a post-Brexit discredit for which all anti-populist codes were ready to be given. Comparable results are sometimes achieved by different procedures. Conversely, the same and unique procedure can produce incomparable results. Moreover, any result is also explained by the negative. Cameron, strategically, by triggering further withdrawal from the EU, and tactically, by seeking to impose an outcome by dramatizing it, provoked Brexit. This is a tactical effect, not a procedural one.

The results of any procedure are obviously worthy of interest, but on condition, as we have just said, of considering all the uses and results or almost all of them and, even more, of being very attentive to the precise aims and practical details. Better to study than to judge.

Is there something stable and constant in the procedures? Yes, but it is only the material operations on which they are based: the operation of voting (adding votes) differs from that of drawing (subtracting names). Both have meaning and effects only according to a chronological sequence of operations that has a programmed purpose, in other words: procedure. Here are some recommendations on the use of procedures to combine, not to oppose. I will only mention sortition and the referendum.

First of all, a procedure must be taken seriously and applied on its own terms. Using the referendum to divide the opposition or to legitimise oneself by obtaining a river score acquired without the slightest suspense is to mock the procedure. Sometimes deceivers deceive themselves or are deceived in return—but it's not for them that I speak. As a former French president said: this procedure is "a good idea provided the answer is yes". He talked about a referendum. This caricature applies to the citizens' assembly as well. At least it is what appears in most of them, especially when they are created by governments.

Do you really want to use sortition? Do you really want to use the referendum? Several obligations arise from this.

5. Making Good Use of Sortition in a Procedure

A/ The purpose of the procedure must be firmly linked to the type of draw required. Using it to represent a population precisely implies a large sample. Consulting a small sample is completely different. Making a collective decision without going through the election of officials is another and very dissimilar use.

B/ Who participates? The whole of a population, or a large large part, or a very small one. These options form almost opposite bases for sortition. Is it compulsory, optional to be in the pool? Then is it compulsory or optional to accept the designation by lot?

So many are the crucial details. The number, qualities and qualifications of people selected by lot must vary according to the goals: representation, consultation, an equal right to participate, who should take the initiative in legislation, the provision of feedback on policies, or the selection of a jury capable of expertise.

C/ A well done drawing of lots makes it possible to know the opinion of a group without convening it in full. It is neither the tyranny of the majority, nor the tyranny of minorities. These two risks must nevertheless be taken into account and prevented by the institutional design.

D/ Regulate the procedure so that the people selected by lot do not behave like voters during a referendum, nor like another type of representatives, nor like a new elite of experts.

E/ Use sortition in small institutions, including non-political ones, sometimes with strong obligations, in order to acclimatise the different strata of a society to this practice.

6. The Referendum

A/ Any referendum is made in good faith and is only useful when, and only when, each option has both advantages and disadvantages, for the initiator or the controller; it is held with a view to determining a common and collective good; no option is impracticable or impossible to execute.

B/ The elected official who thinks, or pretends to think, that an entire programme was approved by the same vote is exaggerating. The voter could only choose between people and attitudes. On the contrary, the referendum decision only rarely relates to the choice and approval of a single person, and in this exceptional case, voluntary or not, it means that the procedure has been diverted from its main function. It is curious to hear leaders regret that voters do not answer the question of referendums in France, when they are the only ones who ask the questions. They can do better.

C/ The easiest way to avoid deviations and bias in a referendum is to ask several questions, on the same day, on different subjects. The number of questions encourages people to take them seriously.

D/ We will choose subjects that affect everyone's life, not very technical issues of varying importance. The big ones are obviously not excluded.

E/ The execution of the decision will be guaranteed, unless expressly stated otherwise.

Everything here is a question of finding a balance between dramatisation and de-dramatisation of the procedure and its issues. The dissemination of information by the government and the parliament, the majority and the opposition, the supporters of the different options, all this counts as much as the feeling of making a respectable decision because it was made in common. The main objective is not collective intelligence, which cannot go beyond an intelligent approximation, but responsibility and legitimacy. We aim to bind people to their political regime, to reduce the gap between "them and us".

Deciding should not be without recourse: a deadline for candidacy is to be specified, but also the possibility of another vote sooner or later on the same question. The acclimatisation, the routinisation are finally done by a popularisation of the tool and its trivialisation: a series of questions is put to the vote every two years, and not every ten or fifteen years. The paradox should no longer be one after reading these pages: the most effective, the most measured and the most democratic use of the referendum presupposes referendums in large numbers.

7. Sortition in France in the Near Future

These remarks apply in many contexts. What about France? Should we develop sortition?

Yes: why do without sortition just on principle, because of anti-randomness values based on education and expertise? Make use of sortition at various levels, do not oppose sortition to the rest of the procedures.

No? the Climate Convention (CCC) had many flaws, but most were avoidable, are correctable.

Maybe: be more demanding, better prepared, do not organise sortition mainly against elected officials, parliament, or instead of a referendum.

Please experiment: if academics are for sortition, let them set an example in their own institution.

On the basis of universal suffrage? Why not, if not for fear of having a precise image of the realities? Politics without a sense of realities is not recommended for amateurs or professionals alike.

8. On Referendum in France

Yes: in the present political process, this democratic breath would limit precipitation and inattention, postures and impostures, indifference and demonstrations, paternalism and radicalisation.

No? The risk, for the time being, is that all those who want it want their tailor-made referendum: initiative for some, ratification for others, consultation for others.

Maybe: if we are ready to acclimatise it by routinising it.

I do not deal here with the type of questions to ask or not to ask, nor the degrees of obligation and abstention, and many other details… which really matter.

9. Current and Urgent Questions about Sortition

To speak of a tendential law of sortition in favour of equality presupposes that several conditions are fulfilled. Once again: efficency and fairness only rely on the details of the procedure.

My typology of political regimes according to procedures leads to combinations and not to confrontations or substitutions in the use of procedures (legacy, vote, test, market, membership, drawing of lots).

This approach, based on various combinations, starts with a few questions to ask in theory and in practice, keeping in mind what has already been done and what could easily be done:

A/ Can we, should we, concentrate the experimental sortition in the sphere of political decision-making? No.

B/ Reserve this use for deliberative tasks and functions? No.

C/ Combine sortition with the classic functioning of parliamentary democracy? In many cases.

D/ Direct or semi-direct democracy? In some cases.

These recommendations are to be studied, included, tried and measured. For scrutinizing of some decisive practical details WE NEED TO DESIGN A PROTOCOL THAT WILL ALLOW CAREFUL COMPARISONS OF MOST CASES.

I conclude: as it has been said so many times — "The people are not the best judge." To what extent? In science, they are not. In art, the answer is rather no, but without excess of aesthetic elitism. In economics, in politics, in administration, everything depends. But in a democracy? Many refusals in the name of democracy are self-inflicted blows or more or less unconscious hypocrisy, even if they are formulated through high democratic values tending to disguise de facto oligarchic power and a condescending attitude. Each procedure is an instrument. Democracy is not just chamber music. Each instrument has its place in the orchestra.

Oliver Dowlen

The Necessity of a Design-Based Discourse in the Evaluation of Random Political Recruitment

Abstract: *The main claim of this chapter is that the value of institutions that include randomly selected citizens can only be usefully assessed if accompanied by a discourse on the design features and desired democratic objectives of the institutions in question. There are some uses of sortition that might extend and enhance democracy while others might prove to be problematic or even undermine existing democratic measures.*

The author starts with three major design principles. The first is that any use of sortition should be based on an understanding of the irrational qualities of the lottery process. The second demands a consideration of those elements of the lottery procedure that are rationally determined. These include the size and nature of the pool from which office holders are selected, the duration of office and the powers given to those selected. The third principle is the need to consider the relationship between institutional arrangements that use random selection and other existing or planned institutions. The main reason for this is to prevent institutions based on random recruitment from compromising the collective rationality of other democratic constitutional elements.

The remainder of the chapter will explore examples of historical and proposed uses of random political recruitment in the light of these principles. The aim is to present a range of design options in a variety of different political contexts. In the

context of the book, this will give a broad and diverse picture of the possible
advantages and disadvantages of using this procedure.

To relate to some of the contemporary approaches to sortition discussed in the
volume, the author is also including a short appendix on the problems of
sampling and how these can be approached from a design perspective.

As soon as we start looking seriously at the use of random selection for
political office, we come across convincing evidence of how, in some contexts, this arational and random method of choice can produce results that
many would regard as favourable or desirable. At the same time, it is
equally clear how other schemes that use random selection can prove to
be dangerously unpredictable and unfair, continuously generating difficulties and problems.

We cannot, therefore, come to any meaningful conclusion about the
value of sortition in the political sphere if we merely restrict ourselves to a
simple binary, generally expressed, question of whether we are for or
against the use of lotteries to select political office holders. I would claim,
on the contrary, that any assessment of the political value of random
recruitment is context dependent, is purpose dependent and, above all, is
design dependent. This is especially important because the design process
seeks to assess the suitability of any procedure according to the task or
tasks in hand and seeks to define the structural and operating features of
the proposed scheme according to this assessment.

In this chapter I start with a brief discussion of the nature of design
thinking and how this might apply to political institution and procedures.
I then set out and define three principles that I judge to be essential to the
design of institutions that include the random selection of citizens. I then
look at nine examples of the use or proposed use of random choice,
mainly, but not exclusively, for political office. I explore these in terms of
the three design principles. I end the main chapter with a discussion of
various democratic objectives and how these might be best served by
institutions that are based on random political recruitment.

1. The Political Design Process

The essence of design is the relationship between what I call a paper-
based exploration of a proposition and the realisation of that proposition
in practice. The purpose of the paper-based element is efficiency: it is a
bringing together of ideas and experience in advance of practice in order

to eliminate those that are unlikely to be successful and focus on those options where success might be likely or possible.[1] In this process there is, of necessity, an element of abstraction as real qualities or examples are considered on paper before they are manifested in their real-world form — whether this be a prototype or a pilot scheme or the finished scheme or object.

This abstraction is only a temporary stage in the design process; but if the links between the paper process and the range of real-life configurations it is based on are strong and thorough, the more likely it is that the end product will be successful. We can see, therefore, how, as a conscious process of evaluation, design thinking has a close, even symbiotic, relationship with more experience-based processes by which a product, institution or procedure is perfected over a long period of experimentation and adjustment. Not to recognise the essential similarity between these procedures and to characterise one as "evolutionary" and the other as "design" is to miss the point. The predominantly practice-based forms are not devoid of conscious discrimination; neither is a paper-led new design by individual designers necessarily entirely separate from previous periods of incremental adjustment involving multiple agencies and multiple contexts.

These considerations are very pertinent to our exploration of random recruitment. In comparison to previous eras and contexts such as those of ancient Athens or late medieval Italy, the use of sortition for the selection of political office holders is a largely discontinued practice. What is noticeable about these earlier contexts is not only the widespread and long-term use of this procedure, but also the way that adjustments were continuously being made to the constitutions and institutions in which it was utilised. Faced with this discontinuity (and, incidentally, an almost complete absence of surviving documentation from those who supported its use telling us exactly *why* it was deployed), design consideration for the possible reintroduction of sortition in politics is somewhat of an uphill task. Not only do we have to reconstruct the political purposes for its earlier use, but we also have to calculate whether and to what extent the original contexts pertain to present-day conditions or problems. Added to this is the important question about how much we should actually be guided by history and whether there is a case for a complete re-

---

[1] This is common practice in all design processes (see, for example Tjalve, 1979).

application of random recruitment based entirely on our modern under-standing of the process.

My response to this is to argue that since ancient Athens and late medieval Italian republicanism (for example) are both key periods in the development of our current political thought and practice, they should not be ignored. At the same time, however, if we are going to look at the future value of random political recruitment, we will need design princi-ples and frameworks that we can assess independently from any particu-lar historical context. The basic framework behind this chapter lies in the tension and the balance between these viewpoints.

2. Three Design Principles for the Consideration of Random Political Recruitment

2.1. The qualities of the lottery process

If we are seeking to calculate whether or not random political recruitment should be used in any specific context, the judgement has to be based, in the first instance, on the qualities of the lottery as a decision-making process. The question then is whether the desired outcome or outcomes of the institution or constitutional measure in question is likely to be hindered or facilitated by this particular procedural element.

In my first major study of this subject, *The Political Potential of Sortition* (2008). I presented a simple diagram to illustrate and define the qualities of a lottery.

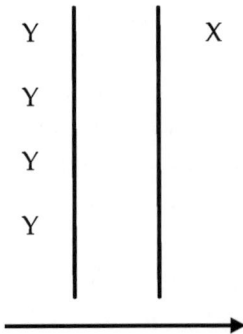

Figure 1.

On the left are the options from which the choice is to be made. On the right is the chosen option. The arrow at the bottom shows the direction of the procedure as a means of choice moving towards a specific outcome. In the centre the two parallel lines indicate a zone in the procedure which I call the "blind break". This is the area in the decision-making process where all reason-based or knowledge-based discrimination ceases to operate. The choice is blind to the comparable qualities of the options from which the choice is to be made. It is also a blind break in the sense that the outcome cannot be known or predicted in advance; and, by the same logic, the choice cannot be controlled by any person or party.

This aspect or component defines a lottery: the procedure cannot be regarded as a proper lottery if the blind break is compromised by manipulation of any sort—in other words if the blind break ceases to be blind. From a design point of view this defining feature enables us to ask a very simple but essential question: "what work is done by the blind break?" in any given proposal. The answer to this question enables us to make a clear decision about how a lottery might contribute to the institution or task in hand, while at the same time it shows us what problems might be created through the use of this mechanism. From an historical point of view this question also enables us to get closer to understanding exactly why this method of political recruitment was deployed in any given constitutional context.

2.2. The rational control over the arational

What the simple procedural diagram also illustrates is the way the lottery process is not arational in its entirety but consists of a number of rationally defined and designed elements that channel or control the actions of the blind break. In the case of choosing political office holders, the membership of the pool is rationally decided, as are the characteristics of the office in question such as its duration, its powers or the rules governing the conduct of office holders. A good example of this is the use of challenges by defence and prosecuting parties to determine the final form of a jury that has previously been selected by lottery. A purely randomly selected jury might not be seen as sufficiently impartial from either of these points of view.

This feature of the rational control of the arational in lottery design is the answer to the so-called capability argument against the random selection of citizens for public office. This is expressed in the idea that those selected by lottery would be unable to undertake the tasks required of them.[2] By restricting the pool to those with suitable qualifications or

---

2   One of the earliest examples of this argument can be found in Xenophon (1940).

experience; by giving training to those selected; or by simplifying the tasks of office, these potential problems can be addressed. All these solutions act as rational adjuncts to the arationality of the lottery process, but they are examples of important practical design elements in the setting up of any project where random selection might be used.

2.3. The relationship between sortive elements and other constitutional and institutional features

This final design principle, although of general value for all types of institutional arrangement, is of particular importance for those advocating the use of random recruitment as an extension of democracy. The major point here is that random selection is an arational means of choice, so care should be taken to ensure that its use does not compromise or devalue institutions or arrangements where rational choice is vital. If we are, as all designers should be, evaluating new models according to longer term or more general desired outcomes, then a democratic desired outcome must involve the ability to aggregate the wishes of the citizens in a meaningful manner. Democratic institutions thus become the means of measuring collective rationality.

In the light of this, it is worth noting that in most of the contexts where random recruitment was systematically used, it was used in combination with other means of selection or democratic decision-making such as voting or direct democracy. The challenge here is therefore to use sortition in a way that complements and improves existing democratic institutions.

3. Examples of Actual and Proposed Uses of Sortition

These examples are chosen to give a wide range of design ideas or options along with a wide range of political and historical contexts. The aim here is primarily to look at examples within the framework of the three principles outlined above, but at the same time to see what else of value these particular applications can tell us about the advantages or disadvantages of using random selection. The idea is that this form of analysis can then contribute to the assessment of future proposals or models in their new individual contexts.

3.1. Lotteries used to allocate commonly held resources: examples taken from Elinor Ostrom's Governing the Commons

This is the only one of my examples that does not deal with the selection of citizens by lottery. Nevertheless, it gives us an insight into the community value of lottery allocation that can inform our understanding of more overtly political uses of the procedure.

Although Ostrom does not analyse the nature of lottery distribution in this work, she mentions several examples in passing (Ostrom, 1990). These include: the allocation of fishing grounds in Alanya (Italy, *ibid.*, pp. 19–20) and in Nova Scotia (*ibid.*, p. 173); the distribution of log piles stacked by villagers in commonly held forests in Switzerland (*ibid.*, p. 65); and water distribution in Spain (*ibid.*, p. 77). To Ostrom's list we can add the allocation of grazing rights on commonly held pasture by lottery. Evidence of this can be found right across Europe (see Grettin, 1910).

The first point to note about these examples is that the lottery is used as part of an agreement between the various stakeholders in order to take the choice, and therefore the power and control, out of the hands of any individual participant. In these contexts, the lottery acts as a type of anonymous mediator and the blind break acts to limit the formation of potentially problematic local rivalries that might occur if the distribution was to be carried out by any identifiable agent.

In respect to the second principle, it is clear that in these examples the distribution by lottery could only operate fairly, and therefore success-fully, if the units to be distributed were approximately equal. It should also be noted that these examples do not designate permanent ownership or permanent use by lottery but are part of a process of temporary alloca-tion, often accompanied by some sort of rotational scheme. Along with the decisions as to who would qualify to take part in the lottery alloca-tions, these constitute the rational controls and design features that surround the arational lottery decision in each case.

In terms of the third principle—how the lottery scheme might relate to other procedures—these examples are what I would term "proto-political" in that they operate largely at the level of the communities in question and are outside the sphere of any form of governmental control. Despite this, they embody many of the principles of shared, rule-governed order that underlie later, more centralised (and therefore more power-based) political forms. The sharing of these resources and the decision to allocate them by lottery indicate the value to these communi-ties of making inclusive agreements and making them in such a way as to avoid antagonisms between individuals, families or other groups.

From a design point of view there is no clear design agent indicated in these examples. We can therefore assume that they were decided upon though some process that involved collective input, consideration and agreement, possibly linked to various means by which the arrangements could be changed or modified in the light of practice.

3.2. The Venetian and Florentine use of sortition in conjunction with voting to promote the ideals of the shared republic

The republics of Venice and Florence provide two of the best examples of the political use of lotteries from the late medieval period in Italy. Both republics combined lottery choice with voting but did so in two very different and distinct ways.

In Florence an arrangement by which the major political office holders were chosen by lottery from a pool of those elected by a limited electorate was the cornerstone of the First Republic which lasted from 1328 until the Medici takeover of 1434. It was also revived in the Second Republic, which lasted (in two phases) from 1494 until 1530. This system was known as the *Scrutiny and Tratte* and its most significant application was for the two-monthly rotating governing executive: the *Signoria* (see especially Najemy, 1982; but also Becker, 1967; Brucker, 1962; Rubinstein, 1966; Kent, 1978). Elections were held amongst the members of key guild and corporate bodies every two or three years and the names of those chosen were not made public but were placed in special bags. This was known as the *Scrutiny*. The *Tratte* then consisted of the drawing of the names of the next six members of the *Signoria* from the bags every two months.

The Venetian system can be described as the inversion of its Florentine counterpart. Groups of nominators were chosen by lottery from the *Consiglio Grande* or Grand Council (see Lane, 1973; Queller, 1986; Finlay, 1980). The *Consiglio* consisted of around 1,200 hereditary office holders whose main task lay in the election of the members of a number of smaller, more powerful, governing bodies. The nominators would be divided into groups who would then discuss and vote on who to nominate. The whole Council would then vote by secret ballot to choose the office holders from these nominations. This model has its origins in a form known as the *Brevia* (relating to the short office-holding responsibilities of those selected, see Wolfson, 1899). It was a system that was commonly used in towns and cities right across Europe in the late Middle Ages. In Venice this system survived relatively unchanged from its inception in 1297 until the fall of the Republic in 1798 following Napoleon's invasion of the city.

Neither of these regimes can be correctly described as democratic. They were ruled by elites from the major mercantile and banking families. The Venetian model provided the city with a stable, shared, but fundamentally exclusive form of government. The Florentine system was more flexible in terms of participation and there were periods, especially during the First Republic, when participation in the *Scrutiny* was open to a wider range of guild representatives than previously. These alternated with periods when participation was more severely restricted (see Dowlen, 2008, pp. 89–92).

The key to understanding both arrangements lies in the idea of bringing powerful, potentially hostile, family groupings into a shared, united political system. In both cases lottery selection was used to inhibit the power of appointment at key stages in the process of selecting political office holders. This made it less likely that one family or grouping could use its influence to dominate election procedures and thus consolidate a potentially despotic power base. In both cases elections were used to introduce some level of meritocracy or merit-based judgement into the proceedings, while the lottery element prevented the rise of hegemonic factions under the guise of this meritocracy.

This use of the blind break coincides with the Ostrom examples in that it creates and interjects an anonymous, uncontrollable element within an otherwise rationally-based process of choice. In both contexts we can understand and characterise the use of the lottery as an anti-power mechanism.

The constitutional and institutional particularities of both these systems are numerous and complex. There are, however, a number of rational design features worth consideration. Here I concentrate on two particular features of the Florentine Republic but use Venice as a contrasting example.

The first of these is the *divieto*. This was the arrangement by which no more than one member of any Florentine family was allowed to be part of the same *Signoria*. If a second member's name was withdrawn from the bag in question, the name ticket would have to be put back in the bag and another drawn out (Brucker, 1962, pp. 67–8). This is an excellent example of how a feature that involves rational choice and differentiation is introduced to cover possible deficiencies in the random selection process. Here the addition of the *divieto* is also a clear indication that the primary purpose of this complex selection procedure was to prevent power being concentrated in the hands of any single family.

The second example of a significant rational design feature in the Florentine system is the ruling that the identities of those whose names were placed in the bags as a result of the earlier vote should remain secret. The extreme nature of this provision is an indication of the level of corruption and patronage and the threat it posed to the inclusive ideal of the republic. The contrast between the unknown pool, or hidden political society, in Florence and the well-established and well-known hereditary *Consiglio Grande* in Venice could not be greater. A key feature of the selection of nominators by lottery in Venice was the openness of the lottery procedure itself. This is an indication of how lottery choice was valued because it was demonstrably fair and demonstrably free from manipulation. Thus, while Florence sought to counter corruption by greater secrecy, Venice did so by making some of its procedures more open to general scrutiny.

If we now turn to the question of how rational decision-making elements relate to the arationality of lottery choice in the overall constitutional arrangements of Florence and Venice, we can immediately see how lottery selection operated at a very different stage in the procedure for choosing public office holders in each of these two cities. In Venice the lottery took place at the beginning of the process of choice by choosing the nominator groups. These then deliberated and made a conscious, collective series of decisions about the names of those who should go forward to be voted on by the *Consiglio Grande*. In Florence, on the other hand, the final decision about who should govern and when was taken by lottery and the act of voting merely established the broad pool or "political society" from which these temporary rulers were to be drawn. The intervention of the blind break therefore comes at the beginning of the chain of rational decision-making in Venice and at the end of that chain in the case of Florence. From a design point of view, then, the former arrangement places a higher value on the collective process of rational deliberation and choice. In the latter case, however, the chain of collective reasoning (such as it is) is undermined because the final decision is taken out of the hands of those who vote in all but the most general of senses.

This is, of course, a very brief exposition of the basic features of these two systems. It should, however, be mentioned in passing that while the Florentine system inhibited forms of direct autocratic control, it operated in a context in which indirect patronage and covert control was rife. The fact that the first Florentine Republic fell to the Medici dictatorship in 1434

(Rubinstein, 1966; Kent, 1978) can be seen as evidence of its vulnerability to these forms of patronage and of its failure to create stronger forms of open accountability.

3.3. Machiavelli's provosts: a proposal for randomly selected tribunes

In his *Discourse on the Re-modelling of the Government of Florence,* a proposal made to Giovanni de Medici in 1520 that features a number of Venetian-style elements, Machiavelli includes the new post of the provost (1989, pp. 111–12). The scheme as a whole is founded on a *Consiglio Grande* of 100 citizens who would elect a Senate plus 16 Gonfaloniers. The main executive body, however, was to be based on a pool of 65 senior office holders, appointed for life, who would elect a single Gonfalonier as a head of state for each two- or three-year period, plus a three-monthly executive group of eight from their number.

Sitting with this executive as silent observers rather than as deliberating members would be four provosts selected for one month only, by lottery, from a group of 16 Gonfaloniers elected for this purpose by the *Consiglio Grande.* These provosts would have the right to veto any measure transacted by the executive. Vetoed measures would then become the subject of consideration, in the first instance, by one half of the grouping of 65 from which the executive had been originally chosen. By appeal the issue could then be considered by the Senate or finally by the *Consiglio Grande* itself if this proved necessary.

In this way, Machiavelli sets out what we could call a form of mixed constitution based on two pools or proposed groupings within the body politic. The higher of these is the group of 65 permanent office holders from which the executive and head of state would be chosen. The lower of these is the *Consiglio Grande,* based on the body of active citizenry. The provosts then provide the active linkage between these two groupings. Based on the Roman Tribune model they act as guardians against the misuse of executive power. Their selection by lottery is primarily to set their appointment outside the competitive electoral process and to inhibit the role of active patronage and manipulation in their appointment.

I have included this scheme as one of my examples because it illustrates the potential value of the citizen witnesses in the protection of inclusive and shared constitutional arrangements. Here those chosen by lottery have a very different role from their elected or appointed colleagues, but it is a role that complements and supports those in government and those who deliberate rather than one that seeks to replace them. I would argue that this type of role could be a very important means by which citizens with a basic minimum of political experience and knowledge might be involved in the oversight of key institutions within a modern elective democracy.

3.4. The Athenian boule: random selection used to prevent an aristocratic takeover of the democratic state

Herodotus tells us that Kleisthenes "took the *demos* into his faction" (Herodotus, 1998, p. 137) in order to resolve a divisive stand-off between two aristocratic rivals: himself, a member of the influential Alkmaeonid family, and his rival, Isagoras, who had recently been elected *archon*. This took place in 508–7 BCE and is regarded as a pivotal point in the development of Athenian democracy. Isagoras called in the help of Sparta, but the Athenians then besieged the Spartan force on the Acropolis and, in what can only be described as a revolutionary moment, forced their retreat (Aristotle, 1986, pp. 163–4; Ober, 1998).

The major structural reforms that followed the resolution of this situation in favour of Kleisthenes considerably strengthened the active role of the *demos* or Athenian citizenry in the political arrangements of this small city-state. We can, I believe, rightly think about this settlement as a form of pact or agreement between the leadership of an older aristocratic family and a new but, I would argue, already organised force on the Athenian scene.

The logic of this conclusion is clearly revealed in the introduction of ostracism by Kleisthenes. We can read this as a condition for support: "yes", says the organised *demos*, "we will support you, but only if we can remove you or any of your successors in the future if we so wish".[3]

Although there is no direct evidence that proves that the random selection of the principle administrative body of the *polis*, the *boule* or council of 500 was part of the Kleisthenic reforms, we can certainly understand this as belonging to the same political trajectory. At this highly critical time in the formation of the new Athenian constitution the *boule* was potentially the de facto centre of state power. An elected *boule* would hand this power straight back to the aristocrats. Lottery selection, on the contrary, would prevent those with money or influence from buying or forcing their way into political office since any aristocratic

---

[3]   This goes some way to explaining why ostracism only started to be used long after it was first introduced.

candidate would be on the same footing as a citizen candidate in the lottery draw. The blind break, therefore, acts in a manner that inhibits the effective operation of existing and future concentrations of power within the context of a shared, inclusive, rule-governed political system.

In respect to the other design features and the overall context of the randomly selected *boule*, several points are worth mentioning. Firstly, the membership of the *boule* was organised according to the *demes* or local wards that made up the Athenian *polis*. Each *deme* had the task of selecting a number of *boule* members determined by a ratio based on the size of its population (Traill, 1975; Whitehead, 1986). This meant that the random nature of the draw was linked to a rational, in the sense of reason or ratio-based, form of representation linked to population numbers and local areas.

Secondly, those citizens selected could hold office for one year only; they could only be members of the *boule* twice; and could not do so on successive years. Thirdly, the role of all public office holders was subject to strict anti-corruption laws and procedures. All office holders would have their accounts checked upon leaving office and anyone suspected of corruption could face prosecution by the people's courts—a process, incidentally, that could be initiated by any concerned citizen.[4] In addition to their selection by lottery, those chosen had to pass a simple citizenship test before they could take up their office. This was known as the *dokimasia*. Although this was very much a formality, during the immediate aftermath of the defeat of the 30 tyrants this procedure was used to prevent those who had supported the tyranny from holding public office (Adeleye, 1983).

While this gives us a brief view of the *boule* selection and its safeguarding design features, we should also remember that ancient Athens was a direct democracy based on the decisions made by a voted majority in the citizens' assembly. Six hundred of the seven hundred magistrates were selected by lottery while the other hundred were elected. Citizens selected in large numbers by lottery also served in the people's courts where they voted by secret ballot on major political issues as well as on general criminal matters. Thus, the randomly selected *boule* can be understood as the administrative centre of the Athenian state because of its

---

[4] For an overall picture of the structure of Athenian institutions, see Hansen (1999) and on the use of lottery selection, see Headlam (1933).

effective oversight of all executive activities and its control over the assembly agenda. At the same time, however, it was also part of whole range of interlocking measures designed to defend the role of the *demos* in the running of the city.

3.5. The seditious libel controversy in eighteenth-century Britain and America

This is an example, not so much of a design process, but of how one constitutional element that has its own developmental path, namely the jury system, assumes a wider role under certain conditions and in pursuit of certain ends. In this case the jury, usually a means of making judgements based on existing laws, assumes a law-making role.

In Britain in the early eighteenth century, publishers and authors could be prosecuted under seditious libel legislation for writing or publishing articles critical of the government (Green, 1985; Dowlen, 2008, pp. 178–81). Their only form of defence was to appeal to the jury to acquit, not because the act of authorship or publication was in doubt, but in the hope that they would consider the criticism to be justified rather than seditious or libellous. Since the Penn, Mead, Bushel case of 1670, jurors had had the right to go against the instructions of the judge, and this precipitated a whole series of jury acquittals in seditious libel cases in both Britain and its American colonies in the latter part of the eighteenth century.

The controversy reached its climax in 1763 when the government attempted to use the act to prosecute Wilkes for the publication of his Junius papers in which he criticised British policy towards its American colonies. The final resolution in legal terms came in 1792 with Fox's Libel Act which recognised the right of juries to bring in "open verdicts" in cases of seditious libel (Aspinal and Smith, 1959, p. 363).

What is useful and instructive about this example in terms of our discussion on design is that it illustrates the process of law-making operating from the bottom upwards: here those subject to the law were able to force changes in the law. In a period where British electoral arrangements were limited, unfair, unequal and corrupt, the jury system acted as the vanguard for democratic change. Its defence of free speech was a necessary prerequisite for the battles for parliamentary reform that followed in Britain in the first half of the nineteenth century.

Juries had been randomly selected since 1730 in Britain and while most of the American colonies followed the British lead, others, such as South Carolina, had introduced lottery selection as early as 1682 (Sirmans, 1966). The 1730 legislation (Cobbett, 1811) was designed to prevent corruption in the choice of jurors and jury participation was still based on property ownership during this period. Nevertheless, the regular acquittals for seditious libel and the capitulation of the state on this matter in 1791 demonstrates how they began to be understood as constituting the legitimate voice of the people. In this context random selection can be understood as an essential part of their defence against corruption from above.

Another important point concerning this example is the context of common law under which these events took place, especially the way that, under common law, rules are modified and adjusted by precedent (Laws, 2014). The right to trial by jury was enshrined in the Magna Carta; the Penn, Mead, Bushel case was resolved by the Court of Common Pleas; and Fox's Libel Act followed the precedent of the jury acquittals as a reflection of custom and practice.

In terms of its lessons for the present and future design of schemes based on random recruitment, therefore, this is an example of a high level of public participation and deliberation at what I would describe as a low, entry-level institution. Of importance is the manner in which multiple decisions over time and space then contributed to a centralised, specific resolution. It therefore contrasts, in design terms, and in terms of legitimacy, with schemes that seek to place randomly selected citizens at a high level within the body politic where they might be asked to make single, major, binding decisions.

3.6. The French Directory of 1795 and Penn's draft constitution for Pennsylvania

The use of lotteries to deselect members of the French Directory in order to start a process of rotation is probably one of the best examples of the ill-considered use of sortition. The Directory was a seven-man executive elected by the National Convention that was set up in the immediate aftermath or the Reign of Terror. The 1795 Constitution specified that one member of this body should be deselected by lottery every year so that the office could be filled by a newly elected member (Stewart, 1951, p. 589; Sydenman, 1974, p. 127).

This is what I would describe at a weak use of the lottery: in other words, it is an application where there is no obvious or pressing need to use an arational means of selection, beyond, of course, that of mere convenience. Because the random decision to deselect followed a process of selection by the collective vote of the Convention, the random decision clearly undermined the considered rational process of choice that preceded it. Any voter who saw their chosen candidate removed from office by lottery after one year would be rightly aggrieved. This random deselection, applied to the top leadership, only created greater uncertainty and instability at a time when the country was attempting to move out of crisis and when, therefore, collective certainty and confidence in the process of collective judgement was especially needed.

A similar proposal can be found in one of the early drafts for the Constitution of the state of Pennsylvania written by its founder William Penn (Penn, 1982). In this draft, one third of the elected state council was to be deselected after one year by lottery to allow a further third to be elected. This process was to be repeated a year later and in the third year the remaining third from the original vote would be replaced by a new batch of elected members to complete the new rotational scheme. In the final version of the constitution, however, this scheme was changed. As part of the initial electoral programme, the council seats (and thus also the candidates) were divided into three equal categories: those for one year, those for two years and those for three years duration.

In the original proposal, as with the French Directory, the electoral choice would have been undermined and devalued by the subsequent lottery process of deselection. Penn's final solution, however, meant that the voters would know how long every candidate would serve on the council in advance of casting their votes. It therefore preserved the integrity and value of the elective process.

Both these examples illustrate my third design principle: that a lottery element should not contradict or compromise the collective rationality of the democratic system in which it was to operate. From a design point of view, a possible use of lottery selection in the context of the French Directory would have been to select an eighth member of the Directory by lottery from the body of the Convention for a shorter time period than the other seven. This member could have had a role similar to that of Machiavelli's provost: that of bringing certain issues back to the Convention for greater collective scrutiny.

4. "Some Problems of Citizens' Assemblies" — an Academic Letter by Keith Sutherland and Alex Kovner

This short chapter sets out an innovative format for parliamentary or assembly decision-making by large randomly selected juries who vote on a range of options presented and argued for by their elected parliamentary representatives (Sutherland and Kovner, 2020). The authors, correctly in my opinion, recognise how the model of the deliberative citizens' assembly can easily fall prey to the organisational power of the agenda setters. The non-deliberating jury element in this scheme follows from this observation. The options on which the jury or juries would decide upon would be decided upon by a "superminority" method, which involves lowering the threshold of acceptance of questions in order to include more options for consideration.

This combination of a jury system for the ultimate decision-making alongside a reduced role for the elected representatives (that of producing the alternatives and arguing for them) is well presented. The scheme does, however, raise some design issues that would need to be addressed if it were to move closer to being implemented in practice.

The key point here is the relationship between the role, or roles, of the elected representatives and the proposal that the final decision should be made by a randomly selected body (or by a number of jury groupings). The electoral process, however flawed by the rhetorical claims and counterclaims of its participants and its domination by internal party politics, is, nonetheless, a process of collective rationality. By way of elections, the conscious preferences of the voting population are, in a parliamentary system, aggregated to produce an executive body and a legislative assembly that is, in some form, a reflection of this conscious preference. Now if we characterise random selection as an essentially arational process, then the model that is put forward here gives those chosen arationally a higher rank in the final decision-making process than those elected by the rational consideration of the voting citizens. In addition to contradicting the effectiveness of the voters' original decisions, the scheme (as it stands) threatens the chain of personal accountability, responsibility and trust that underpins the representative system. The insertion of a blind break *at this level of decision-making* would effectively break this chain.

5. Citizens' Parliamentary Groups

This is a proposal put together by the author in 2017 (Dowlen, 2017). The basic idea is that for each sitting member of a parliament or legislative assembly there would be a group of around 20 citizens randomly selected from the member's constituency. The main role of these citizen office holders would be to protect the fairness and integrity of the political system. This would be addressed through three main tasks. First: to ensure that the member adhered to an agreed code of parliamentary conduct or its equivalent. Second: to act as a link between the sitting member and the wider constituency. Third: to demand action from the member in cases where the fairness and integrity of the political system was understood to be under threat.

The members of the group would attend monthly question and answer meetings with the MP or assembly member. The minutes of these meetings would be posted online. In addition, two members of the group would be on "special duty" for each monthly period. This would involve practical contact with the member's work such as visits to the parliamentary office, attending meetings held by the MP, and attending surgeries in the constituency. They would report back to the monthly meetings. In respect to the third task, any demand for action would have to be endorsed by two other constituency groups before it could be legitimately made. Failure by the MP to act as requested would lead to a recall and therefore a by-election in the constituency. The powers given to these groups, in respect to this task, would have to be carefully controlled and limited to prevent their misuse.

The principle behind this proposal is that since the citizens elect their MP or assembly member, and since the member's salary is paid out of the public purse, it is logical to ask for some level of public oversight in respect to the work that they do. From a design point of view there are two main aims for this proposal. The first is to bridge the gap between the political system and the general citizenry, establishing some sense of the common ownership of the system by the citizens. The second aim is to protect and improve the democratic accountability of the political system. The random element in the selection of the group is to establish their impartiality and their freedom from the complexities and dangers of political appointment. For this reason, members of political parties or similar groupings should not be members of the group. Each participant's term of office would be for one year only.

In overall terms the scheme is designed to complement and enrich the process of active representation. As such it could be seen as fulfilling a state, rather than a governmental or legislative, function. It could also be understood as an important entry-level facility, and those with initial experience as members of these groups could then form the pool for other offices such as, for example, a citizen element in a second chamber.

6. Tom Paine's Proposal for Random Conscription During the American War of Independence

My final design case study is of a proposal made by Tom Paine to recruit members of the American militias during the War of Independence against Britain. The documents relating to this date from around 1780 (Paine, 1945, pp. 208–9). The scheme is based on the idea that pools of 30 possible conscripts were to be drawn up and each pool would then choose one member of the militia by lottery. The other 29, however, would have charges levied against them in order to cover the one soldier's expenses and equipment. In other words, they would be asked to take the role of supporting their chosen colleague.

Conscription by lottery is a common means of choosing who is to be called up for military service once a compulsory element has been introduced. In this context the blind break is a demonstrably anonymous means of choice that excludes any personal, organisational or group preference or prejudice from the judgement.

Why Paine's proposal is important for this discussion is because he pays particular attention to those who are *not* selected by giving them a supporting role. The chosen individual is thus less isolated and the lottery decision less burdensome and less divisive than it would otherwise be. A variation of this scheme might be to give the 29 some level of military training and to hold additional lotteries to see who would serve after the term of service for the first militia member had ended. This would extend the level of group responsibility and their sense of shared service.

7. Possible Conclusions

The first thing that becomes clear from these examples is the diversity and variety of applications of random selection, even within the political sphere. Institutions that rely on this recruitment procedure can be found in different locations within the body politic, they draw from different pre-selected pools of citizens or elected office holders, the tasks assigned to those selected vary considerably, as does the length of time that those selected would hold office. The analysis also revealed how a whole range of rational design elements could be used to control and focus the random element of lottery selection. When considering the value of this means of selection, therefore, we should not restrict ourselves to the consideration of a small number of possible models.

Linked to this is the fact that random recruitment was often used in combination with voting or alongside electoral systems. This is an indication, if one were needed, that we should not think of the lottery selection and voting as systems that should replace each other or exclude each other in practice. It would, I suggest, be more useful and constructive to look at ways that they might complement and support each other.

Perhaps the most important conclusion to be drawn from these examples (and from the form of analysis they were subjected to) is to see them as a range of different *problem-solving* applications, or proposed applications operating in a range of different contexts. In respect to the historical examples, if we understand the qualities of the lottery process, the other design features that contributed to each application and the overall context of each application, we can then begin to understand the problems that necessitated the use of a random process. This is a form of reverse design thinking where we seek to discover the problem by looking at the various acts and measures that contributed its resolution. We can then take this framework of analysis and apply it to future applications where we know the problems and are looking for various measures and devices by which we might resolve them.

Sometimes, however, the process is reversed, and a consideration of the means begins to generate new ideas for new desired outcomes. I would argue that this is very much the case with random political recruitment; and the new ideas relate specifically to the nature of power within the political sphere.

If we start from the simply expressed problem of there being too great a distance between citizens and those holding political office in modern democracies, then the primary desired outcome of using institutions that involve random selection is that of participation. If we then add the important conclusion gained from the study of random recruitment—that lottery selection can act as an anti-power mechanism by inhibiting concentrations of personal or group power—then this changes our overall view of what might, or might not, constitute a successful democracy. Put simply, it focuses our attention on those areas within our current democratic models where concentrations of power have the potential or capacity to act against the interests of the citizenry. If these key areas were to become subject to some form of citizen control or oversight, then we are, in effect, extending and defending our democracies and bringing the political process under a more comprehensive form of citizen control. Within this type of scenario, therefore, we can begin to see the possible value of using institutions that use random recruitment: replacing concentrations of personal or group power with a more diffuse, but more collective, form of power.

Exactly how this could be done is, of course, a difficult question and very much beyond the scope of this chapter. I would suggest, however, that a design process that starts from similar general objectives, is based on an understanding of the qualities of the lottery process, considers the design features that might accompany lottery selection and looks seriously at the way random recruitment can work with other constitutional measures will get us looking in the right direction.

Charles Ramond

Democratic Accounts and Miscounts?

Rancière and Spinoza

Abstract: *Both Spinoza and Rancière are theoreticians of absolute or radical democracy. Spinoza, however, defines democracy solely by the law of "account", while Rancière, on the contrary, defines it by the "miscount". This is one of the reasons why Rancière thinks that the essence of democracy lies in "sortition", and not in "elections". We present and discuss here Rancière's point of view, in the light of a quantitative-extensive-Spinozistic conception of democracy. For this, we ask ourselves in the first section what Rancière means exactly by the notion of "uncounted": which categories of a given population can be considered as "uncounted" in our contemporary representative democracies? We show that Rancière does not mean by "uncounted" sub-parts or subsets of a given population, mainly because he does not adopt an "intersectionalist" point of view. But then, the Spinozist quantitative-universalist position can be opposed to Rancière as an objection: this is what we do in the second part of the presentation, before concluding on the superiority of elections compared to drawing lots.*

1. Introduction

Luke Rhinehart's marvellous novel *The Dice Man* (1971) shows absurdly and tragically the developments of a personal life entirely subject to sortition. Broadening this perspective, I would like to offer here a critical presentation of the very notion of sortition in political matters. The fact that I will refer to the philosophies of Spinoza and Rancière in order to deal with such a question will no doubt come as a surprise. It is justified from my point of view by the fact that both are theoreticians of democracy understood in a radical way, and basically share, in very different contexts and according to very different formulations, the same questioning about the possibility of legitimising the power in general, and democratic power in particular. And sortition is nothing more than a way of legitimising democratic power.

In the last chapter of his very last work, the *Political Treatise*, Spinoza made democracy the "absolute regime", *imperium absolutum*, a statement unexampled in its time and which was to prove prophetic, especially if we consider the fact that democracy has steadily spread across the surface of the Earth over the past three centuries, and today seems to many nations a regime not only desirable above all others, but unsurpassable. Spinoza had an entirely extensive or numerical conception of democracy. As such, he was part of the current of modern philosophy which established "the reign of quantity" (Guénon, 1953) against the "occult qualities" (Spinoza, 2023, part 5) of the Aristotelian and scholastic world: the aristocrat (or "man of quality"; Prévost, 1728–1731) was then giving way to the man of democratic societies ("the man without qualities"; Musil, 2011; the "plus one" of the generalised equivalence of votes). In a particularly striking passage of the *Political Treatise*, Spinoza declares that "we must estimate [...] the power of a State, and consequently its right, according to the *number* of citizens" (Spinoza, 2022, chapter 7, §18),[1] thus, the political, legal and arithmetical planes are folded back exactly one on the other. What I have called "the law of counting", and which I have been trying to highlight for several decades in my readings of Spinoza and in my other works, thus places elections or democratic counts at the heart of a philosophy, a politics and an ethics of immanence (nothing is above accounts), governed by the single conceptual doublet "law of the account/unjustified preferences" (Ramond, 2023).

Jacques Rancière, starting from his fundamental thesis of "the equality of intelligences",[2] also makes democracy the "absolute regime" (even if he does not use Spinoza's expression). According to him, no politics is possible without the implicit postulate of the "equality" of citizens: when I give an order to another person, when I exercise my power over him, I thereby recognise his ability to understand what I command him to do. And, therefore, the very exercise of power (of domination) paradoxically presupposes the recognition of the equality of intelligences, and of a kind of "arche-democracy" present in all forms of political regimes. Unlike

---

[1] *Nam imperii potentia et consequenter jus ex civium numero aestimanda est.*
[2] I developed this fundamental thesis, and its genesis (Ramond, 2019), from which I take up here some analyses from chapter 13.

Spinoza, however, Rancière offers a vision of democracy that would escape the law of counting. I therefore propose to explain, shed light on and finally discuss Rancière's unexpected proposal in favour not of demo-cratic "accounts", but of sortition which, according to him, must accom-pany democratic "miscounts".

2. Rancière: Equality Without Numbers

According to Rancière, the emancipation of a person most often consists of borrowing speeches, attitudes or lives which are not intended for him, and which are not "proper" to him (for example, for a worker, doing poetry or philosophy), which allows him to get out of a path traced in advance, to "reconfigure" a situation that presented itself as frozen. Like this emancipation of the individual, there exists, according to Rancière, collective, political emancipations, which are the result of "collective subjects" (Rancière, 2009c, p. 9), or collective processes of subjectifications, during which a community will monopolise, "usurp" (Rancière, 1999, p. 22), a sermon which was not necessarily made for her, but which allows her to "recut", or to propose a new "distribution of the sensible". These "hazardous subjectifications" (Rancière, 1992, p. 152) — in every sense of the word "hazardous", that is to say, made at random, in a non-concerted way, with an uncertain result, never given in advance — are another way by which Rancière conveys the idea of the "politics" or the "part of those without a part".

The "part of those without a part", being both the "nothing" and the "everything" of the political community, cannot be measured. The "police" is the level of management of current affairs, of exchanges. We sell, we buy, we count, we vote. "Politics", for Rancière, presupposes a qualitative leap that suddenly takes us out of the "reign of quantity" specific to democracies. According to him, "politics", even in a democratic regime, installs us in the "supernumerary" or in the "dis-agreement" — all so many ways of saying that it escapes the law of counting, or quantification.

As Rancière states in the back cover of *The Dis-agreement*, "Politics begins when the natural order of domination and the distribution of parts among the parts of society are interrupted by the appearance of a super-numerary part, the demos, which identifies the collection of the uncounted with the whole of the community. From this initial disappoint-ment, a logic of misunderstanding is established, equally far removed from consensual discussion and absolute wrong." Rancière plays on the proximity between "miscount" (disappointment, disillusion) and "wrong" (injury). Miscounts are not just mistakes in accounts. They cause suffering, as in litigation or conflict. A democracy in which there would be only "accounts" without "miscounts" would be a democracy of "consensus", a democracy (falsely) appeased, pacified, without litigation. For Rancière, it would be a regime of "police" and not of "politics". For there to be politics, it is therefore absolutely necessary that something escapes the "account".

These theses may surprise. On the one hand, the democracies governed by the law of account (those regimes that Rancière would associate with the "police" or the management of current affairs), far from refusing litigation, continue to organise it in all its forms. Elections, election campaigns, demonstrations, party platforms, clashes between candidates, petitions, media enquiries, justice, polls… all of this creates, in our democracies, at many levels and on many occasions, disputes, conflicts, and dis-agreements, sometimes stormy, sometimes violent, sometimes fatal.

It is therefore difficult to see why a democracy of the type that currently exists in Europe and in France would necessarily be "polite" (or policed), "consensual", incapable of reconfiguring its parts as well as its political parties. On the contrary, we are witnessing great surprises in the electoral process, which seem to attest to an undeniable "process of subjectivation" at work. The same goes for certain absolutely unforeseen protest processes (such as the famous "yellow vests", which no one had seen coming before they decided to end their "invisible" status in a particularly spectacular way).

In a democratic regime, it is even difficult to see what could remain "uncounted". Anyone can stand for election, create an association, launch a petition or get together with friends or colleagues to parade or block roundabouts… no doubt there are accounts prohibited by law. There is no right in France, for example, to make "ethnic statistics". Or again, we do not count as "cast" the blank ballots during elections. One could then imagine the "uncounted" designate in Rancière, not as uncounted individuals (because every individual is counted or can be counted in our democratic systems), but as categories which would not have been "taken into account" until then. For example, for a long time the women present in political parties, on the boards of directors of large companies or on the selection committees of universities were not counted. Then "quotas" were established, which means that now we count the members of this categories.

The alliance of certain categories could also create new categories, which previously had not been taken into account, but which could be formed following some event or other. For example, before May 1968, it is unlikely that there were statistics that counted students and workers together. But their alliance during the "events" of May 1968 created a new category that had to be taken into account. The same goes for the recent category of "feminicide": we count them today whereas we did not count them yesterday. So one could think that Rancière, speaking of the "uncounted", designates this kind of category: those which only give rise to a count under some form of possible pressure causing new "categories" to emerge in our societies (new divisions, new "distributions" of the community) previously uncounted or unaccounted for.

But Rancière does not see things from this angle. For him, the "uncounted" are not categories of the excluded or the hitherto unnoticed that should then be reintegrated into the accounts of the community. Because (he thinks) if we proceeded in this way, we would gradually eliminate the uncounted until everyone would be counted or taken into account. And in doing so, we would not have progressed towards "politics", but towards "police". "Police" represents a dream of complete accounts without remainder, a dream of "saturated" (Rancière, 1990; 1999; 2009a) accounts, while "politics" distinguishes itself by maintaining disputes or "miscalculations". Rancière's "miscounts" or "dis-agreements" are therefore not to be thought of as the "exclusion" of those who should be "included", because total inclusion is for him a dream of police and not of politics. As he puts it, "the part of those without a part is not the part of the excluded" (Rancière, 2009a, p. 490).

Rancière did not express a desire for ethnic statistics, or a count of blank ballots in elections, or the generalisation or multiplication of quotas. Neither does he support intersectionality. Moreover, he does not have an immoderate taste for elections in general, which are the very symbol of the democratic law of counting. He explains this in *Hatred of Democracy*: "Democracy", he declares for example, "is not a type of constitution nor a form of society. The power of the people is not that of a people gathered together, of the *majority* [emphasis CR], or of the working class. It is simply the power peculiar to those who have no more entitlements to govern than to submit. […] The drawing of lots is its essence"; "Nor is the vote in itself a democratic form by which the people makes its voice heard. It is originally the expression of a consent that a superior power requires"; "universal suffrage is in not at all a natural consequence of democracy", which moreover "has no natural consequences" (Rancière, 2009b, pp. 46–7 and 53–4).

The "hate of democracy" is certainly not shared by Rancière, who, on the contrary, vigorously defends democracy against a certain type of new criticism that has been addressed to it in recent years. Moreover, Rancière often repeats (this is one of his most striking and endearing theses) that he is not one of the people who believe that the people are "dumb" or "backward". From this point of view, Rancière is very different from Badiou, for example, since he refutes the position of "activist" as well as that of "spokesperson", "leader" or "pedagogue". He absolutely does not conceive of political action as the action of small, enlightened groups guiding the people. As he keeps repeating, emancipation presupposes self-learning, learning by oneself, and can never pass through an instruction delivered by a master.

As a result, one would have expected Rancière to value elections. If people aren't "dumb", why not trust their vote? But Rancière's preference for "sortition" actually stems from his thesis of "equality of intelligences". If everyone has exactly as many rights to govern as everyone else, wouldn't it be the right way to organise democracy if we were to somehow reflect this absolute egalitarianism and constantly reshuffle the election cards to prevent the gradual establishment of a political class which would continuously seek and produce justifications for its own existence, its *perseverentia in existendo*? Higher education, the ability to deal with complex issues, but also rhetorical skill, experience of responsibility… all of this could gradually self-justify the perpetuation of a political class initially composed of "representatives", then soon of "leaders" installed for entire decades who would weave together all the networks of influence necessary to maintain their power. Sortition, on the contrary, constantly reminds us that "anyone" in a democracy is entitled to anything. Equality of opportunity (to be drawn) is here the image of equality of intelligences.

3. Objections and Conclusions

There is, however, an objection to sortition in politics, which Rancière (unless I am mistaken) does not consider. It is very unlikely that several governments drawn by lot would wish to pursue the same policy. Sortition would therefore prevent the implementation of long-term policies, for example: land-use planning, the construction of high-speed train lines or highways, or major infrastructure (canals, forest plantations, etc.) that require continuity of public action. Sortition, for the same reasons, would prevent the conduct of courageous long-term policies: taxing the large international companies, modifying the distribution of the large budgetary masses in favour of the poorest rather than the wealthiest, etc. At the very moment when it would be the perfect image of an entirely egalitarian society, sortition, with its random results, would thus paradoxically prevent us from realising this equality in practice, and could, therefore, hinder the type of resolutely social policy that we might well imagine Rancière would support. The principle of drawing lots is indeed very different from that of polls, which can always (despite/ thanks to their innumerable failures) claim a certain scientificity, due to the "corrections" which are made to the answers according to the previous answers, and to the determination of the standard samples. The drawing of lots, in its nakedness, is much more random, is much more likely not to represent the preferences of citizens and could not fail to lead to absurd policies where laws wanted by most people would not be enforced while laws that the people would not want would be imposed on them.

The very positivity of the sortition (this would be a second objection) further loses the essence of politics, which is the possibility of questioning any rule or decision or direction previously taken, and which therefore has an essentially negative essence. As strange and paradoxical as it may seem, it is indeed impossible to assign a positive end to politics without losing it (just as Orpheus could not look at Eurydice without losing her). To say that the end of politics is "happiness", or "security", or "freedom", or "power", or "wealth", or "the health" of peoples, would immediately take away from the political that which makes it specific, namely the freedom and the capacity for a people to change and give up old aspirations. If, for example, one were to posit that the ultimate goal of politics is the "wealth" of a population, the "growth" of its economy, the increase of its Gross Domestic Product, etc., as is almost constantly the case nowadays, then politics would not be distinguished from economics and finance, and all its transactions would have to be done on the stock market. If we posed life expectancy, or the extension of the lifespan of citizens, as the end of politics, then politics would not be so different from medicine and should be the responsibility of doctors. If it was "security", politics would not be very different from policing, and would have to be the responsibility of the police and the military. If it was "happiness", it would not be very different from a religion or a wisdom and should belong to priests. We can no doubt imagine other justifications or other purposes. But any positive definition of politics will be a way of confusing politics with another practice or art. We can therefore maintain a specificity of politics only as the "negative" of all the ends mentioned above, and indeed of all ends.

Properly understood, politics should therefore be defined, not by this or that end, but by the possibility left to peoples to modify their ends as they wish. "We the people" may one day want security, another day want freedom; one day we might want adventures, even conquests, another day we might want calm and prosperity. In this there is an intrinsically revolutionary dimension to democratic politics. This point, which today haunts the thought of Jacques Rancière (since in his eyes "politics" consists in de-legitimising the forms of power that "political philosophy" has always tried to legitimise) had, in my opinion, been seen by Spinoza in his refusal to subordinate politics (like the order of the world in general) to any meaning, to any purpose, or to any play of values. Indeed, it was this that enabled him to present a particularly pure and exact vision of the very essence (all negative) of politics in the *Political Treatise*. But this absence of finality, this immanence, and this radical equality enveloped by democracy adapt much better to the intentionalities and collective preferences manifested by elections and accounts of all kinds than they do to random draws, which can undoubtedly give absurd results, but precisely not negative results. Rancière never wanted to admit that there was a revolutionary dimension to the accounts themselves. From Rancière's point of view, which I extend in my own way, between the total confidence that could be given to elections because of the equal intelligence that it presupposes among the voters, and the total mistrust of elections, such as we find for example in Badiou and which always envelops the idea of an insufficiently enlightened people, the middle way of sortition does not therefore seem to me practicable as a political way, however scientifically it may be envisaged.

Jason Brennan

Democratic Sortition versus Epistocratic and Statistical Decision Methods

Abstract: *Sortition is the use of lotteries in making political decisions or staffing political offices. Many defenders of sortition claim that sortition is in practice and at the limit more fair and equal than normal democratic elections. Other defenders claim that sortition improves the epistemic quality of democratic decision-making.*

This chapter considers the question of whether epistocratic versions of sortition are superior to and overcome some of the problems of purely democratic versions of sortition. For instance, even democratic forms of sortition are likely to have severe epistemic defects. Further, while a sufficiently large random sample of citizens can ensure that the voting legislature is demographically identical to the public at large, this does not overcome the problem of persistent minorities and majoritarian rule. In contrast, weighted lottery systems in epistocracy can remove demographic bias from the legislature.

The average person believes that voting and elections are essential to democracy. Many democratic theorists demur.

Some theorists have a broader view of democracy: a political system is democratic to the extent to which basic political power is distributed equally among all members of that polity. According to this definition, neither voting nor elections are requirements for a system to be democratic. They are *a* way, not *the* way, to instantiate democracy.

This inclusive definition leaves open when and how the people participate in politics, and also how the democratic government is structured. A
democracy might be big or small. It might meet frequently or
infrequently. It might have separated powers with checks or balances, or
it might not. The people might decide some issues themselves, some
decisions might be made by their representatives, some decisions might
be made by people appointed by their representatives and so on.
Decisions might involve structured deliberation or not. There could be a
bicameral, unicameral or some other kind of legislature. There could be a
unitary executive with lots of power, or not. There might be judicial
review of legislation or independent bureaucracies, or not. There might be
constitutional bills of rights or strong constitutional restrictions on the
scope of government power, or not. Political participation might be
optional or compulsory. They might have first-past-the-fence voting,
Condorcet voting, proportional representation, some other voting mechanism or no voting at all. Instead of having representatives/decision-
makers chosen by voting in elections, they might be selected, or decisions
themselves might be made, through some sort of lottery.

In recent years, many democratic theorists have developed a renewed
enthusiasm for sortition—for selecting democratic leaders or making
democratic decisions through a lottery—over voting. Some claim that
sortition is fairer than elections. Others claim that sortition will produce
better quality decisions—decisions that are more likely to be smart, just,
efficient, cost-effective, stable, or whatever, according to some external
standards.

My goal in this chapter is not to take a final stance on whether sortition
is superior to elections. Instead, I want to describe how certain voting
techniques borrowed from the epistocracy literature can improve democratic sortition. A political system is epistocratic to the extent that, by law,
political power is apportioned according to political knowledge. I will
argue that we should expect certain forms of epistocracy—in particular,
forms which involve some degree of sortition—to outperform democratic
sortition. Further, these forms of epistocracy are not in decisive ways *less
fair* than democratic sortition and, in ways, are likely to be fairer.
Democratic forms of sortition are likely to have severe epistemic defects.
Further, while a sufficiently large random sample of citizens can ensure
that the voting legislature is demographically identical to the public at
large, this does not overcome the problem of persistent minorities and

majoritarian rule. In contrast, weighted lottery systems in epistocracy can remove demographic bias from the legislature.

1. Is Sortition Democratic and Fair?

Thomas Christiano defines a democracy as "a society in which all or most of the population has the opportunity jointly to play an essential if not always very formative role in the determination of legislation and policy" (Christiano, 1990, p. 151). He elaborates:

> To fix ideas, the term "democracy" [...] refers very generally to a method of group decision making characterized by a kind of equality among the participants at an essential stage of the collective decision making. Four aspects of this definition should be noted. First, democracy concerns collective decision making, by which I mean decisions that are made for groups and that are binding on all the members of the group. Second, this definition means to cover a lot of different kinds of groups that may be called democratic. So, there can be democracy in families, voluntary organizations, economic firms, as well as states and transnational and global organizations. Third, the definition is not intended to carry any normative weight to it. It is quite compatible with this definition of democracy that it is not desirable to have democracy in some particular context. So, the definition of democracy does not settle any normative questions. Fourth, the equality required by the definition of democracy may be more or less deep. It may be the mere formal equality of one-person one-vote in an election for representatives to an assembly where there is competition among candidates for the position. Or it may be more robust, including equality in the processes of deliberation and coalition building. "Democracy" may refer to any of these political arrangements. It may involve direct participation of the members of a society in deciding on the laws and policies of the society or it may involve the participation of those members in selecting representatives to make the decisions. (Christiano, 2006)

Based on this definition, sortition is a form of democracy, not an alternative. One reason to have such an inclusive definition is that ancient Athens, which most consider an early and archetypical instance of democracy (despite it excluding over 80% of members from participation), often used sortition rather than voting (Bouricius, 2013).

Let's consider one possible form of sortition as an illustration. Suppose that, instead of holding elections, a country selected members of parliament through sortition. On Selection Day, instead of Election Day, the government randomly selects four hundred citizens to serve two-year terms in parliament. This system exhibits democratic equality because every citizen has an equal basic political standing. By default, no one has any effective power, but they have equal eligibility and a genuinely equal chance of becoming a member of parliament.

Still, there are good arguments against considering sortition as a form of democracy. Some might insist that democracy requires that all citizens have a voice—an *equal voice*—in politics. Or they might say that democratic systems allow members to exercise equal control over political outcomes. Or they might say that it's essential to democracy that members exert equal control and oversight over any appointed decision-makers. In sortition, the objection could go, most citizens have no such voice, control or oversight. Because appointments are made by lottery, the typical citizen has *no say* at all; only lottery winners acquire power.

However, these arguments make a big deal of the supposed principle that having the vote creates the citizen. In a typical democratic election, an individual's vote has a vanishingly small chance of making a difference. How *we* vote matters, but how an individual votes does not. As an individual, voting with the goal of affecting the outcome of an election is like using a water bucket to stop a tsunami.[1] Democracy does not provide citizens equal slices of power; it's more like equal crumbs. Sure, a person with one crumb has more food than a person with nothing, but we should not make much of that.

Still, the person who insists that sortition is not democratic might respond that, in voting systems, the people *as a whole* have power over decisions, even if individuals do not. However, the insignificance of single votes leads to an empirical result which deflates the power of this objection. Because individual votes matter so little, voting is a collective action problem. Individuals have little incentive to become informed and every incentive to indulge their worst cognitive behaviours, or to use their politics for signalling purposes rather than to support policies which actually further their interests. In fact, empirical research on voter behaviour overwhelmingly finds that most citizens possess very low levels of information, few vote on the basis of ideology and irrational cognitive biases abound.

As Christopher Achen and Larry Bartels conclude, "elections [...] turn out to be largely random events [...]" (Achen and Bartels, 2017, p. 2). According to the realist model of voter behaviour, most citizens do not

---

[1] Barnett (2020) argues otherwise (somewhat), but see Brennan and Freiman (2023) for a response.

vote on the basis of policy. Instead, different identity groups become attached to different political parties for social reasons having little to do with the party's platform. Most voters are innocent of ideology. Of the minority who do espouse an ideology, most simply copy their party's platform. They share the party's platform because they vote for the party; they do not vote for that party because they share its platform (Achen and Bartels, 2017).

Elections *could* be a way that the people as a whole exert control over politics and force politicians to heed their will. But, as a matter of fact, people use their votes for other purposes. For most voters, politics is not about policy.

2. Which Form of Sortition?

"Sortition" is an umbrella concept. Different sortitionists have different ideas in mind about how governments should use sortition. Some of these proposals or ideas are better than others. Consider these questions:

1. Which offices should be chosen by lottery? All? Only some?
2. Are selected office holders required to accept some sort of training before taking their positions?
3. How long should office holders retain their positions?
4. Can office holders be recalled by the public?
5. Are there any checks on the power lottery winners have, such as bills of rights, or other branches of governments?
6. What will the constitution of the state look like? How are decisions made?
7. What is the scope of government power?

How we answer these questions determines what kind of sortition we might have.

A conservative form of sortition involves retaining the existing structure of government, but staffing at least some or all offices through lottery. So, for instance, the United States might retain a presidential system with a bicameral legislature, but have the house, senate and president selected through lot. The UK might have its house of commons and even its prime minister selected through lottery. And so on.

More radically, perhaps even the judiciary or permanent bureaucracy have some or all members chosen through lottery as well. I call this more radical because many accept that the judiciary and bureaucracy are supposed to have professional expertise (in law, regulation and so on) as a prerequisite for their jobs.

Even more radically, some deliberative democrats favour eliminating or reducing the role of the legislature altogether. For instance, they might favour Deliberation Day-style proposals, where randomly selected citizens are brought together to discuss an issue and then write laws governing it (Ackerman and Fishkin, 2004; Landemore, 2020). Or they might favour creating long-term lottery-based deliberative boards of citizens who oversee regulation and law in specific domains (Guerrero, 2024).

This is barely a cursory sketch of the possible forms of sortition. I only want to note that there are many possibilities. If someone raises an objection to sortition, we need to ask whether that objection applies to sortition in general, or rather only to specific forms.

For instance, consider an extreme form of sortition called "queen-for-a-day".[2] Imagine that, each day, the government selects at random a new citizen, who for 24 hours has radical dictatorial power over everything within the government's scope of power. We would expect that this would be a disaster. But that does not mean other forms of sortition would be disasters.

3. Why Sortition? The Fairness Argument

There are two main arguments sortitionists invoke. The first is that sortition is fairer than democracy; the second is that sortition could overcome some of democracy's epistemic defects and perform better.

Let's start with fairness. Democracy is supposed to give each person equal basic political power. But, in all actual democracies, de facto political power is uneven. Rich, educated, well-connected, charismatic and physically attractive people find it easier to gain power than others. Ethnic and religious minorities find it harder to win than members of the majority.

Further, in every democracy, voting rates are unequal among different demographic groups, even when de jure these groups have equal voting rights. For instance, in the US, the old vote at higher rates than the young, the rich at higher rates than the poor, and the employed at higher rates than the unemployed. Advantaged groups often enjoy a higher turnout than less advantaged groups. Many democratic theorists think that an

---

2 Estlund (1997, p. 178) discusses this but rejects it.

unequal turnout results from unequal access: perhaps rich people find it easier to take time off from work to vote. This is one reason why some theorists favour *compulsory voting*; they think forcing the disadvantaged to vote will even up the political playing field (Brennan and Hill, 2014).

Worse, equal voting power might itself result in unfair outcomes. Even if democracy equalises inputs for each person, this might lead to outputs which democrats regard as objectionably unequal. For instance, consider the problem of persistent ideological minorities. As Christiano says:

> This problem is the difficulty of persistent minorities. There is a persistent minority in a democratic society when that minority always loses in the voting. This is always a possibility in democracies because of the use of majority rule. If the society is divided into two or more highly unified voting blocks in which the members of each group votes in the same ways as all the other members of that group, then the group in the minority will find itself always on the losing end of the votes. [...] Though this problem is often connected with majority tyranny it is distinct from the problem of majority tyranny because it may be the case that the majority attempts to treat the minority well, in accordance with its conception of good treat- ment. It is just that the minority never agrees with the majority on what constitutes proper treatment. Being a persistent minority can be highly oppressive even if the majority does not try to act oppressively. This can be understood with the help of the very ideas that underpin democracy. Persons have interests in being able to correct for the cognitive biases of others and to be able to make the world in such a way that it makes sense to them. These interests are set back for a persistent minority since they never get their way. (Christiano, 2006)

Political equality is of little value to persistent minorities. It's true that, as individuals, they have de jure equal power, but given how other people vote, this is equivalent de facto to having no political power at all. What good is having an equal say when you never get an inch of your way?

Note, however, that persistent minorities could have outsized power instead of none. Imagine a society split into three groups, A, B and C. Suppose A and B both constitute 99% of the population. Suppose members vote at equal rates. Suppose A and B are always opposed and will not work together. A and B are thus, on their own, always dead- locked. To win, they each need to form a coalition with C, which only has 1% of the population. Here, C will have disproportionate bargaining power. It can win large concessions from either possible partner, since A and B must compete for C's favour, but C need not compete for theirs.

Consider also how majorities could harm, exploit or ignore minorities even in an egalitarian voting system. Imagine a society is 90% white and 10% black. Imagine that full democratic equality has been achieved, and so no white person has any advantage over any black person in getting to the polls. However, suppose all white people hate all black people, and are thus willing to vote for any policy which harms black people. In this case, given these stipulations, we would expect fair and equal political inputs to produce unfair and unequal results, results that are objectionable from a democratic point of view. Of course, these stipulations are unrealistically extreme. However, weaker versions of this dynamic have appeared in the past and perhaps occur even now in some democracies.

Sortitionists claim that lotteries can overcome some of these problems. Lotteries are random; randomness means there is no inherent bias. A lottery provides no special advantage to the rich, the attractive or the well-connected. If there are 1,000 citizens and 10 seats, every citizen has a 1 in 100 chance of winning a seat, regardless of how educated, pretty, rich or well-networked they are.

Further, sortition reduces the problem of persistent ideological minorities. In a democracy, a voting group that constitutes only 1% of the population might have de facto 0% of the power. Sortition instead gives such members a 1% (proportional) chance of winning power.

However, sortition might not solve all problems. Take the case where opposed groups A and B are equal sized, but much smaller group C is willing to form coalitions with either. If we select a legislature through sortition and we get a representative sample, C will continue to have disproportionate bargaining power. If instead we get a non-representative sample (which is more and more likely the smaller the legislature is), then we might overcome this type of deadlock if, by luck, one side wins disproportionate power. Similarly, sortition cannot be expected to solve the problems which arise from a large majority wanting to crush and exploit a small minority. At best, it might *reduce* such problems if it helps ensure at least some minority members get power.

Still, realistically, sortition will always be more fair than electoral democracy. Getting an unbiased lottery is trivial in the real world, but in the real world, getting de facto equal voting power and equal electoral eligibility to all citizens is impossible. However, fairness and equality are not the only values upon which democracy rests. If they were, the case for sortition over voting would be overwhelming.

Consider: the queen-for-a-day proposal is a fair system. Or, for any issue, we could let each citizen write down their favoured policy on a note card, and then select a card at random to become law. Or we could make decisions in a purely random way, by having a computer list all possible responses and then select one at random. These lottocratic decision-making methods are perfectly fair and equal, but most of us (and most sortitionists) oppose them because the chances of passing disastrous laws or producing disastrous outcomes is too high. This shows that, despite many democratic theorists' rhetoric to the contrary, we care not only about *how* decisions are made, but whether the decisions are *good*.

4. Why Sortition? The Epistemic Argument

This brings us to a second argument for sortition. Many sortitionists claim that certain forms of sortition should produce better outcomes than electoral democracy. Here is a brief summary of their main reasons.

First, they claim that *random selection removes pernicious biases*. Right now, in every electoral democracy, the advantaged tend to have more de facto power than the disadvantaged. The rich vote at higher rates than the poor. The middle-aged vote more than the young. Even if people *intend* to promote justice and are not actively voting for their narrow self-interest, nevertheless, such voters are likely to be ignorant or misinformed about what is good for others. In short, sortitionists claim that the de facto inequality — the de facto demographic biases — we see in real-life democracies leads to flawed results. But, they claim, random selection can be expected to overcome this.

Second, they claim that *reducing the number of decision-makers* will in turn reduce or eliminate the problems of voter ignorance and irrationality. If there are fewer voters, their votes will matter more, and so voters will have an incentive to vote intelligently.

Empirical work finds that most voters lack most basic political information and reason in biased ways. The standard explanation for this behaviour is that voters are responding to perverse incentives. Democracy ensures that their individual votes do not matter and voters behave as such.

By analogy, imagine a professor teaching a giant class of 10,000 students, a class which covers introductory political science, economics, history, criminology, constitutional law and so on. Imagine the professor tells the students that, in 120 days, they will take a final exam worth 100% of their grade. Rather than each student receiving their individual score, he will average all scores together and give each student the same grade. With such perverse incentives, you would expect the class to fail.

5. Problems with the Epistemic Case for Sortition

However, sortitionists face a problem here in determining the optimal number of participants. To illustrate, consider the form of sortition which consists of a legislature with elected representatives, but in which the right to vote in elections is allocated by lottery. Randomly selecting 20,000 citizens to vote more or less guarantees that the electorate is representative of the nation, indeed, more representative than what we get under voluntary voting. However, their individual votes would still barely matter, and so it's unlikely this would reduce problems of ignorance and irrationality much.

One might think, then, that the solution is to have even fewer voters selected by lottery. The smaller the number of voters they select, the more any individual vote matters, and so the greater the incentive to vote intelligently. However, a lower number of voters also makes it less likely that the random sample of voters is demographically equivalent to the population at large. This eliminates one of the supposed benefits of sortition.

Further, making individual votes more efficacious might produce another unhappy result. In general, empirical work shows that voters in large elections vote sociotropically, for what they perceive (perhaps incorrectly) to be in the national interest rather than their narrow self-interest. This sounds surprising, given how selfish most people are, until we remember the incentives. Because my vote counts for so little, it's not in my self-interest to vote for my self-interest. However, some empirical work shows that in special cases where individual voters have a high chance of being decisive, they switch from sociotropic to selfish voting (Feddersen, Gailmard and Sandroni, 2009).

So, sortitionists need to find an optimal number of voters, N, where N is sufficiently large to ensure that random selection does not introduce demographic bias, sufficiently large to ensure voters vote sociotropically rather than selfishly, but also sufficiently small that voters are incentivised to be informed and rational rather than ignorant, misinformed or irrational. It's unclear that there is any such N, even in principle. It might be that our only choices are voters who are nice but dumb or selfish but smart.

Now consider more radical forms of sortition. These also face serious problems. Some sortitionists want randomly selected citizens to choose policy, say by selecting 500 citizens at random, requiring them to deliberate for a weekend over an issue, and then requiring them to write regulations or laws to address it. Others want to use sortition to select long-term boards of citizens to oversee regulatory agencies, or to serve as regulators themselves. Still others think that members of parliament should be selected through lottery.

Here are some worries:

1. The massive scope of government and complexity of the world make it unlikely that randomly selected citizens would have the knowledge needed to make smart decisions on the issues they are appointed to discuss. Many such decisions require specialised knowledge which citizens lack and cannot acquire quickly.
2. If citizens have long-term appointments, they might acquire such knowledge, but then might also then behave much like other long-term bureaucrats or members of the state's professional classes. All organisations face principal-agent problems, where the people inside the organisation use the resources and power of that organisation for their own personal goals rather than the organisation's putative goals. A person with, say, a two-year appointment faces these perverse incentives regardless of whether they were hired or appointed by lot.
3. If citizens are supposed to acquire knowledge through some sort of training or deliberation overseen by expert facilitators, then this training and deliberation is likely to suffer from various biases, as special interest groups and others compete to control what training materials citizens receive, who monitors and guides discussions, what the agenda is and so on. In the real world, interest groups will compete and are likely to succeed in controlling the agenda of Deliberation Days and citizens' councils.
4. Whether deliberation "works" in the first place—for instance, whether citizens learn from each other or instead react by polarising—is itself an open question.

I do not intend these to be fatal worries. The reality is that sortitionists are forced to engage in informed speculation. They are responding to problems with real-world democracy with which we have great experience by proposing alternative institutions with which we have little or no real-world experience. They recognise that most new arrangements have intended and unexpected consequences, and so we won't know whether sortition works better unless we try it and see.

6. Epistocracy

A political system is epistocratic to the extent that greater knowledge is a legal prerequisite for holding power or there are legal grounds for being granted greater power through law. Just as there are many different forms of democracy, there are many possible forms of epistocracy. Some are more defensible than others. These include:

1. *Values-only voting*: citizens are allowed to vote on the *ends* of government, but not on the *means* (Christiano, 1996).
2. *Epistocratic veto*: laws are passed through normal democratic means, through an elected representative legislature or direct democracy with universal suffrage. However, an epistocratic council of some kind (perhaps constituted by appointed experts, or perhaps made up only of citizens who can pass a rigorous test of basic political information) retains the right to *veto* demo-cratically passed legislation, though it cannot pass laws on its own. Perhaps the democratic legislature can overturn the veto with a supermajority (Caplan, 2007; Bell, 2015).
3. *Plural voting*: all citizens have one vote, but some citizens, perhaps those with superior educational credentials or those who can pass a political competence exam, are given additional votes (Mulligan, 2018).
4. *Restricted suffrage*: by default, no citizens have the right to vote. However, those who can pass a political competence exam or who obtain certain educational credentials can acquire a right to vote (Brennan, 2011).
5. *Enfranchisement lottery*: immediately before the election, thousands of citizens are selected, via a random lottery, to become pre-voters. These pre-voters may then earn the right to vote, but only if they first participate in and *pass* certain competence-building exercises (López-Guerra, 2014).
6. *Enlightened preference voting*: every citizen may vote. When citizens vote, they (a) indicate their policy preferences or their preferred political outcomes, while (b) indicating their demographic information, and (c) taking a test of basic political knowledge. The government then uses data sets a, b and c to determine, statistically, what a fully-informed electorate would want, while correcting for the influence of race, income, sex and/or other demographic factors on the vote. In short, government-by-

simulated-oracle estimates what a demographically *identical* but *fully-informed* electorate would want, and then implements that instead of what the uninformed electorate in fact wants (Brennan, 2016).

At first glance, one might think that only the enfranchisement lottery is of interest here, as it's the only one which explicitly mentions sortition. However, in previous work, I've defended the idea that the "competence exam" described in forms 2–6 should be written by ordinary citizens who are selected by sortition.

To illustrate, consider enlightened preference voting. In this system, on Election Day, everyone gets to vote as an equal. However, when they participate, they do not merely vote for a candidate, party or position on a referendum. Rather, they have to do three things:

1. Tell us who they are, by indicating their demographic information, such as sex, gender identity, income level, ethnicity, employment status and so on.
2. Tell us what they want, e.g. which candidate or party they support in an election, or which position they support in a referendum.
3. Tell us what they know. Citizens take, say, a 30-question quiz of basic political information.

This test of knowledge is *not* used to determine who may vote. Rather, once we have all three sets of data, the data is anonymised and released into the public domain. A government electoral commission then uses the data to estimate, using existing statistical methods, what the public *would have wanted* if it were demographically identical but had achieved a perfect score in the knowledge test. This result—the public's enlightened preference—is then instantiated. Since the data is public, the government's calculations can easily be verified or challenged. In short, enlightened preference voting is a statistical method which allows us to estimate what a demographically identical but fully informed public would have wanted.

Who gets to write the test is the most common question asked about this proposal. I suggest that a month or so before the election occurs, we randomly select, say, 500 citizens. We pay them to deliberate and design the 30-question battery of questions.

This might seem like a paradoxical view: if I think citizens are so ignorant and misinformed, why would I want a democratic council to write the test? But, on further inspection, it's not paradoxical. Voters know which *questions* should be on the exam, even if they don't know the answers. They understand that informed voters should know things such as what laws were passed, which candidate is incumbent, how the government functions and so on, even though they don't themselves know these things. In the same way, the average person knows a doctor should know anatomy even though this average person doesn't know much anatomy themselves. As a group, voters can deliver a reasonable account of political competence despite not being competent themselves.

7. The Enfranchisement Lottery

Claudio López-Guerra defends an epistocratic system he calls the "enfranchisement lottery":

> The enfranchisement lottery consists of two devices. First, there would be a sortition to disenfranchise the vast majority of the population. Prior to every election, all but a random sample of the public would be excluded. I call this device the *exclusionary sortition* because it merely tells us who will *not* be entitled to vote in a given contest. Indeed, those who survive the sortition (the *pre-voters*) would not be automatically enfranchised. Like everyone in the larger group from which they are drawn, pre-voters would be assumed to be insufficiently competent to vote. This is where the second device comes in. To finally become enfranchised and vote, pre-voters would gather in relatively small groups to participate in a *competence-building process* carefully designed to optimize their knowledge about the alternatives on the ballot. (López-Guerra, 2014, p. 4)

In López-Guerra's scheme, everyone has equal *eligibility* to become a voter. Before the enfranchisement lottery takes place, candidates would proceed with their campaigns as they do in democracy. However, they campaign without knowing which citizens in particular will eventually acquire the right to vote. Immediately before the election, a random but representative subset of citizens is then selected by lottery.

These citizens are not automatically granted the right to vote. If they were, then arguably this would remain a democratic rather than episto-cratic form of sortition. Instead, the chosen citizens merely acquire permission to *earn* the right to vote. To earn this right, they need pass a competence-building exercise. López-Guerra suggests that, to earn the right to vote, these "pre-voters" will be required to participate in various deliberative fora with one another, study party platforms and the like. In order to ensure that voters can succeed in this task, he proposes they be granted paid time off from work and other forms of support.

Lopez-Guerra's proposal is thus, from an epistemic standpoint, likely to be superior to more democratic forms of sortition. Random selection *helps* but is not enough. Further, Lopez-Guerra admits many of the problems I mentioned above (agenda control, etc.) would remain, but his response is that an enfranchisement lottery need not be perfect, only *better*.

8. Using the Enlightened Preference Method to Debias Democracy

A putative goal of sortition is to remove demographic bias from democratic elections. As we saw, though, there are some serious worries about whether we can find some optimal number of voters N which is sufficiently large to ensure demographic matching, sufficiently small to incentivise voters to avoid ignorance and irrationality, but not so small that voters vote selfishly. We do not know if any such N exists in principle.

Another possible way to reduce improper biases could be to used enlightened preference voting to simulate what actual voters *would have wanted* if they were *demographically identical* to the actual eligible voting public. I call this "demographic matching". According to this system, instead of using sortition to determine who may vote, we let everyone vote, knowing we will have an uneven turnout. However, when voters vote, they both (A) indicate what they want (by selecting their choices from the ballot) and then (B) register their demographic information. I leave open which demographic categories should be measured and considered, in part because this will vary from country to country and time to time. The data from A and B can be made anonymous and released to the public. With this public data, it is then possible to estimate what the public *would have* supported if various demographic biases or disparities in voter turnout vanished. Governments could then implement this instead.

For instance, suppose there are two candidates, A and B. Suppose rich people prefer A and poor people prefer B. If we simply hold the election without demographic matching, then suppose A would win. But this result might not reflect the underlying overall preferences of the people; it would instead reflect the bias from higher turnout among the rich. Demographic matching can overcome or at least reduce this problem. We can simulate what would have happened if rich and poor had voted at rates proportional to their population. If B *would have won* under the demographic matching method, then B in fact wins.

Note that introducing such changes can have radical effects. The number and kinds of political parties there are, which candidates the parties run, and what the platforms the parties espouse are not exogenous variables in electoral systems. Parties and candidates want to win, and so they modify their platforms, select candidates and run their campaign strategies in response to the kind of voting system in place, what the voters want and what the expected turnout will be. If parties know demographic matching will occur, they will run different candidates and different platforms. In that way, demographic matching might significantly improve democratic outcomes.

9. Realising the Veil of Ignorance

Demographic matching reduces racial, age, income or other demographic biases introduced by differential turnout. However, it does not eliminate all such biases. It may even reinforce some.

Consider again the hypothetical example from above. Suppose 90% of voters are white and 10% black. Suppose all white voters are deeply prejudiced against blacks, and will actively support candidates who promise to harm black interests. This was an extreme hypothetical example, but weaker versions of this problem remain in place. Demographic matching might reduce, say, white dominance in the Australian elections, but whites are nevertheless the largest ethnic group. Even if, optimistically, whites do not intend to push policies detrimental to non-whites, they might nevertheless do so, in part because their different life experiences and epistemic standpoints cause them to overlook or misunderstand minority interests.

John Rawls famously argued for a procedural mechanism to select the principles of justice to govern the basic structure of society. He said that justice consists of whatever principles properly situated parties would select for themselves under fair and equal bargaining procedures. To ensure that the parties had to choose for everyone, rather than themselves more narrowly, he placed parties behind a "veil of ignorance". Parties had to choose principles which they believe would best support their interests, but they were made ignorant of their own race, gender, income level, employment status, religion, conception of the good and more. Further, they were forbidden from knowing what percentage of society would fall into each category. This prevents the parties from, say, deciding to exploit a tiny ethnic minority because they think they are statistically unlikely to be members of that minority group (Rawls, 1971).

The worries that lead Rawls to defend the veil of ignorance apply to real-life democracies. Even with proportional turnout or demographic matching, we reasonably worry that the electoral results could reflect unjust biases or differences in demographic size that are arbitrary from a moral point of view.

Accordingly, instead of engaging in demographic matching, a polity might do something more radical. On election day, citizens again (A) vote for what they want, and (B) indicate their demographic categories. The data is again anonymised and released, so that any qualified statistician can check the results. This time, though, the government calculates what the polity would have selected behind a veil of ignorance. We measure and then *erase* the independent effect various demographic variables — such as income, employment status, race, gender and so on — have on the overall electoral outcome. We can calculate and then implement what the public would have wanted if it were placed behind the veil of ignorance.

Again, in real-life democracies, which parties, questions and candidates appear on the ballot, and which platforms parties espouse, are to a significant degree dependent upon the kind of voting system in place. In a democracy with "veil of ignorance voting", this will not merely create a post-hoc corrective to racial bias but will discipline parties and candidates (who want to win) to push for different and potentially superior policies.

10. Hypothetical Electorates and Standpoint Epistemology

While veil of ignorance voting can overcome certain problems demographic matching cannot, it might also introduce certain problems. One worry is that erasing the effect of various demographic identities on voting behaviour does not simply erase *bias* or *advantage*, but also erases *information*. For instance, recent advances in standpoint epistemology argue that members of certain groups might possess various epistemic advantages deriving from their experiences (Mills, 2017). They might recognise patterns of behaviour, including patterns of oppression, which are not apparent to members of other groups. As a result, members of such groups might develop policy preferences which reflect their differential and, indeed in this respect, superior epistemic standpoint.

Veil of ignorance voting measures and then erases all differences in ballot preference which result from voters' underlying demographic differences. As a statistical method, it simulates what a public *would* choose if the public were ignorant of their own demographic identities and ignorant of the distribution of such identities. While veil of ignorance voting erases certain biases, it might also erase certain strands of superior knowledge.

Thus, another method — which might be used as a supplement to the other two — would be to calculate what hypothetical electorates of different demographic composition would support. For instance, suppose there is a ballot initiative concerning police reform. Ample empirical work already suggests that police treat ethnic minorities far worse than they treat advantaged majorities. It may be that, under veil of ignorance voting, the hypothetical identity-less public would pick choice A. But suppose we calculate that a hypothetical minority-only electorate would prefer B. In this case, this strongly suggests the veil of ignorance erases valid forms of knowledge instead of merely erasing improper bias and morally arbitrary differentials in power. Accordingly, we might use a hypothetical electorate method as a check on either demographic matching or veil of ignorance voting.

11. Institutionalizing Debiased Democracy

Debiasing democracy in the abstract is easier than debiasing it in practice. Real-life democracies are subject to all sorts of abuse. Politicians rig voting systems and voting districts to favour their parties. Laws limiting advertising and spending are sometimes tweaked to the benefit of incumbents. Rent seeking is common.

Presumably, were a real-life democracy to instantiate any of these three debiasing devices, self-interested politicians, administrators and special interest groups might try to rig them for their own benefit. For instance, suppose demographic identification is voluntary: each time someone votes, they check a box indicating their race or gender. We can imagine, say, a conservative talk radio host enjoining his large white audience to lie about their demographics in order to spoil or influence the outcome. "The left is trying to *inflate* blacks' votes, so you should lie and say you're black."

One possible response is to say that voters must pre-register their demographics and may be subject to auditing. Of course, this introduces its own problems and dangers. What if, for example, many citizens sincerely believe themselves to belong to a particular group, but the auditor disagrees?

While these are significant worries, we note some reasons to be optimistic that such abuse will not be rampant. For one, while Census and other government surveys affect the distribution of government funding and spending, including aid and investment programmes targeted toward certain demographic groups, there is not strong evidence of widespread or even significant fraud or deception of this kind. Further, many universities aim to create a diverse student body in some way representative of society at large, but we do not see widespread student deception, e.g. with students lying about their demographics to rig the admissions process.

Another serious worry concerns information rather than motivation. *Which* demographic categories matter? How fine-grained should they be? For instance, should "white" be a category, or should whiteness be decomposed into finer ethnic categories? When we try to correct for income effects, how fine-grained should the income categories be? What if it turns out that composite identities, such as "Southern white evangelical" have strong effects on voter behaviour, but the individual components of that identity have little independent effect?

These are largely empirical issues. They will vary from society to society but also time to time. How people see themselves affects their behaviour, but which categories are salient is largely a social construct in flux. For instance, it's plausible that being of Irish or English descent mattered more in the US in 1853 than in does in 2023.

We cannot offer a formula for solving this problem. We note, though, that identical versions of this problem exist for every other government or non-government programme that is based on demographics. Government health organisations tasked with studying, preventing and curing disease must make decisions about which demographic categories to use. Similar remarks apply to government educational or housing agencies. They face the same puzzle: in order to assess how much various demographic categories matter, they must first choose and measure categories. However vexing this problem is, few recommend that governments simply stop trying to use demographics in decision-making. For instance, governments need to know whether COVID-19 has differential effects on different races, sexes or income-levels in order to develop proper treatment and containment strategies. In short, when it is difficult to know which differences matter, that does not usually tell us to pretend everyone is the same.

Presumably, then, the problems our proposal faces can be solved, as best they can, with the same kinds of methods used for these other problems. It may take a mixture of both expert and democratic oversight. We might want to use deliberative polling or other democratic techniques. There may be other superior mechanisms.

Overall, though, the issue is not whether epistocratic sortition, demographic matching, veil of ignorance voting or hypothetical electorate voting methods will be perfect or free of problems. Of course not. Rather, the issue is whether, all things considered, they will perform *better* than our current, highly biased systems, and perform better than simple sortition. The issue is: which system, warts and all, will produce the most just outcomes, do the best job respecting and protecting people's liberal freedoms, be the most stable, contribute most to growth and prosperity, and ensure the most fair and unbiased outcomes.

Part II

Sortition and Representation

Clarisse Van Belleghem

Inclusion or Representation?

Questioning the Argumentative Grounds of Random Selection for Deliberative Assemblies

Abstract: *This chapter examines the main argumentative grounds mobilised in the literature on deliberative assemblies drawn by lot. The proponents of these assemblies often present them as the source of a fairer and more democratic deliberation, either for their inclusive or for their representative virtues, without it always being clear what forms of representativeness and inclusiveness are meant. The chapter starts by differentiating the claims of inclusiveness for deliberative assemblies. The supposedly more egalitarian property of sortition is being questioned, as Annabelle Lever and Chiara Destri suggest in their chapter. The inclusiveness understood as cognitive diversity is also questioned, in line with the analysis provided by Jessy Bailly, also in this book. This chapter explores the capacity of deliberative assemblies to respond to the deliberative requirement of inclusion of all points of view – a question largely addressed in Stefan Rummens and Ralph Geenens's chapter. The contribution then addresses the representativeness claimed for deliberative assemblies, which is mainly descriptive. The author argues that this type of representation is not without its problems in terms of the democratic legitimacy of the representatives. The author then argues, as does Didier Mineur, that the socio-demographic categories used cannot claim to reflect the diversity of political views within society. More generally, the chapter seeks to highlight the lack of solid theoretical foundations for legitimising deliberative assemblies in terms of theories of political representation and democratic deliberation.*

For more than twenty years, many democratic innovations have been conducted around the globe. In recent years, we have witnessed a "deliberative turn" in this field (Blondiaux and Manin, 2021), emphasising citizen deliberative processes. Many actors coming from the academic and political world, as well as the public at large, are supporting these deliberative forums. Because they attempt to give more voice to the citizens within the public policy process, the supporters of these experiments often present them as an essential source of empowerment for our democratic systems, restoring the bond of trust between citizens and politicians.

This ambitious objective has been translated in recent years through various evolutions and experimentations from deliberative polls with an advisory role (Fishkin, 2009) to mini-publics such as the G1000 in Belgium or the Irish Constitutional Convention in Ireland. Deliberative assemblies are also envisaged in bicameral systems to complement and control the legislative chambers (O'Leary, 2006; Gastil and Wright, 2018; Owen and Smith, 2018; Vandamme 2019). More recently, deliberative assemblies have been moving in the direction of increasing institutionalisation and empowerment, as recently illustrated in Belgium by the establishment of mixed deliberative commissions composed of elected members and citizens drawn by lot in the regional parliaments of Brussels-Capital, and a "Permanent Citizen Dialogue" in the German-speaking part of the country (known internationally as the *Ostbelgien Modell*) (Niessen and Reuchamps, 2019). A growing body of literature supports a more direct role for these assemblies (Sintomer, 2018). Various formulations exist along these lines, from experiments in law reform (Warren and Pearse, 2008) to constitutional review (Reuchamps and Suiter, 2016). Some authors go even further and argue that democracy can do without elections and rely exclusively on deliberative assemblies to make political decisions (Guerrero, 2014; Van Reybrouck, 2016; Landemore, 2020).

Deliberative assemblies are composed of citizens, usually drawn by lot, initiated to deliberate on specific policies. The increasing popularity of deliberative forums, and their potentially significant political role, incites us to consider their conceptual grounds rigorously. Proponents of these experiments often enumerate the various properties of sortition to justify them. Among these is the claim that they produce a better democratic quality of discussion. However, the conceptual references used to make these arguments sometimes need clarification. For example, arguments for inclusiveness or representativeness often come up without it being clear what inclusion and representation mean and what their implications are. To prevent confusion between these lines of argument, the different claims about random selection should be more explicit.

This contribution aims to clarify the entanglement of concepts mobilised in the literature on deliberative assemblies by distinguishing their different pretensions and formulating some reflections to nuance the scope of these arguments. The point here is not to put these mechanisms on trial but to contribute to a critical and constructive analysis of their democratic claims: on what grounds are they inclusive or representative? And what can we say about this from a theoretical perspective as we look at the theories of political representation and democratic deliberation that underpin these proposals? In what follows, I will distinguish three argumentative registers on deliberative assemblies (epistemic properties, inclusion and representation) in order to see how they are related in the argumentation.

1. The Benefits of Random Selection for the Deliberation

One of the main arguments for promoting deliberative assemblies as an interesting complement or alternative to more traditional political processes is the superior epistemic quality of their results. The use of random selection as a mode of designation of participants would improve the quality of deliberation according to two main arguments generally put forward: on the one hand, sortition would have the advantage of designating citizens who are more politically disinterested and less corruptible than those established by our traditional elective system. The citizens drawn by lot, not being preoccupied with their future re-election and not being bound to respect a specific political line, would be less likely to defend particular interests and would be more predisposed to listen to divergent arguments and thus also to see their opinions change. Therefore, they would be more impartial (Sintomer, 2018, p. 352) and more inclined to a deliberative attitude (Vandamme, 2018, p. 4). The second argument mobilised is the more significant epistemic diversity made possible by sortition. By selecting any citizen and exempting itself from any selection criterion, random selection allows the deliberative process to have a social and cognitive diversity that would be much more difficult to obtain via the elective process. This epistemic diversity is valued as favouring a more rational and fairer deliberation because of greater informational diversity and a better consideration of the different existing social perspectives (Landemore, 2013).

These arguments (impartiality and cognitive diversity) belong to the tradition of the deliberative theory that emerged at the turn of the century. Deliberative theorists, including authors such as Jane Mansbridge, Jürgen Habermas, Bernard Manin, John Rawls and more recently Simone Chambers, Stefan Rummens, Loïc Blondiaux and Charles Girard, maintain that democracy cannot be satisfied with a system that is merely representative of the aggregate of individual preferences, but that it is necessary to find a system in which these different preferences can be confronted and tested by the discussion process in order to reach a decision that is more well-reasoned and oriented towards the common good. Democracy is, therefore, not a matter of a fair representation of the willingness of all, but of the general interest, which results only from the confrontation of points of view through dialogue. This school of thought maintains that deliberation, as a rational, discursive process reflecting universal reason, does not require a specific representation (statistical or majority) of citizens. It needs only to be collective, which means that all the existing points of view have been heard and defended within the discussion.

This last point could be one of the most problematic elements within the argumentation about deliberative assemblies and the use of sortition. Apart from the fact that the epistemic arguments we have mentioned may be a matter of debate (can we guarantee that citizens designated by lot are more disinterested and less corruptible than elected officials, knowing that it is primarily self-interested individuals who take part in deliberative processes and that these, although anonymous, can also be carriers of partisan or particular interests?), it remains that these arguments only refer to the enhancement of the quality of the discussion. They do not guarantee that drawn assemblies are inclusive and egalitarian in themselves. To do so, it would be necessary to ensure that all social perspectives could be considered and heard in the deliberation process. To that end, we can find some arguments in the literature that seek to value these experiments as capable of expressing the citizens' expectations on a small scale and in a regulated framework. Therefore, there is a shift in the argumentation, which no longer focuses on the epistemic qualities of the sortition but valorises the panels as being intrinsically inclusive and representative. In what follows, I try to identify these different forms of justification and interrogate them from a theoretical perspective.

2. More Inclusive Assemblies?

Proponents of deliberative assemblies frequently use the notion of inclusivity as a key criterion to justify the democratic character of the deliberation (Gastil and Wright, 2018, p. 6; Caluwaerts and Reuchamps, 2012; 2015; 2018). However, there are many ways of arguing that an entity is "inclusive" in a democratic sense. Indeed, inclusion can refer to the better inclusion of something (citizens, cognitive diversity) but can also signify a requirement of exhaustiveness (inclusion of all citizens or all existing points of view within society). Therefore, inclusiveness can be related to greater epistemic inclusion, but, here again, different meanings are possible: one may value the fact that different perspectives existing within society are included in the process and that these improve the deliberation's quality. But deliberative processes can also be described as more inclusive because they promote the participation of marginalised people. Second, inclusiveness can also refer to the principle of equal participation of individuals in the deliberative process. Promoters of deliberative assemblies describe random selection as particularly inclusive for two reasons: first, because this mode of selection does not restrict the designation to anyone in particular, and second, because it grants an equal chance to citizens to take part in the deliberative process (O'Flynn and Sood, 2014, p. 43). From this perspective, sortition is presented as particularly inclusive because it allows ordinary citizens to participate in the debate.

In this regard, Dominique Leydet (2019) wonders if this political equality, understood as an *equal probability* of participation, is not sometimes confused with *equality of participation*. This confusion would be possible because of the random selection process, which ideologically induces a series of elements. Sortition is associated with a remarkably egalitarian mode of designation because, unlike elections, it does not require that individuals possess certain qualities or resources to be selected. This mode of appointment considers all individuals equally for participation. As the French philosopher Jacques Rancière would express it, sortition is the only genuinely democratic appointment process because it recalls the very principle of democracy: that power to govern cannot suffer from any rules or criteria (Rancière, 2009b). It is always fundamentally anyone's power. In this way, sortition restores the ideal of an equal distribution of political competencies and recognises citizens as the *locus* of politics. Therefore, it gives, in a symbolic way, power back to the people.

According to Leydet, the inclusiveness of sortition as *equality of chances* to participate should not be confused with equality of participation:

> [...] equality of opportunity supposes that everyone is provided with the opportunity to secure the desired position. Sortition does not aim to realise that form of equality: it is not the case that all those who have the willingness to achieve a certain position or to participate in a given process will have the opportunity to do so, formally or substantively. Access depends on the luck of the draw. Unlucky individuals have no possibility to participate even if they would have wanted to, given the opportunity (Brown, 2006, 212–213). Participation, to use Lynn Sanders' (2010) words, is "by invitation only". (Leydet, 2019, p. 352)

Sortition is often associated with Athenian direct democracy because in the ancient city this mechanism effectively operated within a system that allowed for the democratic inclusion of all citizens. This inclusion was made possible because of a system of rapid rotation of political offices. The number of citizens was limited, so every citizen was assigned a political office at least once a year (Sintomer, 2018). In contrast, current deliberative arrangements cannot claim this form of direct participation as recent deliberative events are few and the number of citizens is too large. The previous considerations suggest that the equality of opportunity made possible by random selection is primarily formal and should not be confused with other forms of political equality, such as equal participation.

Referring to the principle that "every person who can be affected by a political decision should theoretically be involved in the decision-making process in question" (Caluwaerts and Reuchamps, 2018, p. 67), some authors argue that the deliberation process must include the *diversity of perspectives* existing on a policy to achieve this goal.[1] Besides this conception, others understand the notion of democratic inclusiveness as the inclusion of an *epistemic diversity* that matters for the quality improvement of the deliberation. These authors add that epistemic inclusivity within

---

[1] In their book discussing the legitimacy of citizens' assemblies and more specifically the experience of the G1000 in Belgium, these authors recognise that the demographic diversity of the panel favoured by random selection cannot be sufficient to reflect all perspectives on a specific policy. The authors suggest various possibilities for increasing the panel's "ideational comprehensiveness": for example, through the distribution, prior to the deliberation, of informative booklets containing all the arguments "for" and "against" a given political subject, or through the inclusion of experts of all kinds (Caluwaerts and Reuchamps, 2018, pp. 68–9).

the deliberative assemblies is more likely to produce "smarter" results than less inclusive ones. These last considerations reveal how ambiguous the notion of inclusion can be. Understanding this ambiguity immediately exposes some of the misleading aspects of this literature. The following section explores the connections between the arguments favouring inclusion and the pretensions of representation present in deliberative assemblies, along with the potential confusion those associations can cause.

3. More Representative?

Theorists of citizen forums all defend forms of representativeness in the composition of these deliberative arenas. Their claims regarding the representativeness of these assemblies, however, are many and varied.

Some of them (Fishkin, 2009; Courant, 2019; Gastil and Wright, 2018) advocate the "statistical" representativeness of the assemblies drawn by lot. They defend the idea that emerged in the 1930s with opinion polls, according to which it is possible to form groups of citizens that are representative of the population according to statistical standards. Through an equitable and cross-sectional distribution of the main socio-demographic characteristics, in terms of social class, age, gender, etc. sortition would thus be able to select a microcosm of the population, a sort of "mirror" reflection of the *demos*. From this point of view, such a group of citizens would be statistically representative because it would contain the same percentage of men, women and minorities as would be found in society.

Among the proponents of statistical representation, there is sometimes confusion between the principle of inclusion as a principle of *quod omnes tangit*, which establishes that everyone must be able to feel included in the decision process, and the representation of the whole. For instance, in Gastil and Wright's 2018 article on the possibility of a second legislative chamber drawn by lot, we can read:

> The first principle is inclusion, which requires that a democracy make every effort to include all the persons within a political unit, save those who are transient (e.g., non-residents and tourists) or incapable of representing their own interests (e.g., children and the most severely mentally ill). For our legislative design, this principle means that the body's membership should be as representative of the citizenry as possible. Representational legitimacy hinges on meeting this criterion. (Gastil and Wright, 2018, p. 308)

There is an equation here between the representativeness of the panel and its inclusiveness. The confusion consists in affirming that the representativeness of the group allows the (virtual) inclusion of any citizen within the deliberation. There is no concrete evidence, however, that every citizen's interests and political views would be represented in these panels if they were judged solely on the basis of their statistical representativeness.

Some authors, such as Dimitri Courant, add that the representativeness obtained through random selection finds its legitimacy in other resources that most theorists would not have understood (Courant, 2019, p. 242). They argue for legitimacy by "similarity": the social diversity obtained within the panels allows the represented citizens to feel "closer" to their representatives. This "feeling" of legitimacy would constitute the expected value of these assemblies.

In general, theorists who support these probabilistic conceptions of representation are more supportive of direct decision-making roles for deliberative assemblies because they estimate that these microcosms can reflect the aspirations of the whole. However, some proponents of random selection do not claim to obtain this type of representativeness of the whole as it can easily appear out of reach, especially in the case of limited samples of citizens. For this reason, they are more concerned with obtaining representativeness understood in terms of diversity and epistemic inclusion (Leydet, 2019, p. 355), using quota and stratified sampling techniques. The representativeness envisaged here does not consist in representing the entire society (inclusion of all) in the manner of a socio-demographic "screenshot", but rather in ensuring that all possible opinions on a given subject can be taken into account (Caluwaerts and Reuchamps, 2012; Devillers, Vrydagh, Caluwaerts and Reuchamps, 2020, p. 151). The promoters of this conception generally request that they operate in an advisory role, primarily on the grounds of their cognitive diversity.

The same kind of confusion between epistemic diversity within the panel and inclusiveness as the exhaustive inclusion of all points of view is present among the promoters of "cognitive diversity". As Caluwaerts and Reuchamps' 2015 contribution on the issue of the legitimacy of deliberative assemblies stated:

> [...] As such, in order to make citizen deliberation viable, it is usually scaled down to a mini-public, taking into account that the participants are in some way representative of the larger population. For this selection process, forms of descriptive representation through random sampling are

considered to be ideal (Landemore, 2012), because they offer each citizen an equal chance of being part of the mini-public, and they increase cognitive diversity. Rather than being selectionistic and choosing only the most able citizens, deliberative organizers should include an epistemically diverse set of participants (Page, 2007). This allows for a thorough process of argumentation in which all public positions are represented, which eventually leads to more legitimate decisions (Thompson, 2008). After all, only when all ideas are heard, can the best idea be identified. (Caluwaerts and Reuchamps, 2015, pp. 153–4)

In this quote, descriptive representation is promoted as increasing cognitive diversity, but then this cognitive *diversity* is assimilated with the inclusiveness of "all public positions". However, this creates confusion about the notion of inclusiveness since the epistemic inclusion of cognitive diversity does not mean including all the existing points of views about one particular question.

Furthermore, it is sometimes difficult to understand the real added value of this epistemic diversity. Some researchers limit themselves to describing epistemic diversity as a *sine qua non* condition for genuinely democratic and inclusive deliberation without further questioning the plausibility of this inclusiveness (can it be guaranteed? How do we define this diversity in the selection?). In contrast, others place greater emphasis on the epistemic properties of this diversity. According to the latter, cognitive diversity would increase the overall quality of the decisions. These authors generally refer to empirical experiments showing that cognitive diversity facilitates the resolution of complex problems better than deliberation among experts. According to them, the quality of discussion would be much better in a representative sample drawn by lot than in an elected assembly (Landemore, 2012; 2013, p. 1210). In other words, it is more likely that the results of deliberation from a randomly drawn assembly would be directed towards the general interest and would avoid the shortcomings of the argumentative process (interests, partisanship, ideological posturing) within elected bodies.

Beyond the fact that some criticisms are formulated against these alleged epistemic qualities (see the contributions of Keith Sutherland and Alex Kovner in this book), it remains that these authors should distinguish between the better epistemic conditions of deliberation and the better political representation of interests. From a procedural perspective, the alleged "greater reliability" of the results for the deliberative assemblies still does not guarantee that these deliberative processes are democratically inclusive, in the sense that each citizen can feel that his or her point of view has been taken into account in the deliberation process. As we shall see below, the question remains as to how, from a more systemic perspective, the recommendations made by deliberative assemblies can contribute to improving the quality of public deliberation.

4. The Problem of Descriptive Representation

Most proposals on deliberative assemblies have in common the fact that they all claim, in some way, the possibility of representing the political interests of citizens through a descriptive representation based on socioeconomic categories. However, this approach that makes essentially descriptive criteria the vehicle of political representation needs to be revised. Does selection according to socio-demographic criteria guarantee the inclusion of the diversity of political opinions? Can a purely descriptive form of representation act as a substitute for the political interests of the citizens?

If we refer to the theory of representation, this last proposition raises several problems. According to the supporters of collective representation, the descriptive representation of randomly drawn assemblies would give citizens the impression that there are "at least some individuals on the panel who will represent their interests". Parkinson describes this argument as a "slippage" between representation in the statistical sense and representation in the principal-agent conception (Parkinson, 2006, p. 79). Indeed, there is no evidence of a necessary link between the descriptive representation of a social group and a better representation of political interests. This is notably what some theorists argue in their research. Carol Swain studied the impact of descriptive representation on the interests of the people represented. She has shown that the increased presence of African American figures in the House does not necessarily lead to increased advocacy for African American causes (Swain, 1993). In sum, sortition designates individuals who hold particular political opinions, but these do not *necessarily* have any connection with the various social categories to which they belong. This suggests that it is difficult to assume that all existing opinions on certain political regards can be included via a sociological representation of the individuals.

The problem with the descriptive approach resulting from sortition is that it only represents the persons in a symbolic and theoretical way and that there is no possibility of affirming that a representative will act in the interest of the persons he represents (attributional representation). Parkinson also agrees with this point, stating that random selection only allows for the *representativeness* of the panel but not for representation in the political sense of the term (Parkinson, 2006, p. 79). Sortition thus allows for some kind of representation, but it is not strictly political. A model involving a principal-agent relation (such as that obtained through the elective process) allows agents to demand that representatives pursue the interests of those who elected them in their actions. The relationship of accountability of representatives for their behaviour can only be made possible by this type of relationship. In the case of *active* representation, therefore, representatives do not in any way need to reflect the identity of their constituents: they must only be able to reflect their interests (Griffiths and Wollheim, 1960; Pitkin, 1967).

Even if the descriptive representation succeeded in gathering citizens representing all the current political interests in society, such a descriptive representation would not guarantee that political interests would be defended during the deliberation. Indeed, citizens who did not participate in the discussion could not know whether their views had been supported and could not hold their representatives accountable for defending their interests. This is problematic in terms of the systemic legitimacy of these assemblies. The lack of visibility of the debate prevents the mechanisms from being sources of democratic reinforcement of the public debate by not allowing the rest of the citizens to appropriate the questions and issues at stake. From this point of view, citizens would thus feel that they were excluded from the sphere of public deliberation at large (Pourtois, 2013; Rummens, 2016). This seems to be the most fundamental problem facing proponents of deliberative assemblies. Some more critical authors (Chambers, 2009; Rummens, 2016; Girard, 2021; Blondiaux and Manin, 2021) regret the fact that, with these assemblies, mass deliberation is set aside. In the end, citizens drawn by lot only may appear as nothing less than a new form of "participative elitism" because the rest of the population is not allowed to identify the arguments and the interests supported by those citizens.

It follows from the above that deliberative assemblies do not resolve the tension between the ideal of well-reasoned deliberation and the inclusion of the largest number of citizens in public deliberation because a truly inclusive deliberation presupposes that all citizens should be able to develop their views on the policy discussed.

4. Conclusion

The new procedures of citizen deliberation are today experiencing the equivalent of a great plebiscite. There is no doubt that the mobilisation of certain words (participatory, representative, inclusive, citizen empowerment) plays a preponderant role in this respect, along with the references to the image of the Athenian democratic use of sortition. All of this can contribute to the foundation of a powerful ideology concerning these democratic innovations. However, this chapter shows that the argumentative grounds mobilised for these assemblies are still too weak and wavering. Moreover, important issues can appear concerning their compatibility with theories of democratic representation and deliberation: what is the value of deliberative assemblies if the discussions within them cannot be representative or inclusive of all citizens' interests in any way? Can different considerations be made depending on the nature of the issues these assemblies address and the scale at which they take place? The arguments around inclusiveness and representativeness within the literature on deliberative assemblies are generally either mobilised to combine some ideals (i.e. the ideal of the deliberation and participation of all) or just listed one after another to densify the argument. However, even if sortition has inclusive, epistemic and egalitarian properties, it does not have the property of promoting collectivity in the debate, either directly or indirectly. This raises the fundamental question of its relevance to the task of strengthening the democratic character of public debate.

Besides this, these experiments do not seem to resolve the fundamental problem of elective representation but only circumvent it. While they may strengthen citizens' confidence in the system *in general*, they do not increase confidence in their representatives. In this regard, we should not lose sight that the strengthening of our democratic system can also involve the strengthening of both the transparency and the control procedures of the decision-making process.

Annabelle Lever and Chiara Destri

Equality of Opportunity, Equality of Outcome and the "Democratic" Case for Lotteries

Abstract: This chapter argues that the egalitarian defence of lotteries rests on two versions of political equality that are at odds with each other. As some advocates of lotteries claim, random selection is supposed to achieve both equal opportunity for political influence and equality of outcome in the form of descriptive representation (see Geoffrey Grandjean's introduction). This chapter shows not only that these two forms of equality are distinct, but also that sortition cannot realise both at the same time.

As a matter of fact, equality of opportunities is only achieved if sortition is <u>unweighted</u> because this is the only way they can offer all citizens the same chance of being selected as members of a deliberative assembly. On the other hand, <u>weighed</u> lotteries, which constitutively give unequal chance to citizens of being selected, are necessary to have descriptively representative assemblies. This is easy to see by looking at two important factors. Firstly, the size of randomly selected assembly is too small to ensure that all relevant ascriptive features of the population at large are duly reflected in the assembly. Secondly, in so far as citizens can and do refuse to serve in office, pure randomisation ends up selecting for an assembly skewed towards those social groups that are more likely to be politically interested and active.

The authors conclude the chapter by observing that randomly created assemblies have a democratically important role as complements to, though not substitutes for, elections, because they provide a useful way to engage citizens as equal deliberators in matters of public policy. This chapter is a continuation of Gil Delannois' arguments.

1. Introduction

Contemporary proponents of randomly selected assemblies believe that elections are an aristocratic, not a democratic, way to select people for political power and responsibility, enabling the same people to be chosen repeatedly on the grounds that they are "the best" (Abizadeh, 2021; Landemore, 2020; Manin, 1997; Owen and Smith, 2018; OECD, 2020; Sintomer, 2007; Smith, 2021). Following Aristotle, Montesquieu and Rousseau, they claim that random selection is as an especially democratic way to select people for political office because it gives citizens an equal chance to be selected. In addition, they argue, random selection also achieves a form of equality of outcome that elections cannot achieve — namely, *descriptive representation* (Abizadeh, 2021; Buchstein, 2010; Landemore, 2020; Manin, 1997; Owen and Smith, 2018; Guerrero, 2021a,b; Chwalisz, 2021). We think it is urgent to test the cogency of these arguments, because lotteries are increasingly used politically and advocated by theorists and activists alike.[1] Hence, in this chapter, we aim to disentangle these two elements in contemporary claims about the egalitarian character of lotteries, and to show why they cannot both be true simultaneously.

Our conclusion should be no surprise to egalitarians, familiar with the difficulties of generating egalitarian results from formally equal opportunities. It is, however, at odds with current efforts to promote lotteries as peculiarly democratic. As we will show, creating mathematically equal opportunities to be selected for office will not produce substantively equal opportunities to serve, however we understand these, so long as people do not want to take up the opportunities that they are offered, are unable to take them up even if they would like to, or doubt that the offer is meant for people like themselves (Jacquet, 2017; 2020; Phillips, 1995; Williams, 1998). In short, the reasons why formally equal electoral opportunities regularly fail to generate descriptively representative assemblies apply also to lotteries.

The chapter is organised as follows. The next section (Section 2) introduces what we consider the standard "democratic" argument in favour of

---

1   See for instance the recent plea for sortition: https://www.progressives-zentrum.org/en/another-democratic-future-is-possible/ or van Reybrouck (2016) and see also Chwalisz (2022), whose work with the OECD and, now, with *DemocracyNext* aims to combine activism and scholarship in favour of random selection.

lotteries as opposed to elections. That argument has two parts: (1) the claim that lotteries guarantee equality of opportunity and (2) that they secure descriptive representation. In other words, all citizens have an equal chance of being selected and by selecting people randomly the resulting assembly will be a microcosmic reflection of society at large, thereby realising a form of substantively equal representation. In Section 3 we show that *unweighted* lotteries are incapable of constructing a descriptively representative legislature whether we look at them through the lens of ideal or of non-ideal theory. Hence, to the extent that lotteries realise equality of opportunity they will fail to be descriptively representative or to meet minimal and well-established criteria of equality of outcome. On the other hand, to the extent that random selection generates descriptively representative assemblies using *weighted* lotteries that over-sample disadvantaged social groups, it will not offer people an equal opportunity to be selected for office. We then show how these problems affect Abizadeh's recent argument for replacing Canada's appointed second chamber with one that is randomly selected, rather than elected, before concluding with some alternative suggestions about the democratic significance of randomly selected citizen assemblies, once one rejects the idea that they are suitable for legislatures.

2. The Standard Egalitarian Argument: Two Strategies

In *The Principles of Representative Government* (1997), Bernard Manin noted that until recently elections were assumed to be aristocratic, not demo-cratic, ways of selecting people to political office. However, no one seems to have thought that the Greeks were right to suppose that elections, even with universal suffrage, were less democratic than sortition, or that it would be a gain for democracy if people replaced one or more of their legislative bodies with a chamber created by random selection—until recently (Zakaras, 2010; Vandamme and Verret-Hamelin, 2017; Gastil and Wright, 2019; Owen and Smith, 2018; Landemore, 2020; Stone and Malkopoulou, 2021; Abizadeh, 2021).[2] Yet, as democratic proponents of randomly selected assemblies like to emphasise, suitably constructed

---

[2]   For those interested in the militant use of Manin's book in France, and his reaction to it, see Hayat (2019); Chollet and Manin (2019).

lotteries[3] answer to the democratic idea that people are equally entitled to participate in politics, and to take part in ruling as well as being ruled. Equality of opportunity to hold office, created by unweighted lotteries, and the rotation in office they encourage, seem to capture in an intuitively appealing way the democratic idea that citizens are entitled to take part in the government of their society as equals and are, in principle, interchangeable, in their claims to political power and responsibility. As Hélène Landemore puts it, "Random selection, unlike election, does not recognize distinctions between citizens, because everyone has exactly the same chance of being chosen once they have been entered into the lottery" (2020, p. 90). As a result, she submits, "given enough rotation and a small enough population, actual access to power is strictly equalized over the long term" (*ibid.*, p. 90).[4]

Where it is impossible to share a good equally, and no compelling claims of desert or need obtain, random selection makes it possible to treat claimants as equals by avoiding invidious, destructive and unfair comparisons amongst them (Dworkin, 2002). When justified by randomisation, unequal rewards do not impugn the virtues, capacities, status, needs or desires of those who lose out and therefore provide no grounds for arrogance or preening on the part of winners, or of self-abasement on the part of losers (Delannoi, 2019, pp. 95–7; Montesquieu, 1748, Book II, Ch. 3). As Alex Zakaras states, lot treats "all adult citizens as equals in their capacity as candidates for representative office", therefore expressing "respect for their capacities and judgment" (2010, p. 461). Hence, it might seem, unweighted lotteries are the democratically ideal way to distribute goods, including political office, to which all have equal

---

[3] "Suitable construction" is important because historically lotteries, in conjunction with elections under a restricted franchise, have propped up oligarchical rule in the renaissance republics of Venice (Harivel, 2019) and Florence and, even as late as the nineteenth century, in Swiss cantons like Berne (Mellina and Dupois, 2019; Mellina, Dupuis and Chollet, 2021; Stone, 2021a,b).

[4] Owen and Smith (2018) are more circumspect, referring to the "equal probability of being invited" as the form of equality that lotteries create (p. 423). The difficulty with this conception of equality, however, is the question of why citizens should have to wait for an *invitation* to have the chance to present themselves for office—something that alternative formulations, such as Landemore's, avoid.

claim but which it is impossible or undesirable to share amongst everyone at once.

A second egalitarian argument in favour of sortition-based assemblies reflects the possibility of realising a descriptively representative assembly that answers to an ideal of equality of results in the constitution of a democratic legislature. Where a randomly selected body is sufficiently large relative to the total population, and where everyone selected participates, unweighted lotteries create assemblies that are a microcosm of the larger population. That is, the randomly selected assembly, though smaller than the whole population, will be made up of different groups in proportion to their numbers in the population. This will be true for the invisible as well as visible attributes of citizens and it will therefore be possible to treat the smaller group as an exact replica of the larger one, and an accurate replacement for it for certain purposes. To quote Gil Delannoi, "whereas universal suffrage brings equality by voting and potential equality in eligibility (anyone has the right to be a candidate for election), selection by lottery brings more equality in eligibility and more equality in terms of the result" (Delannoi, 2010, p. 14). In other words, random selection generates what Hannah Pitkin has called "mirror representation" (Pitkin, 1967, pp. 71–5).[5]

Randomisation then can be compatible with microcosmic selection, or descriptive representation, as it is now usually called. Thus, without having to make any politically controversial decisions about who or what deserves to be represented, those who have not been selected by a random draw can be confident that there will be people like them in their assembly, and in numbers proportionate to their total in the population. In these ways, individually equal opportunities to be selected will coexist with, and generate, equality of results in the representation of everyone's visible and invisible, ascriptive and voluntary characteristics. Put otherwise, while randomisation in these circumstances still means that many — perhaps most of us — will not be part of a legislative assembly, we will know that we had the same chance to be selected as everyone else, and

---

[5] The distinction between indicative and responsive representation made by Pettit (2010) is often mentioned in support of the idea that randomly selected representatives would fail to be responsive but would still be indicative of the broader people's views and interests in virtue of their statistical mode of selection. See for instance Zakaras (2010); Landemore (2020). For criticism of this view see Lafont (2015; 2019).

that, despite our absence, we will be represented by others who think, feel and live like us in numbers that fairly represent their frequency in the population (Guerrero, 2014, p. 167).

3. How the Two Egalitarian Strategies Conflict

Unfortunately, for reasons both of relative size and of people's willingness and ability to participate, it is impossible to create deliberative assemblies that preserve both an equal opportunity for individuals to be selected and a microcosmic or descriptively representative character. Unweighted lotteries standardly create assemblies that don't look at all like the citizen body. This is in part because if citizens can refuse to serve in office, unweighted lotteries will generate assemblies skewed towards those social groups that are more likely to be politically interested and active than others—namely, the socially advantaged (Blais, 2006; Kostelka and Blais, 2021).

Firstly, even under relatively ideal circumstances, citizens may find political engagement unappealing, inconvenient or inconsistent with their conscientious conditions. Evidence from the larger citizen assemblies, such as the Scottish assembly on climate change, suggests that on average only 3.7% of people respond positively to an invitation to join such assemblies; and while much higher proportions have been found for smaller and less onerous assemblies, the existing average positive response rate for all assemblies is a bare 15% of those invited (Jacquet, 2017; 2020), which is the same as the current exemption rate from compulsory jury service in France (Fourniau, 2019, footnote 11, p. 386). Alex Guerrero hopes that high salaries, help relocating and other forms of support and encouragement might persuade people selected at random to take on the onerous responsibilities of a legislative body (2014, p. 156)— but realism suggests that most people are unlikely to want to devote large amounts of their time to politics, even for a relatively finite period, and to disrupt their professional and private relationships in order to shoulder responsibilities for which they may have no taste or affinity.

Secondly, under non-ideal circumstances, such as those that currently attain, structural inequality affects people's interest in, and ability to take up opportunities for, political participation. While financial incentives might combat some of the obstacles that poverty and economic inequality place on political participation, they do not address the other consequences of social inequality and subordination, as both John Rawls and Iris Marion Young describe them: a lack of self-confidence and of the belief that one deserves the same opportunities as others; or the expectation of being silenced, mocked or denigrated because of one's appearance, accent, beliefs and experiences (Rawls, 2005; Young, 2011). Financial incentives will not adequately address the sexually inegalitarian division of labour in our societies that leave women predominantly responsible for unpaid labour and the care of others (Okin, 1989); nor will they neutralise the racially inegalitarian burdens of chronic illness due, in part, to unequal and inadequate access to medical care.[6] Indeed, the number who are excused jury service in England and Wales for factors ranging from insufficient linguistic competence through ill-health, the need to find work or having the responsibility of caring for others suggests that voluntary participation in randomly selected legislatures is likely to be profoundly affected by a variety of forms of structural inequality. Hence, an equal probability of being selected is no guarantee of a substantively equal opportunity to serve, nor is it a guarantee that the probability of serving will indeed be equal.[7]

The third reason why an equal opportunity to be selected is unlikely to result in a descriptively representative assembly is *intrinsic* to the nature of deliberative assemblies themselves, namely, their very small size relative to the total eligible population. As Hélène Landemore acknowledges, randomly selected assemblies are too small for all the different characteristics of citizens to be represented proportionately. Even under ideal circumstances, in which people's political differences do not reflect past injustice, it is likely that people will differ from each other in politically significant ways that are too numerous to be represented proportionately in a small assembly. After all, in a free society we can disagree with others without fear. Hence, it is possible that descriptively representative assemblies will be harder, not easier, to create the more our societies approach to justice.[8]

---

[6] https://www.ncbi.nlm.nih.gov/books/NBK24685/.

[7] As a matter of fact, supporters of lotteries tend to conflate probability and opportunity in ways that lose sight of how one's social and economic conditions affect one's substantive opportunities for political participation. Giving all citizens the same probability of being selected does not generate equal probability of serving exactly because it does nothing to improve disadvantaged people's (lack of) substantive opportunities to take part in politics.

[8] Perhaps in such circumstances the significance of departures from descriptive representation will matter less, at least to an egalitarian, but if everyone

Faced with the predictable consequences of unweighted lotteries, it is scarcely surprising that most citizen assemblies use *weighted*, not unweighted, lotteries to determine their membership. But of course, weighted lotteries fail to give people formally equal opportunities to be selected, as they oversample certain subsets of the population to ensure their presence in the assembly. It therefore seems that we must choose amongst the two forms of equality that make random selection look so appealingly democratic, as we cannot have them both. Advocates of lotteries must then give up the claim that these are democratic because they give everyone the same chance to be selected to the assembly, and instead rest their democratic credentials on the claim that stratified sampling means we can construct randomly selected assemblies that look like the general population, at least in certain respects.

Unfortunately, clarity about this trade-off, and the need for political choice which it implies, is uncommon in the literature, where it is still customary to assert that sortition-based assemblies are both descriptively representative and examples of individual equality of opportunity.[9] Yet not only does the philosophical literature on equality suggest the impossibility of reconciling formally equal opportunities with equality of results is normal—and not something that replacing elections with lotteries will change—but it also casts doubt on the assumption that lotteries are democratically preferable to elections because they give everyone the same chance of being selected to office whether they want it or not.

Unweighted lotteries were used in ancient Athens to select from a pool of volunteers for *supplementary* offices, given that all citizens were entitled to take part in the primary political body—the assembly that, prior to the reforms of 403/2 BCE, which initiated the distinction between laws and decrees, was responsible for passing both. Lotteries, therefore, were used to distribute a scarce good that volunteers desired, and to which they

---

deserves to see people like them in their assembly, it is unclear why this should be the case.

9   For example, Alessandro Bellantoni, Claudia Chwalisz and Leva Cesnultaityte, for the OECD, claim that "The participants should be a microcosm of the general public. This is achieved through random sampling from which a representative selection is made" and then require that "Everyone should have an equal opportunity to be selected" (Bellantoni, Chwalisz and Cesnulaityte, 2020, p. 6). This confusion pervades OECD publications on random selection and "the deliberative wave", reappearing in their accounts of "good practice principles" since (OECD, 2020, p. 118; see also Chwalisz, 2022).

were thought to have equal claims. In those circumstances, lotteries may have been a fair way to treat equals, just as they can be a fair way to distribute burdens among a group of people who are equally liable to bear them (Saunders, 2008). However, when we are dealing with a population who disagree about the value of the good to be distributed, in that some desire it whereas others see it as a burden, the egalitarian rationale for random selection vanishes. Giving everyone the same opportunity to be selected for office, regardless of their attitude to office-holding, is more likely to illustrate Michael Walzer's worry that "equality as sameness" (Walzer and Michael, 1983, p. xi) renders the ideal of equality "ripe for betrayal", rather than illustrating the democratic appeal of lotteries.

Arash Abizadeh's recent article on the introduction of a sortition-based second chamber in Canada is indicative of the confusion between weighted and unweighted lotteries (2021). On the one hand, he declares that random selection allows for descriptive representation, while also claiming that, unlike elections, sortition "treats all candidates as equals" because "each has an equal prospect of being selected" (2021, pp. 798, 800). It is unclear how Abizadeh can justify the use of weighted lotteries, given his concern that, since someone must decide which individuals/ groups should have greater chances of being selected than others, they risk undermining the impartiality that gives *unweighted* lotteries their democratic appeal (2020, p. 800). Stratified sampling is inconsistent with people having the same chance to be selected for office and, once one abandons the idea that everyone should have the same chance to be selected, there seem to be a variety of ways of creating a descriptively representative assembly without using lotteries — including the use of quotas in elections and appointments (Mráz, 2021).

On the other hand, Abizadeh also appears to recognise the difficulties of maintaining that equality requires people to have the same chance at office, whether they want it or not, as well as the difficulties of reconciling formally equal opportunities for individuals with equality of result, understood as the descriptive representation of individuals as members of ascriptive as well as voluntary groups. Thus, he notes that the use of lotteries does not preclude the need for self-selection in the creation of an assembly for reasons both of principle and practice — thereby agreeing with Guerrero, who rejects the possibility of mandatory participation, as distinct from Graham Smith and David Owen, for example, who endorse it (Owen and Smith, 2018, p. 431). Abizadeh notes that self-selection threatens impartiality because "those willing to serve may tend to have unrepresentative features" relative to the rest of the population (2020, p. 799), but believes that the resulting departures from descriptive representation can be justified if they are "*germane* to the ability to serve — such as having the status and powers of a representative, but also political engagement or willingness to serve" (*ibid.*, pp. 799–800).

However, this begs the question of why political engagement and a willingness to serve are relevant to having the status and powers of a representative, and how it is then possible to reject elections as undemocratic, because they do not give us all *the same* opportunity for office, regardless of our willingness to serve. After all, the *willingness* to serve has no evident relationship to the *ability* to serve, or adequately to represent others. If, nonetheless, it is taken as relevant grounds for departures from descriptive representation, this needs to be explained[10] and justified in ways that explain why lotteries are egalitarian democratically in ways that elections are not.

In short, while Abizadeh clearly believes that some forms of self-selection are consistent with democratic forms of equality of opportunity, as are some forms of quota-based randomisation, it is unclear *what* forms of descriptive representation and of self-selection he believes to be consistent with equality, and how far they reflect his belief that randomly selected legislatures are more egalitarian than elected ones.

When one considers the two forms of equality that gave sortition its democratic appeal — the equal chance to be selected, and the equal representation of voluntary and ascriptive groups — one must conclude that this appeal is more apparent than real. There are all sorts of ways in which we can create assemblies that look like the general population out of a very small and atypical bunch of volunteers. The use of weighted lotteries is merely one, as we can use reserved seats, quotas, variants of cumulative

---

10 That lotteries take all citizens to be equally *able* to serve is clear; less clear, however, is how lotteries should treat citizens whose willingness to serve is different. Abizadeh's distinction between "germane" and "non-germane" departures from descriptive representation obscures rather than illuminates this issue. As a matter of fact, the distinction itself is either redundant (if the difference between lay citizens and representatives is that only the latter hold office) or unjustified (because if political engagement is likely to be higher in certain groups, such as the educated, then what Abizadeh unproblematically classifies as germane departures from descriptive representation are non-germane and problematic).

and proportional voting and the use of affirmative outreach and support as well. It is an open question, then, what moral, political or epistemic virtues we should attribute to randomly selected assemblies even if we can create them to look like us—given that at their base we are dealing with a handful of people whose willingness to take on the burdens of office is no guarantee of their ability to do so, or of their ability to gain the trust of those they are supposed to represent.[11]

4. Descriptive Representation, Equality of Results and Lotteries

Just because randomly selected assemblies do not combine equality of opportunity and equality of result, it does not follow that they cannot be democratically appealing. At a minimum, they enable citizens who are strangers to each other to come together as equals to deliberate on matters of collective importance, based on shared access to the best available evidence. The democratic appeal of these features is considerable, as is their specifically egalitarian appeal, given the ways that socio-economic inequality affects people's access to politically relevant information.

Sortition has many virtues if one wants to distribute benefits and burdens amongst equals where neither rotation nor sharing are possible. Its unpredictability makes favouritism harder, even impossible—and this can be true even when weighted lotteries are used to distribute benefits and burdens amongst a large group of people (Stone, 2011). Unweighted lotteries give everyone the same chance of being selected, and that can be appealing in cases where formal equality of opportunity is a pre-eminent good (Stone, 2010). Weighted lotteries enable forms of proportionality which can be appealing in cases where formal equality of opportunity is either irrelevant or seems less significant than ensuring certain types of equality of outcome (Broome, 1990). However, while weighted lotteries can enable us to pattern random outcomes in ways that reflect our values, they cannot ensure substantively equal opportunities for individuals or groups, as they do nothing to change the unfairness in people's circumstances which prevent them from taking up the opportunities that they

---

[11] Our objection to lotteries, here, is different from the one famously raised by Cristina Lafont: that mini-publics cannot claim simultaneously to be *representative* of the broader population and a deliberative *amelioration* of it (2019), as we are concerned only with the conflict between descriptive representation and equality of opportunity.

are offered — or from correctly recognising something *as* an opportunity. Thus, it is important to be clear that descriptive representation is no proof of equality of result absent substantively equal opportunities, and therefore to beware of confusing an assembly created using differentially weighted statistical samples to look descriptively representative with one that embodies equality of results.

It is important that citizens have numerous and varied opportunities to participate with others in considering public policy, and in providing a considered opinion on the performance of their government, of other public officials and of the common institutional framework within which they operate. Citizen assemblies can therefore make important contributions to informed public opinion, or to the deliberation of others (whether professional or lay); and can provide a means for using public resources to educate and engage citizens in ways that help to instantiate the idea that government is there to serve citizens, and not the other way round. There are lots of different ways in which citizen assemblies might be constructed, their deliberations organised and the results of their efforts formulated and made available to others, especially once we are clear that there is nothing especially egalitarian about current ways of constructing and organising them (Lever, 2022; 2023). There is huge room for progress and experimentation in these matters, and this is exciting. But from what we have seen, democratic principles do not justify ascribing significant decisional power to randomly selected assemblies, and there is no reason at present to suppose they can substitute for elections in the creation of democratic legislatures.

Indeed, surprising as it might seem, the questions about secrecy, voluntariness, accountability, equality and legitimacy that characterise the philosophical literature on the ethics of voting are likely to find their place in the theory and practice of sortition assemblies — once more progress is made in considering their democratic appeal and limitations (Vandamme, 2018; Engelen, 2013; 2009; Lever, 2010; 2007; Lever and Volacu, 2018).[12] Unanimity in deliberative assemblies is unlikely when people are free to dissent and have no prior reasons to agree with each other, as is the case for people selected at random, as well as those chosen for their competing and partisan beliefs and experiences. The willingness publicly to accept or

---

[12] For the importance of accountability for relations of political equality see Destri and Lever (2023).

reject a particular decision, opinion or person, therefore, remains, and with it the need to consider the merits of majority rule and even minority and majority reports, as compared to other ways of closing deliberation (see also Lafont, 2019). Above all, in so far as citizen assemblies, however constituted, seek to contribute to public debate on behalf of all citizens, deeper reflection on the relationship between their procedures and their outcomes is unavoidable, as is the evaluation of both procedures and outcomes in terms of democratic values, aspirations and experience.

The ready reference to Athenian democracy, by proponents of sortition such as Owen and Smith (2018) or Landemore (2020), can obscure the importance and difficulty of deciding what constitutive and operative rules sortition assemblies might use. In democratic Athens all citizens were entitled to participate in the law-making body. The use of lotteries was therefore reserved for additional public offices for which citizens could volunteer, and these offices were largely individual, except for juries, in which many could participate. These points are important, because lotteries, appointment and election (Sintomer, 2023) in Athens coexisted with the pre-eminence of a law-making assembly in which all could participate as equals, even if they could also volunteer for other offices. Thus, the equal citizenship and rights of citizens were protected despite the existence of positions of power and responsibility which could only be filled by relatively few people at any time.

Nowadays, however, there is no such politically pre-eminent body in which all citizens can assemble as equals. Some other way must therefore be found to make plain the political equality of citizens despite their differential access to political office. It is therefore worth considering whether it might be possible to use randomly selected assemblies to model the diversity of citizens and the different ways in which they can be equal, in addition to using them to support the deliberative, communicative and advisory work that democracy requires, and on which democratic legislative, executive and judicial bodies depend.

One approach to the problem is suggested by Anne Phillips' idea that equality of outcome can provide a test for equality of opportunity (Phillips, 2004), serving as a critical heuristic for when our political opportunities are, or are not, equal. As Phillips argues, there is no obvious reason morally why men, rather than women, should constitute the majority of our governing bodies; nor why these should be dominated by the wealthy, the elderly and by people who are racialised as "white". So, though assemblies created by weighted randomised samples, as we have seen, cannot render people's opportunities equal, they can help to make visible what an egalitarian assembly might look like, how it might differ from those with which we are familiar, and what it might take to realise them by equalising people's opportunities for office. Moreover, even in the absence of equality of opportunity, more descriptively diverse assemblies may be able to shed a critical light on the relationship between *who* gets to be an assembly member and the *type of conclusions* they reach, given that different forms of randomised strategic sampling can be used to form assemblies while holding the *other* aspects of their constitution, procedure, information and expertise fixed.

Seen in this way, descriptively representative assemblies — however imperfect the mirror they create — can offer a variety of images of deliberative equality in circumstances where neither substantively equal opportunities nor equality of outcome are possible. Achieving more descriptively representative assemblies in some respects, even if failing to answer to ideals of equality of opportunity or outcome, can offer a contextual and functional conception of who "we" are and of the relevant features of "us" that it is helpful, even necessary, publicly to highlight in particular political settings. For example, when deliberating about welfare, an assembly that aims to be descriptively representative of those on welfare can answer to ideals of inclusive and egalitarian deliberation in ways that supplement, but also throw a critical light on, our best efforts to create democratically egalitarian legislative, executive and judicial bodies via more familiar combinations of election, appointment and self-selection. Such an assembly can remind those who are not on welfare that "we" nonetheless include many who are, and remind citizens — whether on welfare or not — of the importance of adequate representation of disadvantaged members in our governing bodies, as well as in other deliberative and participatory settings.

Weighted lotteries enable the constitution of assemblies with quite different social profiles, which can be designed cumulatively to illuminate the breadth and depth of our differences and similarities as citizens. Hence, randomly selected assemblies might be used deliberately to help citizens envisage the demands of formal equality of opportunity, even as they contribute to the deliberative reflection and information necessary for citizens substantively to treat each other as equals. If so, a democratic perspective on sortition and election may improve our ability publicly to recognise ourselves as equals, while increasing our political opportunities as citizens.

Pierre-Étienne Vandamme

Democracy Without Elections and the Value of Political Parties

Abstract: *The best way to appreciate the value of elections for democracy is to imagine a democracy without it. This chapter therefore outlines the model of democracy without elections that seems the most robust. This would combine representation by lot with participatory mechanisms such as the rights to initiate legislation, to recall the House of Representatives or to hold an abrogative referendum. The next step is to assess what would be missing in such a counter-factual system. And the original contribution of the chapter, in comparison to the critiques of sortition that are put forward in other chapters, is to argue that political parties would be missed more than elections themselves. Indeed, representation by lottery offers much less room for parties than elections. Yet, in the absence of stable political groups presenting citizens with clear alternatives between different political projects, the representative system would lose much of its readability. It would be much more difficult for non-selected citizens to understand how decisions were made – by whom, for what reasons and who could be held responsible for them. As a result, such a system would run the risk of alienating less informed citizens, who would also be less likely to accept an office conferred by lot or would make less use of participatory mechanisms to influence the decision-making process. In contradiction with the egalitarian aims of many proponents of sortition, such a system would therefore risk producing very unequal effects. What is more, it would bring to positions of power people who may not have a high awareness of injustices. It would thereby also fail as an instrument of social transformation. This chapter responds directly to Didier Mineur's chapter and to Alex Kovner and Keith Sutherland's chapter.*

There are at least two ways of assessing the democratic value of sortition. One can consider it as a full-blown alternative to elections, or as a complementary institution to be embedded in a democratic system that remains election-centred. Many objections to sortition fall when it is considered in the latter way, as an add-on, which is also the most often advocated use of sortition. Hence, arguments against the most radical use of sortition have a limited strength and do not in fact disqualify all uses of sortition. There is nevertheless some interest in the exercise of imagining the strongest version and thereby picturing a democracy without elections, for it helps us to form a better appreciation of elections. We tend to value them because we have cultivated the habit of associating them with democracy and because existing political regimes without elections are not attractive at all. Therefore, it takes a thought experiment to see whether there is more to elections than a useful way of pacifying political conflicts (Przeworski, 2019) to which we are accustomed and to which we know no plausible alternative.

In this chapter, I start with a brief presentation of what I take to be the strongest alternative to electoral democracy: a hybrid of sortition and direct democracy (Section 1). I argue that it can stand up to the most powerful criticism that has been levelled against a democracy exclusively based on sortition. From there, I then examine what would be missing under such an arrangement and argue that it is political parties that we might miss more than elections as such (Section 2). I end with a balanced assessment of the value and limits of parties (Section 3).

1. Democracy Without Elections

When theorists consider sortition as a full-blown alternative to elections, there is one objection that immediately rises: in a mass democracy, the use of sortition for the distribution of political offices would disenfranchise a large part of the population — the non-selected — or at least reduce importantly their opportunities for continued participation (Chambers, 2009; Lafont, 2015; Malkopoulou, 2015; Abizadeh, 2021). I see this as the most powerful objection to a pure lottocratic model.[1] Admittedly, non-selected citizens would not be fully disenfranchised, because they would face the prospect of being selected in turn. However, in the period in which they

---

[1]   The second most powerful being probably the accountability objection, which can be accommodated to some extent, as discussed in Vandamme (2023).

do not occupy any political office, they are disenfranchised in the sense that they would have no institutional means of conveying their political preferences or of influencing the decision-making process. They would still have all the extra-institutional means such as the right to take part in public debate, to protest, to strike, to sign petitions, etc., but it is hard to deny that they would face a major loss of *agency* (Abizadeh, 2021) compared with the agency offered to them by the reiteration of elections.

Some might argue that this loss is compensated by the major gain of agency *when selected* and by other benefits of sortition, such as the equalisation of opportunities to access positions of power. This, however, is implausible. First, it runs against the principle of political equality to justify the disenfranchisement of some by the greater power conferred to others. Second, equality—especially understood as narrowly as the mere equal probability of access to positions of power (Leydet, 2019; Destri and Lever, 2023)—cannot be taken to be the only democratic value. The participation of all, or at least all of those who want to participate, seems at least as important for democracy as equality. The best way to see it is to imagine a single decision-making body selected by sortition, with 500 people making decisions for a population of several millions. The harm to participation and agency, in that case, is clear. It is arguably less clear in a multi-body and multi-level sortition system (Bouricius, 2013) where several allotted bodies exist at all layers of power and where rotation is frequent. In such cases, the chance of being selected would be higher and agency might be conferred to all *through time*.

The harm to agency, however, should also be appreciated in light of its likely consequences. Even if agency were fairly distributed through time thanks to the principle of rotation that characterised classical Athens (Manin, 1997, chap. 1), the loss of "permanent" agency would be dangerous in several respects. First, citizens would lose control over the decision-making process. As deficient as they are as an instrument of popular control (Achen and Bartels, 2017), elections have the comparative merit of keeping everyone involved at regular intervals and to offer citizens a "permanent"[2] opportunity to shape representatives' decision-making structure. Arguably, elected representatives enjoy an important degree of

---

[2] *Permanent* is to be considered here in contrast with a pure lottocratic model where citizens have the opportunity to act within institutions only when they are selected. As we shall see later, rights to initiative and recall would make citizens' agency even more "permanent" than elections.

discretion in their decisions, but the set of options available to them is constrained by the combination of electoral results and public opinion— which is why they spend millions in confidential opinion polls (Bronner, 2023). Thus, citizens may not perceive it, but in some respect they are constantly involved in the decision-making process, if only by acting as a judge with the power to switch the result of the next election. This relative control offered by elections is extremely valuable because, even if it often fails to secure adequate responsiveness to the demands of the majority, it contributes to making electoral democracies better protected against authoritarian backsliding. In a pure lottocratic model, other institutional safeguards can probably be imagined, but this means of control would be lacking. As a result, non-selected citizens would also have fewer reasons to trust the whole decision-making process. Because if something goes wrong, if a random selection is manipulated, or participation rates are extremely unequal, or civil society groups achieve excessive influence in the deliberations of an allotted body, non-selected citizens cannot act institutionally to bring in a remedy. All they can hope for is either to be selected soon or that an allotted "control" body (which they cannot con- trol), in charge of fixing these problems, does its work correctly. In a very egalitarian society with extremely high mutual trust, this could work smoothly. In an unequal society with vested interests, it seems very dangerous.

Besides, the permanent involvement of citizens through elections has a pacifying virtue: it means that those who are on the losing side of legisla- tive decisions know why they are defeated and what they can do to try to shape decisions in their favour: garnering more electoral support (Przeworski, 2018; Abizadeh, 2021). In a pure lottocratic model, in the absence of political parties, the divide between majority and opposition is likely to be less clear. Majorities are indeed likely to fluctuate from one issue to the other. This is beneficial in one respect, because it could increase overall satisfaction with policy by increasing the number of citi- zens who see *some* of their preferences satisfied. Nevertheless, there are still likely to be people whose preferences are almost systematically defeated, who would therefore be highly dissatisfied with the system and find themselves incapable of acting *within* that system to defend their aspirations. They might thus face higher incentives to act *outside* the system, leading to higher instability and higher risks of social unrest (Rummens and Geenens, 2023). Admittedly, social unrest is not necessarily negative, but once again, in a scenario where things would go wrong in the political process, the risks of revolt against the system would be higher.

There is a way, however, in which these problems can be avoided without resorting to elections: this would involve the pairing of sortition with mechanisms of direct democracy such as the citizen-initiated referendum and the right to recall representatives from office before the end of their term. Both mechanisms work in the same way: if citizens collect a sufficient number of signatures, a referendum must be organised by public authorities. This referendum can bear on a diversity of questions (Cronin, 1989; Magni-Berton and Egger, 2018): whether a legislation or constitutional change promoted by some citizens should be adopted; whether a legislation or constitutional change approved or considered by representatives should be abrogated or rejected; whether a given representative should be recalled from office; whether the whole legislative assembly should be dissolved.[3] All of these options would make high sense in a political system where representatives would be randomly selected, because it is a significant way of preserving agency and control for the non-selected. If the representative process runs smoothly and things go well, the non-selected do not need to make use of these participatory opportunities, but if they are unsatisfied with the way they are represented, they can. They are therefore not powerless spectators of a process over which they have no control. In a way, they would even benefit from more significant opportunities of agency and control than in a purely electoral democracy without these instruments of direct democracy.

This, I believe, is the most credible alternative to electoral democracy, and it shows why elections should not be part of our definition of democracy. A democracy without elections is conceivable at a large scale, and it would not by necessity entail a major loss of agency for citizens. Hence, if elections are necessary, it is not by definition; it must be because they offer democratic goods that we would miss without them and that are not compensated by goods offered by alternative systems.

---

[3]   I have argued elsewhere (Vandamme, 2023) that the right to recall the whole assembly is probably better suited to sortition than the individual recall, which would be particularly harsh for people who have not asked to be there, and which could further reduce acceptance rates, which are already a source of worry for sortition advocates and critics (see Jacquet, 2017).

Would we miss elections under such hybrid arrangement (let us call it SDD, for sortition + direct democracy)? I am not sure we would have reasons to miss *them*. Provided that there are some guarantees that the system is organised sufficiently well,[4] it seems that citizens might be better-off in SDD in several respects. In terms of agency, the average citizen would certainly be better off than in a pure lottocratic system, and they might also be better off than in a pure electoral system. This comes from the fact that their opportunities to shape public policy would be increased. They would be increased, first, by the higher probability to access a position of power at least at one point in time. Secondly, they would be increased by the significant opportunities for political influence offered by direct democracy mechanisms, which reach further than the influence offered by elections. True, they would lose the opportunity to choose their representatives. But is this not compensated by the gains of agency?

Suppose we were asked to choose a political system under a veil of ignorance, to borrow Rawls' (1971) thought experiment. We know general facts about politics and sociology, but we ignore the system in place and are free to choose an entirely new system. Now, imagine a further constraint: we must choose either mechanisms of direct democracy (+ sortition) or elections; we cannot have both.[5] What would be our reasons to choose elections? I do not think that, in such circumstances, a case for elections can be based on agency or popular control. If we really want to secure continued agency and a significant control over the decision-making process, I think we are better off with the opportunities to set the agenda, to repeal unacceptable legislation and to dissolve the representative assembly than with the mere opportunity to choose representatives among the available options. Both agenda-setting and decision-making power are increased, and one avoids the risks of closure and misrepre-

---

4   In other words, if the random selection of representatives is properly organised, with stratified sampling, strong incentives to accept the mission, a sufficient number of representatives for the sample to count as sufficiently representative, statistically speaking, a fair audience process, etc. The threshold for citizens' initiatives to lead to a referendum should not be too high, so that these instruments can be considered as meaningful options. Nor should it be too low, for a certain legislative stability needs to prevail (without systematic cancellation of laws by organised minorities).

5   This constraint is added to focus the comparison and see whether the benefits of direct democracy mechanisms can compensate for the loss of elections.

sentation generated by the monopoly of political parties over the appointment of candidates and the making of final decisions.

Instead, one could try to build a case for elections based on political equality. This, however, is not entirely straightforward either. Sortition offers, in two respects, a more egalitarian selection procedure than elections. It strongly equalises the chance to access positions of power and hence to exercise genuine influence over legislation (Abizadeh, 2021). And more symbolically, its underlying message that no one has a special title to rule (Rancière, 2009b) and that everyone is at least sufficiently able to rule[6] is much more egalitarian than the aristocratic message conveyed by elections. Nevertheless, there is at least one important aspect in which elections might score better than SDD in terms of equality:[7] taking extra-institutional means of influence as constant, elections make the popular control of representatives quite egalitarian. Every vote in election counts equally, and it is this moment of egalitarian expression that structures the choice set faced by representatives. Under SDD, things would be different, because although every vote counts equally as well in a referendum, there are likely to be significant inequalities at the initiative stage. Although starting an initiative is formally open to all, it takes self-confidence, time, motivation and organisational resources to launch initiatives and mobilise one's fellow citizens in support of it. As a result, some social groups are likely to make a much more intensive use of participatory mechanisms than others, achieving a significantly higher influence. To be sure, organised groups already enjoy more influence under electoral democracy, but the argument is that the problem might be deepened by the replacement of a simple participatory mechanism such as elections by more complex and optional ones like direct democracy mechanisms. Whether overall, this would weigh more in the balance than the egalitarian benefits of sortition is not obvious, though.

Are there other considerations that might make electoral democracy more attractive than SDD? I think there are, and they are related to the democratic value of political parties. Let me explore these in the next section.

---

[6] Rancière claims that sortition is premised on the *equal* capacity to rule, but such a strong claim is not necessary to support sortition: assuming a sufficient capacity is enough.

[7] For a broader egalitarian argument in favour of elections see Destri and Lever (2023).

2. The Value of Political Parties

Let us start by briefly considering the place that there would be for political parties in a democracy without elections. Parties are highly tied with elections. Indeed, they are often defined with reference to elections. In Sartori's classical definition, for example, a party is described as a "political group identified by an official label that presents at elections, and is capable of placing through elections (free or non-free), candidates for public office" (Sartori, 1976, p. 63). What is more, it seems that parties in the contemporary sense of the world did not exist in the main historical alternative to electoral democracy: the Athenian proto-democracy (see Hansen, 2014). Finally, the absence of political parties in a lottocratic form of government is sometimes considered as one of the desirable aspects of sortition (see for example Burnheim, 1985, pp. 101, 116).

Nevertheless, one cannot exclude the formation of parties in a democracy without elections, for the simple reason that they are the natural product of pluralism and freedom of association, while offering major organisation advantages to people seeking political influence (see Lucardie and Vandamme, 2022). As Bouricius (2019, p. 314), who defends a model of democracy without elections, rightly points out, "parties have organized across the globe under nonelectoral regimes, even when out-lawed". It therefore seems plausible to expect political alliances to form within allotted bodies to coordinate action and gain influence. However, the absence of elections and the frequent rotation among representatives would be likely to impede a stable partisan structure from emerging and prevent parties from achieving enough influence to discipline their members. By not counting on anyone for election or re-election, randomly selected representatives would enjoy a significant independence that elected representatives lack and that would make party discipline much more difficult to achieve. Parties having lost their grip on the political system would also be unable to promise nice jobs to allegiant representatives. In sum, it is likely that some kinds of parties would form within the legislative assembly, but they would be much weaker parties. One might also expect political associations to emerge with the "aim to influence the general public, who would form the minipublics" (Bouricius, 2019, p. 314; see also Burnheim, 1985, p. 162). This, however, would bring them closer to pressure groups or civil society organisations than parties in the usual sense, as they would seek to influence public opinion rather than compete for access to political offices. Hence, parties might exist in SDD, but in a quite different, much more modest role, and this would entail some losses.

2.1. Parties and the executive

Let us start with what may be the least important of the three arguments about the value of political parties. It is one, nonetheless, that is worth considering given the frequent neglect of the executive in these debates. As Rosanvallon (2015) argued, political theory has been neglecting the executive branch of government even though power has massively shifted towards that branch in many political contexts. In debates on sortition, the focus is clearly on the legislative branch, because sortition seems much better suited to compose an assembly than to appoint a minister for example. Its virtues play out when a plurality of people is selected, each bringing the benefits of a situated perspective. As a result, partisans of sortition are usually either in favour of preserving elections for the selection of the executive, or in favour of a shift of power back from the executive to the legislative branch. In the few instances where the case is made for abandoning elections altogether, either the fate of the executive is left undiscussed (Guerrero, 2014; Landemore, 2020) or the executive is reduced to a purely administrative role (Bouricius and Schecter, 2014; Bouricius, 2019, pp. 330–31).

Even a purely administrative executive in charge of applying decisions made in the legislature or via a referendum would need an appointment procedure. Bouricius and Schecter (2014) propose to entrust an Executive Hiring Panel, randomly composed, and paired with another randomly composed Performance Review Panel. Two things might be lacking in such a framework in the absence of political parties. The first is the loss of the inside knowledge about the merits of different candidates for executive functions and their performance at lower ladders of power (Malleson, 2018). Candidates would presumably be assessed and appointed by people with no inside knowledge at all. It is hard to imagine how that would work. There could be a kind of certification process or exam narrowing the set of candidates for executive positions. Yet such a procedure is unlikely to single out *one* ideal candidate. There will be choices to be made and, without the accumulated knowledge within parties, it is unclear on what basis such arbitration would be made. The most likely scenario is a kind of self-regulation by the administration, under the external supervision of an allotted body. It is likely that members of the

Executive Hiring Panel would trust senior officials of the administration to come forward with appointment recommendations.

The second element that would be missing is a form of symmetry and continuity between the legislative and the executive. The latter is likely to be composed of people with a high experience in the public administration, while the former would be novices and would be constantly renewed. As a result, an important amount of political power, such as the power to influence decisions or appointments or to implement choices, etc. would reside in the hands of the administration. And in that respect, the value of parties is that—especially where they have the power to appoint the heads of the administration—they supervise the whole process and take in charge the continuity between legislation and execution.

This asymmetry and the uncertainty about the functioning of the executive probably do not count as decisive objections to SDD, but they count at least as points of attention, requiring further thought, and they highlight a function of political parties that is often lost from sight.

2.2. Parties and readability

More significantly, it seems that a major loss indirectly resulting from the abandonment of elections would be the structuring function of political parties. The presence of strong parties highly reduces the complexity of political processes (Manin, 1987; 2017; Rummens, 2012). It does so, first, by reducing the number of players. Although party members may disagree on many issues, parties are usually able to secure some cohesion and consistency in the decisions of their members. For citizens, this means that the plurality of political actors can be apprehended more easily. They can take it for granted that parties will usually act, in a way that can be predicted, based on their ideology. And this makes politics much easier to follow than if citizens had to follow the uncoordinated actions of individual representatives acting in unpredictable ways.

Second, when decisions are made by the parliament or government, they can quite easily be attributed to a party or coalition of parties that is known to have the lead during a given legislature. Under representation by lot, as mentioned above, majorities would be changing from one vote to the other. To be sure, this happens within party democracy as well, in cases of minority government, but this is quite exceptional and still more readable than highly liquid majorities. For citizens, again, a clear majority/opposition divide makes the legislative process much more readable. At the end of a legislature, it is easier to know who can be held accountable for what decisions. Admittedly, many of us are poorly informed about passed legislations and insufficiently equipped for a meaningful retrospective voting—yet the point is only that following the legislative process would be *even more* difficult and less likely in political arrangements that lacked strong and relatively stable parties.

Defenders of lottocracy might nonetheless insist that monitoring the majority in power and keeping it accountable is so defective in electoral democracies that we would be better off in a system that does not rely on it. With randomly selected representatives, one could argue that monitoring and accountability would be less necessary, because the random process would be more likely to select what Jane Mansbridge (2003) called "gyroscopic" representatives, who would be "collectively disposed to act in constituents' interests because random selection tends to produce an assembly that, if large enough, is descriptively representative of them" (Abizadeh, 2021). As a result, citizens would have more reasons to be trustworthy and the need to monitor representatives would be lower. Empirically, it might be true that random selection, properly done, produces a better congruence between the preferences of citizens and representatives than elections. However, taking this for granted would be very dangerous. One should not trust a political process requiring citizens to blindly defer to their representatives (Lafont, 2019). Some degree of popular control over the process and a means to hold decision-makers accountable seem necessary under any democratic arrangement. And from that perspective, the structuring function of parties is essential: it allows citizens who do not participate in the decision-making process to have access to a better knowledge of who defends what and who is accountable for what.[8]

Finally, the structuring of political divisions and the staging of the main lines of political conflict achieved through the media have another beneficial effect: they arguably help citizens build their own political judgements (Rummens, 2012). When dividing lines and positions are clearer, it is much easier to *take part* and thereby form political judgements. Without this reduction of complexity, more citizens might become alienated by a process they do not understand than is already the case.

---

[8]   This is not meant to minimise the difficulty and loss of readability created by the multiplication of actors and unaccountable institutions in contemporary democracies (see Papadopoulos, 2013).

2.3. Parties and ideological mobilisation

A third contribution of political parties that might be missed in a democracy without elections is their capacity to mobilise and raise consciousness among the population—an argument that will particularly speak to those who think the status quo is deeply unjust. In contrast with partisan electoral competition, sortition brings people who are potentially not at all politicised, and who do not necessarily have a deep consciousness of injustice, into positions of political power.[9] The latter must be understood as a revision of the Marxist notion of class consciousness, which refers to the awareness of belonging to a class, located in a struggle, an awareness that generates a desire to act with a common purpose to promote the interests of that class. In other words, class consciousness points to the ability of the oppressed classes to see that they are being oppressed and to form a united front to stand against their oppression, in spite of the ruling ideologies that attempt to conceal it and create what Marxists called "false consciousness". Yet, in a world where divisions have multiplied and where workers' interests have become very disparate, the binary opposition between two classes, capitalists and proletarians, is no longer sufficient to understand social dynamics and conceptualise social change.[10] Furthermore, injustices that are not reducible to class relations must also be taken into account, such as patriarchal domination, racism, homophobia, social contempt (Davis, 1981; Fraser and Honneth, 2003) or the injustices that will be incurred by future generations. Therefore, what matters is perhaps not so much people's class consciousness but their ability to identify all types of injustices, the sources of these injustices and how they can be resolved—what I call the consciousness of injustice.

The limitation of sortition, in this respect, is that, as a selection process, it takes no account whatsoever of whether or not people are interested in politics, are active in civil society organisations or are conscious of existing injustices. This is in contrast to the process of selecting

---

[9]   The following paragraphs borrow some passages from Vandamme (2021).

[10] Not all salaried employees are part of the oppressed class or capitalism's losers: "interclass" households now exist; some workers are also shareholders; self-employed people have their own concerns; the concerns of the most precarious members of society are not those of the middle class; the concerns of unemployed people are not the same as those of people who are in work (see Offe, 1987; Van Parijs, 1987; Wright, 2010, pp. 103–05).

representatives via elections. In an electoral democracy, people who believe they have ideas about how society should be organised compete publicly with each other. They are invited to explain how their political projects are fairer than those of other candidates, and to highlight the injustice in their opponents' plans. With party competition, gaining political office therefore assumes a certain degree of politicisation, in the sense of having an ideological[11] vision and strong beliefs about the way in which institutions should function.

That does not mean that elected officials all have a strong consciousness of injustice. Their political commitment may be based on less noble motives. Their strong beliefs may be wrong or unjust. Not everyone shares the same understanding of justice, and many people care little about inequality. In addition, since the general public has a low level of consciousness of injustice, the most conscious candidates are not the most likely ones to be elected. The argument is not, therefore, that elections necessarily bring to power people with a greater consciousness of injustice than sortition. Nevertheless, it could be argued that electoral democracy is potentially more suitable than sortition from that point of view. First, because it does at least provide citizens with the *opportunity* to be represented by the people with the highest levels of consciousness — the avant-garde, in Marxist language. Second, because it involves more than the selection of representatives via elections: it also enables political parties to mobilise citizens with low levels of consciousness and similarly allows highly conscious civil society organisations to have a significant influence in shaping public opinion and public decisions.

Now, whereas I believe that this is a strong argument against a pure lottocratic model, a hybrid like SDD somewhat mitigates the problem for it would still be possible for parties (and associations) to try to shape political decisions by starting "citizen" initiatives and advocating issues in referendum campaigns. As a matter of fact, that is how parties behave under hybrids of electoral and direct democracy such as Switzerland or several US states (Smith and Tobert, 2001). Nevertheless, by being deprived of the access to institutionalised positions of power, parties are much less likely to strive under SDD than they do in these existing

---

[11] Ideology is understood here not in the pejorative sense of a closed system of thought meant to justify the status quo (Ricoeur, 1997), but in the sense of a set of ideas reflecting an understanding and an evaluation of the existing world and of its alternatives.

configurations where they are still prominent actors. As a result, their impact on initiatives and referendum campaigns is likely to be much less significant. However, one could expect civil society organisations to take up the task and play this role of ideological mobilisation. And, in that respect, SDD scores much better than pure sortition because it creates incentives to mobilise the whole population and to bring it to act against injustices.

It remains true that under SDD, as a result of the rather atomistic nature of lottocratic representation and of the marginalisation of parties, there would be a loss of ideological confrontation between encompassing projects for the whole society.[12] At the heart of the legislative process, this dimension would largely be absent. One could imagine parties or associations playing that role from the outside and trying to influence the randomly selected representatives. However, it is not clear that they would be permitted to undertake the latter role in full. There would be grounds for "protecting" randomly selected representatives from outside influences, in the manner the organisers of the Citizens' Convention for Climate in France sought to do (see also Rummens and Geenens, 2023). The first reason would be on epistemic grounds. If the members of a group formed via sortition are selected because of the value of their diverse viewpoints, the greatest benefits would be expected to come from their internal deliberations, not from outside influence. The second, on grounds of perceived legitimacy. If a citizens' assembly is presented to the general public as representative of the population's diversity, people are more likely to trust the assembly's opinions and judgements. But if it is also told that the assembly works closely with a range of unelected civil society organisations and other self-appointed representatives, trust will probably be more fragile. If, during deliberations, it is not clear who is defending what point of view or who ultimately influences the group's decisions, there is a risk that the process will seem too opaque to generate trust and perceived legitimacy. Hence, it is plausible to expect interactions between militants and decision-makers to be lower in a democracy without elections than in electoral democracy.

---

12   In a similar spirit, Malkopoulou (2015, p. 247) evokes (in a context of sortition, not SDD) a "form of depoliticization, which eliminates the political socialization and action enabled by partisanship. It also undermines the spirit of group formation on common ideological goals (i.e. parties) and breaks down collective power into purposeless individualistic inaction".

In sum, there are grounds for believing that the move from electoral representation to lottocratic representation may reduce the opportunities for influencing and mobilising the most conscious sections of the population, either through political parties or civil society organisations. This problem is arguably weaker with SDD than it would be with pure sortition, but it still ought to be taken into account.

3. The Right Dose of Parties

Obviously, one should not idealise political parties. A full assessment should put the benefits highlighted in the previous section in balance with their many drawbacks. Among these, one could mention their tendency to pursue partisan interests at the expense of the public interest.[13] Thus, it has been argued that dominant parties have in many political contexts become agents of the state, alienated from civil society and betraying their original principles and ideologies for the sake of keeping their power and privileges (Crouch, 2004, pp. 70–77; Mair, 2013, p. 87) — what I call *partisan interests*. As a result, parties increasingly fail in their linkage function and thereby weaken democracy to some extent (Ignazi, 2017).

Parties' dominance in electoral democracies also generates a form of "closure" of the representative system. It does so, first, by excluding valuable candidates for office that are unaligned with existing parties or have failed to win the favours of party leaders — a problem that is arguably deeper in two-party systems. Second, the monopoly over empowered representation[14] enjoyed by parties results in the exclusion of popular demands which are not taken up by parties — and cannot be "imposed" from the inside by committed citizens because parties' structure is usually extremely oligarchical (Michels, 2017/1911; Ostrogorski, 1964) even when they claim to democratise internally (Cross and Pilet, 2015, p. 173; Ignazi, 2020, pp. 12–13). This gatekeeping power may be beneficial in some cases, for example when anti-democratic or

---

[13] This is to be distinguished from the traditional criticism according to which they defend private, factional interests at the expense of the general or public interest (see Sartori, 1976; Rosenblum, 2008). Nowadays, this criticism has lost most of its past strength. It has become more common to see parties as offering competing interpretations of the common good or public interest (White and Ypi, 2016; Bonotti, 2017), although these interpretations can obviously largely be based on hidden private interests.

[14] To be distinguished from more spontaneous and non-institutionalised forms of representation, by associations typically (see Montanaro, 2012).

illiberal demands are excluded (see Levitsky and Ziblatt, 2018), but regrettable in other cases, for example when the main parties act like a cartel (Katz and Mair, 1995), deliberately leaving aside some policy issues, at the cost of responsiveness.

Another problem related to parties' dominance in the political system is a loss of impartiality in institutions where this virtue is valuable. Parties' influence over the selection of office holders in the administration or in supposedly independent institutions like constitutional courts may lead to an excess of partisan politicisation, often pointed at as "partitocracy" (De Winter, della Porta and Deschouwer, 1996). It is probably naïve to expect pure impartiality from civil servants or constitutional judges, who, as with every other human being, are partly moved by personal values which are not neutral. Nevertheless, a willingness and freedom to act or judge impartially might be valuable even if full impartiality is unachievable. And it remains true that the spheres of the administration and of justice derive part of their value and perceived legitimacy from their independence from partisan logics (see Rosanvallon, 2008). Hence, an excess of politicisation of these institutions is regrettable.[15]

Finally, there is a deep tension between partisanship and deliberation, which manifests itself both in the political and in the public sphere. If parties discipline MPs, debates in parliament have no chance of leading to position changes. They become merely addressed to the electorate. This can help voters make up their mind by staging major political conflicts (Rummens, 2012) and exposing citizens to a plurality of visions, but it also creates frustration if people have the feeling that elected representatives are incapable of changing their mind or that the opposition is incapable of recognising a good policy enacted by the majority. Epistemically speaking, the strong incentives to keep the party line also inhibit collective progress through argumentation and correction of errors (Leydet, 2015; Landemore, 2020). Furthermore, the logic of electoral competition creates incentives for parties to discredit political opponents, attack straw men, or even to demonise some parts of the population when the distinction between legitimate opponents and enemies becomes blurred. This "plebiscitary rhetoric" (Chambers, 2009), again, makes

---

15 One could nonetheless make the case that the politicisation of the administration is less problematic than that of the judiciary, for it secures the kind of continuity between political decisions and their application mentioned above.

reasoned public deliberation more difficult and explains how the problem spills over to the public sphere. This dynamic of mutual discredit between parties creates polarisation (in two-party systems at least), ossifies political identities and impedes the development of a public culture of reason-based political discussion. Thus, the French philosopher Simone Weil (2017/1950) blamed parties for being exclusively concerned with their own growth and capturing their members into a partisan logic "killing in the souls the sense of truth and justice" (p. 33).

All of this means that democratic reformers must identify the "right dose" of parties. We do not want them to capture democratic processes entirely, nor to colonise the judiciary and the administration (at least not too much, for the latter). Yet, at the same time, we have reasons to value them, highlighted in the previous section. This, I believe, is what makes hybrid bicameralism (one elected and one randomly selected chamber) particularly attractive (see Gastil and Wright, 2019, for a wider discussion). A political system in which the main chamber would be elected and form the executive, but whose legislation would be checked by a randomly selected chamber playing a role of popular review would have the potential to combine the benefits of ideological confrontation and the structuration of the political process on the one hand, and non-partisan deliberation and wide social inclusion on the other. And if we added to this combination some of the mechanisms of direct democracy considered in the first section, we might find a new equilibrium that would keep partisan confrontation centre stage, yet leave room for non-partisan deliberation at the heart of the legislative system, and leave the representation process open to citizens' input, thereby somewhat loosening the grip on the political system exercised by parties.

4. Conclusion

The main thesis of this chapter is that the reasons that make a democracy without elections unattractive are only indirectly related to the value of elections. In an alternative model of democracy that would combine representation by lot and mechanisms of direct democracy, it is not so much the opportunity to elect our representatives that we might miss; it is more the structuring of political processes by a reduced plurality of collective agents, parties, that have the capacity to mobilise and raise consciousness among the population, to structure and stage political conflicts, to make decision-making processes more readable and controllable for citizens, and to care for the continuity between the legislative and the executive. In these respects, parties are a desirable by-product of electoral competition. They might still exist under alternative arrangements that did away with elections, but they would be likely to be marginalised and come closer to acting like simple pressure groups (among the many others).

As we have seen, however, parties can also harm democracy in many ways. This is why the status quo is not attractive either. We must find a way to preserve the benefits of political parties while mitigating the diversity of the problems that they create. In this respect, a right dose of sortition could play an important role. As argued in the third section, combining partisan confrontation with spaces for non-partisan deliberation (and mechanisms of direct democracy) could be an appealing way of reaping the benefits of sortition (in particular in terms of deliberation and inclusion) without marginalising political parties.

Didier Mineur

Drawing Lots in Politics

A Matter of Democratic Legitimacy

Abstract: *Advocates of the thesis according to which sortition is more democratic than mere election put forward two main sets of arguments. The first one is related to the allegedly better representativeness of an assembly created by lottery; the core of this assumption is that an assembly of this type would resemble the people like a miniature portrait and would make the same decisions that the people themselves would make. The second set of arguments considers that sortition matches the equality principle better than election. The contribution challenges both sets of arguments.*

The argument of representativeness raises at least two major objections. First, the chapter argues that it is the society considered as a whole that is represented, whilst individuals as such are not. Second, the assumption that a majority decision-making system would match that of representatives chosen by lots needs to be verified. Without validation by referendum, the rule of an assembly drawn by lot would amount to that of an oligarchy; if ever a referendum was to take place, it would either invalidate the assembly decision's alleged legitimacy, or make it meaningless, since democratic legitimacy cannot stem from any better source than from the whole people's decision. This part of this case echoes the chapter of Stefan Rummens and Raf Geenens as well as the ones of Jessy Bailly and Pierre-Étienne Vandamme.

Against the argument of equality, the chapter argues that, given the fact of disagreement, equality isn't likely to be achieved by sortition, but rather through voting and majority decision-making, which alone allows everyone to give his say on public matters. That section of this argument is related to the introductive chapter by Geoffrey Grandjean and the chapter by Annabelle Lever and Chiara Destri.

Advocates of the thesis according to which sortition is more democratic than mere election put forward two main sets of arguments. The first one is related to the allegedly better representativeness of a randomly selected assembly. One may call it "the argument of representativeness".[1] Following this argument, sortition would increase the social diversity of representation (see Sintomer, 2011a, p. 149; Courant, 2017, pp. 272-3). Representatives chosen by lot would resemble the population more than elected ones. Besides, because they would be independent from political parties (to the extent that they wouldn't have been designated by any party), they would also be freer in their judgements, and would make decisions only by considering the general interest instead of their own electoral one (or the directives of a political party, which are dictated by its electoral interest). Otherwise put, they wouldn't act as political professionals, but as any disinterested citizen would do. Consequently, it follows that an assembly which would resemble the people as in a miniature portrait and would make decisions similar to the those made by the people themselves. In that sense, *the argument of representativeness* promotes drawing lots on the basis of the political results to which it would pave the way. This argument defends the democratic legitimacy of sortition from a **substantial** point of view.

The second set of arguments, which one may call "the argument of equality", considers that sortition complies with the equality principle better than election (see Rancière, 2005, p. 54). Actually, all have an equal chance to be chosen by lot and to gain a position of power. Moreover, sortition would make representation closer to direct democracy, since all citizens, even if they were not actually participating in the decision-making, could have been invited to do so (Delannoi, 2010, p. 19). Thus,

---

[1] I bring together several arguments that can be distinguished (see, for example, Pourtois, 2016, p. 419). By contrast, I leave aside the hypothesis of a greater epistemic quality of deliberation based on the argument of a greater diversity produced by sortition, in so far as my goal is only to assess the alleged democratic legitimacy of drawing lots. The epistemic argument is only acceptable if the democratic character of the procedure is set; one can't assume that the supposed epistemic added value of sortition compensates for its lack of democratic legitimacy.

compared to that of elected representatives, the democratic legitimacy of the representatives chosen by sortition would be increased. *The argument of equality* argues that sortition is a *designation mode* more democratic than election; in that sense, it promotes drawing lots as a **procedure**.

To assess the democratic added value allegedly brought by sortition, compared to election, I shall first review the *substantial* hypothesis of a greater representativeness of the representatives chosen by lot. This comes in two sub-arguments, the minipopulus argument, and the independence argument. I shall then review the procedural argument of equality.

1. Substance: The Hypothesis of an Increased Representativeness

1.1. The minipopulus argument

Sortition would ensure a greater diversity amongst the representative's assembly than elections, and would, therefore, achieve greater representativeness. Thus, it would be more democratic than election, since an assembly which exactly represents the people in its diversity would allegedly act in a closer way to one in which the people themselves would act, as compared to a socially more homogeneous assembly. In short, it would bring representative democracy closer to direct democracy. Robert Dahl made that assumption explicit: "the judgment of the minipopulus would represent the judgment of the *demos*. Its verdict would be the verdict of the *demos* itself, if the *demos* were able to take advantage of the best available knowledge to decide what policies were most likely to achieve the ends it sought. The judgments of the minipopulus would thus derive their authority from the legitimacy of democracy" (Dahl, 1989, p. 340). The hypothesis according to which the democratic virtue of sortition would be greater than that of election, since the assemblies it gives rise to are more representative, raises at least two major objections. The first one regards representation itself, and the second one is related to the democratic legitimacy of the decisions made.

Representation of sociological diversity is called "mirror-representation". Such a representation can be organised in multiple ways. In a society in which individuals are categorised by their birth, or by their activity, or by both, as in the Ancient Regime and its General-States system, individuals are represented by persons who belong to the same category as themselves. These categories constitute the structure of society, and the individuals don't choose entirely which one they will belong to. Nevertheless, they choose their representatives from amongst their order. In such a mirror-representation, the "mirror effect" stems from the orders-driven structure of society, over which the individuals have no control, except for the fact that they still have a say, but only amidst their order. In the case of a panel stemming from drawing lots, the "mirror effect" is produced by the means of survey techniques in the hands of experts, based on pre-established socio-professional categories. The representative sample constituted by lots isn't representative except at the statistical level. Thus, I am "represented" in such a sample only in so far as my social characteristics categorise me in a pre-established group (worker, agriculturist, civil servant, etc.), and to the extent that the number of persons drawn by lots within that category is proportional to its numerical importance in the general population. To put it another way, I do not have a say about who will represent me. As a single unity amongst a set of aggregated data related to the composition of the population, I can only record the fact that some individuals are identified as my representatives completely beyond my jurisdiction. I don't have any clue of who these persons are and how they came to be selected. In other terms, *while society considered as a whole is represented, because it is reproduced in miniature, individuals as such are not*. The claim to representativeness of sortition can only be supported at the costs of breaking with the classical conceptions of representation, which all presuppose a direct representation of *persons*. One might say that, in some sense, the notion of representation is being substituted by that of representativeness.

The second problem concerns the democratic legitimacy of the decisions being made. The assumption of democratic legitimacy of the decisions made by a sample of persons drawn by lots is grounded on the presupposition according to which individuals don't act except in terms of who they are. Accordingly, similar characteristics, be they social, cultural or even ethnical, are assumed to imply similar behaviours. The survey technics consist of anticipating the result of an election from the statements of a panel of individuals representative of the population, which proves that there actually is a statistical correspondence between sociological profile and political behaviour. As Yves Sintomer puts it, "sortition is today narrowly linked to the notion of representative sample, used in a routine way in science, in statistical surveys or in polls. It is the calculation of probabilities which makes it possible [...]" (Sintomer, 2011a, p. 132; 2011b, p. 170; Fishkin, 2005, p. 288). The only trick would be to ensure that the citizen's panel is sufficiently numerous for the corres-pondence to be assumed. Otherwise put, this statistical correspondence should be given sufficient importance because it makes possible the assumption that *the decision of the population's majority would be the same as the one of the representatives chosen by lots,* provided that the same level of information is ensured.[2] But then, the assumption of democratic legiti-macy of the decisions made by a sample of persons chosen by lot, socially representative of the whole population, relies implicitly on a fictive test by which the decision is validated by the whole electoral body. It is grounded on the hypothetical result of a "ghost" vote. In the absence of an effective vote of the population, intended to validate or reject the decisions made by representatives chosen by lot, the assumption of demo-cratic legitimacy remains an assumption, depending on the correctness of the method used by the experts of survey techniques in charge of con-stituting the representative sample. Sharing that assumption and con-senting to the decisions made by the representatives chosen by lot, both depend on the trust of the citizens in the survey techniques (Lafont, 2015), about which most of them as yet know nothing. Otherwise put, sortition, despite the appearance of giving the power back to ordinary citizens, presupposes a kind of epistocracy. The experts of survey techniques are the only ones to know how the assembly of representatives chosen by lot, which constitutes a "minipopulus", was established. Moreover, its com-position depends on the categories which were used to divide up the population. Experts hold a decisive power over the constitution of repre-sentative assemblies, whereas the citizens have none. Unless they make a considerable effort to understand the technique carried out in order to create a representative sample, they have no choice but to entrust them-selves to the experts. The people's act of sharing the assumed democratic legitimacy of the choices made by the representatives stemming from lots, i.e. accepting the idea that they would act as the people would have had they been consulted, depends on that surrender.

---

2   Hervé Pourtois claims that the presupposition according to which the sample does what the electoral body would do if it were put in the same conditions of information and deliberation forbids every form of accountability: the public can't disavow the representatives drawn by lot, because "even if the positions taken by the members of a mini-public don't match with the actual convictions of their fellow citizens, it is these positions and decisions that these would have adopted if they had been in the representative's shoes" (Pourtois, 2016, p. 430).

A solution to this problem does exist, one might say. It is given by the
referendum validating the decisions made by the representatives chosen
by lots. One may stress, as Pierre-Étienne Vandamme does, that "the fact
that assemblies drawn by lot need to rely on a referendary validation
shows that the perception of their legitimacy is not guaranteed and
probably not sufficient" (Vandamme, 2018, p. 883). But one can argue that
when the proposals made by an assembly drawn by lots are ratified by
referendum, the assumption of democratic legitimacy they presuppose
will prove either to be wrong, in the case of a rejection by a referendum,
or empty, in the case of an approbation. Both cases, rejection or approbation, must be distinguished and more precisely analysed.

(1) The people reject the decision made by representatives chosen by
lot. Does it go against the presumption of democratic legitimacy of the
decision, based on the social representativeness of the persons who made
it? One could probably object that the population doesn't benefit from the
level of information that is provided to the sample of persons drawn by
lot, and that they didn't deliberate before making their decision in the
way that those persons did. For such an experiment to be conclusive, the
information that fuelled their deliberation should be made public and
available to the voters.[3] Provided that the electoral body receives the same
level of information as that of the representative panel, and supposing
that, still, its proposal is rejected, the assumption of democratic legitimacy
of its decision is indeed being contradicted — and it will be every time that
a referendum in good information conditions rejects the conclusions made
by a sample of persons drawn by lots.

(2) The electoral body approves the proposal made by the sample of
persons drawn by lots. In this case, two scenarios are possible.

> (a) The output of the draw has influenced the electoral body
> summoned to settle the issue by referendum. One couldn't

---

[3] One can of course be sceptical about the possibility that the electoral body
might have access to the same information as the representative sample. But in
that case, one must acknowledge that it isn't possible to know if the electoral
body would have made the same decision as the panel, on the basis that it
would have been in the same situation regarding information and deliberation, since it has to be considered that it can't be put in that situation. It is then
to be concluded that the assumption of democratic legitimacy of any decision
made by the persons drawn by lot is impossible to assess. In that case, sortition
should be abandoned as a designation procedure for a legislative assembly.

say, in that case, that the assumption of democratic legitimacy was correct, since it was self-validated. The presumption of the democratic legitimacy of the decisions made by a
panel of persons drawn by lots relies on the idea that they
acted as the people themselves would have done. The
verification of that assumption implies the independence of
the two different actors, i.e. the representative sample and
the body of people itself. In other words, it can be verified
only if the electoral body is not being influenced by the
sample drawn by lots.

(b) The electoral body wasn't influenced by the sample drawn
by lot. In that case, the assumption of democratic legitimacy
is being validated, since the sample has indeed acted as the
people would have, but it is still an empty proposition. What
makes the decision eventually democratic is the fact that it
was made by a referendary vote, not the fact that it was
based on a proposal elaborated by persons drawn by lots. A
referendum decision based on the outcome of a sortition procedure is no more democratic than a referendum decision
based on a proposal put forward by deputies, experts or
jurists. One can at most consider that the democratic added
value isn't linked to the *decision,* but to the *content* of the law,
since it was put forward by ordinary citizens rather than by
specialists. Their role, all things being equal, could be compared to that of the Athenian *Boulé,* an assembly of citizens
drawn by lots tasked with the recollection of the proposals of
the citizens and with their transmission to the *Ekklesia,* the
assembly of the people. Undoubtedly, it wouldn't be
neglectable. But the fact remains that the exemplary democratic character of the Athenian legislation process relies on
the fact that laws were voted directly by the people.[4] Similarly, in the case of an assembly drawn by lots, whose proposals are validated by referendum, the democratic legitimacy

---

[4] It isn't accurate in that sense to say that "the Athenian democracy was mainly
founded on drawing lots" (Courant, 2018, p. 258).

of the law to which the process leads depends on its ratification by the people, and only on it.[5]

1.2. The independence argument

The second argument often invoked in favour of the hypothesis of an
increased representativeness of deputies drawn by lots is that of their
independence. This argument is mostly used in favour of the alleged
epistemic quality of the deliberations taking place among people drawn
by lots (Vandamme, 2018, p. 878). Nevertheless, it can also be mobilised to
support the hypothesis of a better level of representativeness provided by
those persons and, thus, of an increased democratic legitimacy of the
representation based on sortition. Since they aren't linked to any party (in
so far as they aren't designated by any political organisation), they aren't
bound by any party discipline, and they may settle as they deem wise to
do. Moreover, they don't have any electoral interest to vote in any one
direction instead of another since they don't have to worry about their re-
election. That independence of judgement of theirs strongly distinguishes
them from elected representatives; it makes them similar to ordinary
citizens. One can even consider whether it is specific to ordinary citizens,
compared to professional politicians. Briefly put, thanks to the independence of judgement of persons drawn by lots, concern about the general
interest would be restored, and politics would be removed from the
interest logics that parasitise it when it is in the hands of elected representatives. Representatives drawn by lot would be representative because
they are independent as are all other non-professional citizens.

This argument has a major flaw. If representatives are independent
from political parties, then they are also independent from the citizens.

---

[5] It is possible to consider that the deliberation which takes place in the
assembly increases the quality of the proposition eventually submitted to a
referendum (even if that quality is unverifiable in the absence of any
independent criterion of rationality and justice: on that point, see Mineur,
2015). But that added epistemic value doesn't increase the democratic legitimacy of the decision. Supporting the opposite argument would amount to
postulating a scale of democratic legitimacy, according to which a popular
decision would be more or less legitimate depending on whether it was preceded by a public debate, or even whether the public debate was of good
quality. In so far as that quality can always be discussed, the legitimacy of
every popular decision would become in turn contestable. A full democratic
legitimacy would then become an uncertain and unreachable ideal.

Independence can still be a problem in respect to the democratic ideal. Paradoxically, it brings drawing by lot back to the aristocratic origins of political representation where a deputy was a "trustee", according to Burke's words, chosen to deliberate freely, and to substitute his will to the one of his electors.[6] One remembers Condorcet's words: "mandatary of the people, I'll do what I'll believe is the most consistent with their interests. They sent me to expose my ideas, not theirs; absolute independence of my opinions is the first of my duties towards them."[7] That deliberative conception of representation took representative government away from the democratic principle of the people's government. From this viewpoint we can see how political parties and the new dependence they imposed upon the deputies on behalf of their programmes and ideologies strongly contributed to the democratisation of representation. Party and programme, indeed, forge a link between representatives and their electors: voting for the candidates of a party is considered as being equivalent to an approbation of its programme, which, from that moment on, amounts to the will of the party's electorate. So much so that the dependence shown by the deputies towards the programme on the basis of which they have been elected is the equivalent to an act of fidelity to the people's will. In this way political parties created a connection between representative government and the principle of the people's sovereignty which had previously been absent (Mineur, 2010). In addition, the test of their re-election maintains a minimal link between the representatives and their electors, imposing a certain accountability upon the former.[8]

---

[6] Burke expresses that conception in his famous *Letter to the Electors of Bristol.*

[7] "Discours sur la deputation", which was his profession of faith for the election at the *Convention.*

[8] One can conceive certain mechanisms of accountability—for example that the members of an assembly drawn by lots present their work and conclusions to the public, that the citizens may recall a member of this assembly (on that point see Vandamme, 2018, p. 879). Yet those mechanisms are all contestable. The fact that the members of an assembly drawn by lot should present their work to the public is obvious if one wishes to give a democratic value to their achievements, but it doesn't establish a dependence link between them and the citizens. As for the recall, even if it would incontestably restore some accountability, by putting the deputies at risk of losing their position it raises some serious criticisms. Naming and publicly blaming somebody is very close to the Athenian custom of ostracism. Although it belonged to the regime which was the birthplace of democracy, it is not desirable to go back to such an institution

The assertion that representatives drawn by lots are more representative than elected ones because they are freer in their judgement makes no sense except on the basis of an extremely narrow comprehension of representation from which every political dimension has been evicted. They are more representative only in so far as they bear more resemblance to ordinary citizens because they aren't directly linked to a political party, but not in the sense that they defend the wills or the interests of the citizens in a more authentic way than their elected representatives do. One of two things should happen then: either the argument of the independence of representatives drawn by lots is considered in itself and should be rejected as being anti-democratic — the independence of such representatives indeed appears to be a democratic regression rather than a progressive factor — or it is linked to the minipopulus argument and to the assumption that the sample's decisions are democratically legitimate. Each sample member's independence of judgement is indeed a *sine qua non* condition needed to validate the assumption that the sample can decide as the people would, should they both be asked to determine on the same question. Without it the statistical correspondence between the deliberation of the sample and that of the electoral body would be flawed. Put in this way, the argument based on independence should be rejected because of the objections to the assumption raised above (without verification by referendum, it makes sortition similar to epistocracy: if it is verified, it will either be invalidated or rendered meaningless).

2. Procedure: The Argument of Equality

Bernard Manin insists on the paradox that even though sortition had been associated for centuries with the equality principle and with democracy, American and French revolutionaries, one generation after Montesquieu and Rousseau, didn't for one moment consider returning to it. For them, election was the natural foundation of political legitimacy. As Bernard Manin explains, the reason lies in a single principle: that of consent, conceived as the only foundation of legitimate authority by all natural law theorists. Consent implies the vote or the election. Thus, the crucial question of the contractarian theory, that of political obligation amongst human beings held to be equals, supplanted the questions of the

---

whose history shows that it was casually used as a weapon of settling of scores between rival political factions.

distribution of power and of the best regime which had been the traditional political questions since Antiquity. As Manin puts it, "it didn't matter anymore that public functions were distributed in a more or less equal way between citizens" (Manin, 2012, p. 123). Provided that we haven't renounced the modern ideal of collective autonomy, the principle of consent, dear to natural law theorists, has lost none of its importance to us. It constitutes a strong justification for elections. However, it is worth examining the idea that sortition allows an equal distribution of charges. The principle of *modern* democracy, i.e. autonomy, can't be separated from the election; still, the other principle of democracy, *both ancient and modern*, i.e. equality, might be better carried out by sortition.

The arguments linking sortition to the equality principle are well known. They go back to Plato and Aristotle. The Stagiritian writes that "democratic justice consists in equality according to number, not to merit", and that, in a democracy, "each citizen must have an equal part". Equality relates to liberty: all citizens, as opposed to slaves (as well as to metics, and, to some extent, to women), must be equally free. This norm of democracy is based on the "will to be commanded, at best, by absolutely no one, or else, only in turn" (Aristotle, Book VI, 1317 a 40–b 27). It is in the following sentences that Aristotle mentions sortition as one of the characteristics of democracy. However, the link made by the Athenians between democratic equality—which Aristotle considers to be a fallacious application of arithmetic equality to individuals—and sortition is uncertain. As Bernard Manin reminds us, sortition doesn't give each an equal say on the desired good; the link between sortition and the equality principle is bound to the notion of probability—each one having an equal chance of being designated by lots—which wasn't known as such in Antiquity. The Greeks probably had "an intuition approaching the notion of mathematically equal luck despite the absence of instruments allowing [them] to conceptualize it". Anyway, modern philosophers casually reassert that link between equality, or democracy, and sortition, and the famous sentence of Montesquieu linking them gets very close to the notion of equal chance: "suffrage by lots belongs to the nature of democracy. Suffrage by choice belongs to that of aristocracy. Lots are a way of electing which doesn't afflict anybody; it leaves every citizen a reasonable hope to serve his homeland" (Montesquieu, 1979, p. 134). Is there a lesson for us to draw from the tradition running from Aristotle to

Montesquieu,[9] according to which sortition makes the equality principle real? One must remember here, after Patrice Guéniffey, that sortition presupposes a strong homogeneity of the social body, whose members share more or less the same beliefs, the same values and the same interests, so that "the decision can fall indifferently on anyone of them" (Gueniffey, 1993, p. 123). Rousseau does not differ from this view: "elections by lots would have less disadvantages in a real democracy where, everything being equal, both by customs and talents and by maxims and fortune, the choice would become almost indifferent" (Rousseau, 2001, p. 150). In short, even if the Athenians didn't resort to sortition to appoint decision-making bodies (members of the *Boulé* were only in charge of proposing the laws to the *Ekklesia*), they were sufficiently close to consider that ordinary citizens were interchangeable in the functions they were tasked with. In the contemporary uses of sortition, each person isn't considered as interchangeable with *any other*, since the modalities of constitution of the panels aim at guaranteeing their resemblance *vis-à-vis* the society in its diversity. Nevertheless, the representativeness of the assembly is produced through pre-established social categories, within which the choice of one person or another is indeed indifferent. Yet modern democracy, as opposed to ancient democracy, is based on the legitimacy of disagreement.[10] It is characterised, conversely to Rousseau's assertion, by a variety of customs, talents, maxims and

---

9   Rousseau, even if he confirms the link between random selection and democracy put forward by Montesquieu, forges it in a very different way. He understands democracy as the regime where the people exert the executive power in addition to the legislative power. In such a regime the risk is high that the general aims which should lead the legislative body might be contaminated by particular goals. Using lotteries to appoint executive magistrates is a lesser evil since it allows the people to appoint them without having to choose them personally. Rousseau doesn't consider using lotteries to appoint, from amongst the people, citizens in charge of legislating on behalf of the whole people, since "every law that the People in person hasn't ratified is nil; it is not a law" (Rousseau, 2001, p. 134).

10 It is first the religious division that led, after an agitated historical journey, to the principle of state neutrality and to the correlative definition of citizenship as independent from religious attachments that is constitutive of the modern liberal democracy. As Moses Finley stresses, the First Amendment of the Constitution of the United States ("Congress shall make no law respecting an establishment of religion or abridging the freedom of speech") would have been unintelligible, or even would have seemed abominable, to an Athenian (Finley, 1976).

wealth levels. It is trivial to remember that all women, youngsters, civil servants, workers, etc. are not politically identical, even if there is a statistical correspondence between the political behaviours of the different social categories and those of their "representative" samples. The correspondence between the aggregated votes of the members of the diverse social groups and those of the members of the samples of these groups doesn't allow us to postulate the same correspondence as regards their thoughts, their values, their interests, no more than it regards their contributions to the collective deliberation. There is no guarantee that the representative sample of a social category would put forward the same reasons and arguments as would the members of that category if they were to deliberate directly. One can of course say the same thing about elected deputies, who probably don't deliberate as the electors would do; but at least they were chosen by the majority of the electors.

If the fact of disagreement is taken seriously — which, at the same time, in modern democracy, is a norm — one has to admit that it can extend to almost everything — except the principles of free speech, conscience and opinion, which are precisely commanded by the legitimacy of disagreement. Therefore, in politics, equality isn't carried out by sortition but by the vote and by the majority decision, which alone grants everyone the possibility of having his or her say on public matters and gives each the same weight in the collective orientations.[11] One could certainly argue, as Arash Abizadeh (2021, pp. 5–6) does, that election only guarantees equal participation in the choice of the power holders, whereas the equality of sortition is based on the equality of the chances to participate in power. Abizadeh considers that, since there are no imperative mandates, the equality of the electors' votes can't be considered as equality of participation in power. Accordingly, sortition, though it doesn't distribute the power to the individuals equally, is nevertheless more egalitarian than election because it gives everybody an equal chance to have a share of it. Yet, this argument is puzzling. The assertion that election does give an

---

[11] In modern democracy, sortition remains effective in the judicial field to appoint court juries: the democratic axiom of the equal ability of judgement implies that the individuals are interchangeable in the pursuit of truth. By contrast, in the political field, they are not. As Yves Sintomer puts it, "once their ability is verified, their random selection in court juries is justified because of the interchangeable judgement, but in politics, such a legitimization seems impossible" (Sintomer, 2011a, p. 141).

equal part to everyone in the selection process of the power holders but
no access to power itself seems exaggerated: in contemporary representative democracies, the choice of a legislative majority or of the holders of
the power paves the way to the main orientations of the public policies
that are to be conducted—even if, of course, deviations or reversals
during the mandate are common practice. Therefore, why should a
system which gives everyone an equal chance to partake in power, but no
effective participation at all to those who aren't favoured by the lottery, be
considered as being more egalitarian than the one which gives everyone a
real say, even if it is restricted, in respect to decision-making? There is *a
priori* no reason to prefer sortition-based equality, the output of which is
that a very few people take part in power, to that equality of participation
(although limited) that elections guarantee.[12] By contrast, there is a clear
reason to give preference to the latter: in a democratic society divided by
different values and confronted by collective choices, the supreme value is
the autonomy of the individual.[13] As regards that notion, the relevant
equality is not the luck-based equality to participate in the decision-
making, but the equality of effective contributions to the decision. However, in sortition, those who are not selected by lots are indeed deprived
of any autonomy. Election in the representative system, on the other
hand, gives every elector an equal but restrained contribution to the
determination of the great collective orientations.[14]

---

[12] This objection to the egalitarian character of drawing lots is already formulated
by Pourtois (2016, p. 425).

[13] One objects sometimes to the invocation of the autonomy principle (or the
consent principle) in the argument that many institutions endowed with
power aren't elected. The idea that the power holders have been chosen would
be an illusion. See for example Pourtois, who seeks to defend election but
doesn't mainly refer to consent for that reason (2016, p. 421). One can simply
answer that judges, independent administrative authorities, etc. aren't representatives. They aren't supposed to decide upon the fundamental orientations
of the society. Besides, even if their power increases to the point where this
becomes the case, it would be peculiar to draw a moral argument from a
democratic deviation, and to conclude that because more and more non-
elected institutions do exert de facto political power, it would be legitimate to
insist that authorities endowed with political power should not be elected.

[14] One can, besides, put forward that, even in the case where the members of the
samples of the different social groups would think and speak in the same way
as the members of the different social categories they are expected to represent, it doesn't amount to the same to choosing by oneself. This choice of the
one who will represent us because his or her political commitments match

***

The goal of the above reflections is not to deny any interest to the drawing of lots, but only to disqualify it as a legitimate democratic foundation for decision-making. Democratic legitimacy adheres to the equal right of every citizen to express a political will. So much so that it would disappear if sortition were to be substituted for elections. Nevertheless, that doesn't mean that election is the paragon of democracy. It only means that, if the election principle was to be compared to another, putatively more democratic principle, it would be to that of the direct government of the people, not to that of sortition. If it is agreed, by contrast, that representation is necessary, then election appears as the only possible democratic way to designate representatives.

---

ours is an act of will and it differs from knowing that there is a statistical probability that another person will behave politically as we would do. In the first case, the individual exerts his judgement and takes a decision on public matters; in the second, he renounces his judgement and his right to express his political choices on behalf of others he hasn't appointed to that office.

Stefan Rummens and Raf Geenens

Democracy as a Collective Process

A Constructivist Critique of Hélène Landemore's Lottocratic Proposals

Abstract: *This chapter compares the lottocratic paradigm with a more traditional understanding of representative democracy. It does so by focusing on the lottocratic model proposed by Hélène Landemore, who is one of the dominant authors in this growing literature. The authors address two elements in her model.*

First, they investigate the epistemic assumptions on which Landemore's model is built. Landemore evaluates the performance and the legitimacy of political procedures in light of their ability to reach "correct" decisions. She thereby assumes that the good or true answer exists independently of the decision procedure. If randomly assembled panels are preferable for Landemore, it is because they are most likely to find the best possible answer. From a constructivist perspective, as defended by Jürgen Habermas and others, these assumptions are questionable. There is no procedure-independent standard. The best interpretation of the common good can only be found through a procedure in which all views and sensitivities are included, and which offers participants the possibility to transform their views in light of the arguments offered by others.

Second, the authors investigate Landemore's conception of representation. According to Landemore, political representation should be understood narrowly: a body is representative if the composition of its membership corresponds to the sociological diversity in the population. This allows her to say that we should strive for a "pure" representation, where the representative body is a "mirror image" of the people it represents. This narrow, descriptive understanding of representation overlooks the richer and more complex role political representation plays in the collective self-understanding of citizens. It also overlooks that every representation is, inevitably, a construction. Recognising the constructed nature of collective representations is crucial in a democracy. As Claude Lefort and others have pointed out: it is precisely because there is no "pure" or "correct" representation that debate and contestation become legitimate.

Proposals for a democratic system based on sortition rather than elections are gaining ground among both academics and activists (Abizadeh, 2021; Gastil and Wright, 2018; Guerrero, 2014; Landemore, 2020; Owen and Smith, 2018; Van Reybrouck, 2016). Advocates of these proposals believe that legislative chambers composed of randomly selected citizens will prove superior to the elected chambers we are accustomed to. Three main arguments are generally invoked to support this belief. First, sortition is deemed to generate *epistemically* superior outcomes. Elected politicians often cater to short-term, particularistic interests. They are influenced by lobby groups and campaign financiers. And in the context of competitive, highly mediatised elections they are inclined to make unrealistic promises that are at odds with the common good. Sortition chambers are supposedly isolated from such pressures. As a result—and with guidance of social scientists—they can deliberate more reasonably and make better decisions. A second argument pertains to *representation*. In contrast with the elitist bias of elections, stratified sampling guarantees that a sortition chamber faithfully "mirrors" the composition of society in terms of pre-determined categories like gender, class, education or ethnicity. This so-called "descriptive representation" gives ordinary citizens an opportunity to participate in the legislative process, replacing electoral elitism with genuine democratic equality and inclusion. The third main argument, building on the previous two, is that allotted chambers, because of their epistemic and representative features, will be accepted by citizens as *more legitimate* than traditional elected parliaments. The use of sortition will, therefore, overcome the distrust and resentment that increasingly undermines existing democratic systems. When citizens know that political decisions are made by "people like us", they will feel confident that these decisions align with their own beliefs and preferences.

Elsewhere, we have argued that the democratic hopes projected onto sortition are misguided and that the lottocratic model faces serious shortcomings on all three accounts—epistemic quality, representation and legitimacy—when compared to our traditional parliamentary system (Rummens and Geenens, 2023). Our argument revolves around the *visibility* of the decision-making process as a unique feature of electoral politics (Rummens, 2012; 2016). Electoral competition creates a mediatised staging of democratic conflicts. This allows the audience of citizens to read the political process and to see who has decided what and which alternatives were favoured by the opposition. This public staging of conflicts gives focus and structure to a wider public debate in which civil society organisations and ordinary citizens can also participate so as to influence collective decisions. In contrast, the sortition chamber lacks visibility and appears to outsiders as a black box. Randomly selected citizens have no electoral incentive to face public scrutiny and the media have no interesting adversarial story to tell. Citizens might be interested to learn what goes on inside the box, but will find it hard if not impossible to understand which decisions have been made for what reasons over which alternatives. And they will feel frustrated by their inability to hold their randomly selected representatives to account. In sum, the lack of visibility implies that the allotted chamber cannot connect with the wider audience of citizens on the outside and cannot support the collective opinion- and will-formation processes that are essential in a genuinely democratic society.

The purpose of the present contribution is not to simply rehearse our criticisms of lottocracy but to focus, instead, on Hélène Landemore (2013; 2020). Her "open democracy" is one of the most elaborate models for a sortition-based system and is a major reference point in ongoing debates. We aim to show how our general arguments against sortition also apply to her specific proposals. Our critique is structured around the three arguments presented above. (1) We argue, in *epistemic terms*, that Landemore mistakenly reduces deliberation to a search for truth that can be pursued within the closed context of the allotted chamber. Instead, democratic deliberation is a public learning process in which all citizens can participate and in which our understanding of the common good is jointly constructed rather than merely discovered. (2) Landemore's descriptive understanding of *representation* makes her downplay the role of political representation in the construction of society's self-image as an autonomous collectivity. She also overlooks that the democratic distribution of political power and the authorisation and accountability of power-holders depend on the electoral mechanism. (3) In consequence, Landemore's lottocratic model suffers from a serious legitimacy deficit. Deliberation as a collective learning process does not only serve an epistemic purpose but is also crucial for the *legitimacy* of the resulting decisions. Without an electoral relation between citizens and representatives, it is not clear how the distribution and exercise of political power could ever be legitimate.

1. Deliberation as the Collective
Construction of the Common Good

Landemore's defence of lottocracy builds on an epistemic argument that she first developed in *Democratic Reason* (Landemore, 2013). This book's central claim is that democracy, understood as a combination of deliberation and voting, leads to outcomes that are epistemically superior to outcomes reached through other decision-making procedures. Her arguments in *Democratic Reason* especially target those who advocate expertocratic procedures. Landemore admits that, in some specific situations, experts might be better at finding the right solution. Yet we should acknowledge that politics, as "the domain of questions where human beings deal with the risk and uncertainty of human life as a collective problem", is such that "expertise is difficult to determine *ex ante*" (2013, p. 13). When there is a wide variety of unpredictable problems, it is more effective to select the members of our decision-making bodies in such a way that the *cognitive diversity* within the group is maximised, rather than to focus on the supposed *ability* or expertise of its individual members.

To defend the importance of cognitive diversity and explain why "diversity trumps ability", Landemore heavily relies on general formal proofs regarding the role of cognitive diversity in the context of problem-solving procedures as presented by Lu Hong and Scott E. Page (2004; 2012). When translating these formal results into a practical democratic context, Landemore argues that democratic representation (rather than, for example, oligarchy or expertocracy) is the best guarantee for cognitive diversity: "the function of representation is to reproduce the cognitive diversity present in the larger group on a scale at which simple deliberation remains feasible" (2013, p. 106). Importantly, this epistemic argument favouring democracy over expertocracy can also be used to argue that a democratic system based on sortition is superior to one based on elections. For Landemore, elections are inevitably elitist and, thus, undermine the "cognitive diversity" needed for adequate political decision-making (2020, pp. 3, 7–9, 40–52). Whereas "elections tend to bring to power socially and economically homogenous people" (2013, p. 108), "descriptive representation achieved through random lotteries [...] would preserve the cognitive diversity of the larger group" (*ibid.*, p. 109).

It seems to us, however, that Landemore's story relies on two related assumptions about the nature of political decision-making that are deeply problematic. Landemore assumes, first of all, that political problems are *factual* rather than *normative* and that an agreement about values and goals can be supposed to exist *prior to* the decision-making process. And she assumes, secondly, that politics is about *discovering* procedure-independent political truths rather than about collectively *constructing* the common good.

The fact that Landemore reduces political problems to factual issues is already clear from the metaphor with which she starts her book *Democratic Reason* (Landemore, 2013, pp. 3–9). Here, she compares politics to a situation in which a group of people has to find its way out of a maze by decoding clues written all over the walls. She plausibly argues that a variety of cognitive skills and perspectives in the group would prove useful for such a task. When she later discusses more concrete examples of how cognitive diversity enhances the problem-solving ability of a group, she first talks about a (fictitious) trial in which the jury discovers, on the basis of facts, that the accused could never have committed the murder she is charged with. Later, she turns to the real-life example of a New Haven neighbourhood where citizens jointly found a way to prevent recurrent muggings on a bridge by installing solar lamps subsidised by the federal government (*ibid.*, pp. 98–101). In each of her examples, the problem to be solved is a factual one and a consensus on the goal — getting out of the maze, discovering the truth about the murder, stopping the muggings — can be presupposed.

The fact that Landemore chooses such examples is not accidental. Her more general claim that diversity trumps ability essentially relies on the formal results presented by Hong and Page (2004). Yet Hong and Page (2004, pp. 16385–7) emphasise that, for them, cognitive diversity refers to a diversity of cognitive techniques and perspectives brought to bear on a well-delineated factual problem and therefore explicitly *not* to a "diversity of values or goals" (Landemore, 2013, p. 102). Jason Brennan, in his scathing critique of the potential political applicability of Hong and Page's formal results, rightly emphasises that the formal proof assumes a prior consensus on values as one of its main premises (Brennan and Landemore, 2022, pp. 251–61; Hong and Page, 2004, p. 16387) and is therefore inapplicable in contexts where normative disagreements are at stake. As Landemore acknowledges, a diversity of values or goals "would actually harm the collective effort to solve a problem" (Landemore, 2013, p. 102).

Landemore is aware of the fact that her bracketing of normative disagreements might pose a problem (*ibid.*, 213–19; 2014, 200–06).[1] She tries to rescue the situation by relying on a distinction introduced by Gerald Cohen (2003) between "fact-dependent principles" and "basic principles". She argues that it is plausible to assume that democratic societies agree on basic principles, such as "freedom, equality, solidarity, human rights, and democratic procedures" (Landemore, 2014, p. 204) and that all remaining disagreement therefore pertains to fact-dependent principles and could, thus, be solved by a better knowledge of the facts (Landemore, 2013, pp. 215–17). Her reference to Cohen's distinction is, however, unconvincing and goes against the grain of his argument. Cohen's central aim was to show that the justification of fact-dependent principles always relies on more basic fact-independent principles and that the facts, therefore, *never* suffice to settle normative matters. The idea that a widespread normative agreement on more basic principles can be assumed to simply exist and would be robust enough to settle normative questions on the basis of factual knowledge alone is completely absent from Cohen's argument.

In reality, the idea that political decision-making is simply a fact-finding matter is unambiguously rejected by all prominent democratic theories. True enough, most democratic models assume that some kind of prior consensus on basic principles is needed for a democracy to function properly. Even Chantal Mouffe's agonistic model assumes a prior consensus on the "principles of liberty and equality for all". As she emphasises, however, this consensus remains a *conflictual consensus* in that our main political quarrels concern normative disagreements about how these core values should be properly interpreted, applied and weighed against each other (Mouffe, 2000, pp. 102–04). A similar view characterises more deliberative models of democracy. For Jürgen Habermas (1996, pp. 118–31), a prior consensus on the equal protection of the private and public autonomy of all citizens is a condition of possibility for democratic deliberation. Yet in their deliberations citizens give these abstract ideas a more concrete, context-specific content. Empirical matters are relevant in this process, but the primary arguments are moral (*ibid.*, pp. 162–8). And although democratic deliberation is consensus-oriented, the full

---

[1] For similar criticisms of Landemore's inability to account for value diversity and normative disagreements, see Muirhead (2014), Stich (2014), and Levinson (2014).

normative consensus is only aimed for as its *outcome* and not presupposed as its premise.

Landemore's second assumption—that political decision-making is about "discovering" or "predicting" procedure-independent truths—is less outlandish and also endorsed by several other authors working within the deliberative paradigm (e.g. Estlund, 2008). Landemore's version is based on the widespread idea that, in morality and politics, we have to choose between either pure proceduralism—according to which the contingent outcome of the procedure *ipso facto* determines what is right—or the objectivity of procedure-independent standards (Landemore, 2013, pp. xvii–xviii, 44–6, 219–20). As argued elsewhere (Rummens, 2007; 2018), this false dichotomy fails to capture how, for instance, Habermasian discourse theory combines procedural and substantive commitments in an inextricable manner (Habermas, 2003). Through his principle of morality (U) Habermas acknowledges that there is an objective standard of rightness stating that norms are valid only if they are impartial in the sense of "giving equal consideration to the values and interests of all people affected". At the same time, this objective norm is not procedure-independent: deliberation between those affected is needed to determine which norms actually satisfy this requirement of impartiality. Actual discourses thereby serve both heuristic and transformative purposes. This means that the relevant values and interests cannot be known from a third-person outsider perspective but need to be brought into the debate by the people affected themselves. It also means that deliberation is a transformative learning process in which people try to understand the perspective of others through a process of role-taking and possibly adapt their own values and preferences in view of the legitimate values and preferences of others.

The importance of deliberation as a collective learning process is widely accepted and does not depend on the specifics of Habermas's framework. From the earliest days of the deliberative paradigm, the aim to *transform* rather than simply aggregate preferences has been identified as a defining feature of deliberative democracy (Elster, 1986). In addition, the *heuristic* need for the actual participation of potentially affected people has been connected to the need to take seriously the specific and historically situated preferences and needs of citizens as what Seyla Benhabib (1992, 158–70) has aptly called "concrete others". In contrast, Landemore's conceptualisation of political deliberation as a value-free fact-finding process, in which citizen participation serves the purpose of enriching the cognitive tool-box, completely misses the point of the deliberative turn and fails, more generally, to capture the nature of political decision-making.

The heuristic and transformative function of actual deliberation explains why the lottocratic restriction of democratic deliberation to the controlled environment of sortition chambers is a bad idea. Democracy as a collective learning process is only possible if citizens are mentally "plugged into" the ongoing political decision-making debates and if these debates happen in constant interaction with civil society and the wider public sphere (Rummens and Geenens, 2023). To illustrate this, think of essential learning processes our societies have gone through in the past century, such as the feminist or ecological movements. These take a tremendous amount of work and time and the protracted commitment of generations of activists. These processes cannot be reproduced on the tiny scale of short-lived sortition chambers. The epistemic efforts needed require a constant and mutual interaction with civil society and the wider public sphere. The legislative body has to be open to the influence of arguments generated outside it. And the debates at the core of the political system have to provide structure and focus to the wider public debate. And these debates need to be visibly staged so that claims made by, for instance, feminist or ecological advocates are heard by the entire citizenry. This allows citizens to critically test these new claims and gradually incorporate them into their own worldviews. In this process, these initial concerns do not remain unchanged either. In other words, complex issues require permanent interactions between citizens, civil society and decision-makers in which arguments, demands and, ulti-mately, proposals for legislation are circulated back and forth.

Landemore, like other advocates of sortition (e.g. Guerrero, 2014, p. 177), is rather disparaging about civil society. She writes that we should not expect "a series of haphazard, unregulated, and decentralized deliberations among groups of different sizes and compositions" to pro-vide "the proper way of setting up the agenda" and rhetorically asks whether the "deliberation in the wild" of the public sphere "even amounts to proper deliberation" at all (Landemore, 2020, p. 38; also 2020, pp. 8, 206). Even authors who are more aware of the importance of civil society and the wider public debate, like Jane Mansbridge (2019; 2020), fail to explain how the interaction between a sortition chamber and the wider public sphere could be organised. This is not a coincidence. In the electoral system this interaction is supported by the visible staging of political conflicts. The oppositional debates amongst parties and politicians provide structure and focus to the wider public debate. At the same time politicians, eager to be re-elected, provide clear targets for civil society organisations trying to have an impact on the decision-making process. The absence of a staged political conflict in a sortition system makes it unclear how the wider public debate could be structured or focused. And since sortition chambers are intentionally shielded from outside influence, civil society actors no longer have politicians or other decision-makers they can try to convince. As Mansbridge (2020, p. 21) admits, it is unclear whether civil society as we now know it would continue to thrive or even exist at all in a sortition system. Without the hope of influencing the democratic process, civil society action and the wider public debate would simply lose their main *raison d'être*.

Some lottocratic authors propose to enhance the interaction between the sortition chamber and civil society by organising consultations with civil society actors or by having the participating citizens reach out to the public sphere (Mansbridge, 2019, p. 198). Such interactions would, however, generate a *sortition dilemma*. The more they are stimulated, the more the initial motivation for sortition—creating an environment for deliberation that is shielded from outside influence—loses its force and the more sortition starts to reconstruct—in a less visible and hence democratically inferior way—the mechanisms of interaction and accountability that characterise the electoral system (Rummens and Geenens, 2023).

2. Constructive Representation
and the Legitimation of Power

In this section we investigate Landemore's conception of representation in *Open Democracy*. For Landemore, a body is democratically representative if its membership is composed through an *inclusive* and *equal* process. Importantly, this does not mean that all citizens should have an equal say in appointing representatives. It rather means that all citizens should enjoy an equal probability of being included in the representative assembly. Landemore defends this by stating that inclusiveness and equality are the most fundamental democratic values and by claiming that these values naturally point to the ideal of "descriptive representation". When the principles of inclusiveness and equality are perfectly realised, "we should see a representative body that is statistically identical with the demos" (Landemore, 2020, pp. 88–9). This ideal of "identical" representation is to be achieved by combining sortition and rotation (*ibid.*, pp. 90,

142). Sortition gives all citizens an equal chance, no matter how low, to sit in the assembly. Rotation is needed to prevent these ordinary citizens from morphing "into a class of professionalized politicians" (*ibid.*, p. 142), as this would break the identity between representatives and citizens. Landemore defends this ideal of identity in very explicit terms. A lotto-cratic assembly, she writes, comes close to offering "a *mirror image* of the people it represents" (*ibid.*, p. 96, italics added). The aim is a "*pure* lotto-cratic representation" which offers a "*pure* demographic mapping of the population" (*ibid.*, p. 90, italics added). In her earlier work, Landemore had rejected stratified sampling and advocated fully random sampling as the best way to guarantee the identity of the representatives and the represented (Landemore, 2013, pp. 110–13). In *Open Democracy* she concedes that stratified sampling might be needed. If a citizens' assembly is to be genuinely representative of the entire population in its full sociological diversity, it would have to be unworkably large. Thus, in actual practice, stratified sampling (typically on the basis of markers like age, gender, geography, ethnicity, education or socio-economic status) is needed to obtain a representative sample (2020, p. 92).

In what follows, we put this narrow, descriptive account of representation into question. We believe that Landemore relies on assumptions about the nature of political representation that are deeply problematic. The relation between democracy and political representation is richer and more complex than she acknowledges. We will point at three specific shortcomings. First, we address the notion that sortition could lead to a "pure" or "identical" representation of the citizenry. Second, we explain that democratic representation should be understood as an interactive and constructive process, something Landemore overlooks. Finally, we point out that she disregards the deep connection between representation and the distribution, authorisation and accountability of political power in a democratic regime.

Landemore's belief in an "ideal" or "pure" representative sample, composed by scientists on the basis of sociological markers, strikes us as suspiciously undemocratic. If democracy gives ultimate decisional authority to the citizens (as expressed by such concepts as "popular sovereignty" or "collective autonomy"), it seems to follow that citizens can decide for themselves by whom they wish to be represented. Landemore divests citizens of this possibility as it is the social engineer (the statistician, sociologist or demographer) who, prior to the democratic process, decides on the basis of purportedly scientific arguments what constitutes a faithful mirroring of the *demos*, basing herself on descriptive markers like age, gender or ethnicity. This premature foreclosing of the democratic process is incompatible with the autonomy of the citizens. The citizens' political freedom includes the right to decide which considerations are salient in appointing a representative, and these considerations will often be political or ideological rather than descriptive.

Landemore might object that citizens are not particularly good at appointing representatives. If elections are inevitably biased towards certain elites (cf. Landemore, 2020, p. 89), citizens end up being represented by people who are decidedly not like them. As to the interventions of the social engineer, she would likely object that these interventions are necessary for logistical reasons only. A purely random selection of, say, 10,000 citizens would be truly representative, without any need for stratified sampling. Unfortunately, a meeting of 10,000 citizens is unwieldily large, so some decisions are needed as to who can sit around the table. But this objection is moot. The only sample that would be truly identical to the set of all citizens is the entire set itself. This is precisely what Jorge Luis Borges was after in his famous short story "On Exactitude in Science". A map, in order to be of any use, needs to be substantially smaller than the terrain it represents and needs to bring out its most meaningful features. Yet it is never obvious which features are meaningful and how they are to be represented: what is most relevant to a walker is useless for a truck driver. Nor is it obvious how a curved surface is to be projected on a two-dimensional plane: every projection is a distortion. Morever, one needs to decide which way is up. The scientist wishing to produce a map that is truly identical to the land it represents would end up—as in Borges's story—with a map as large as the land itself. If a neutral map is impossible, a neutral representation of the entire citizenry is certainly impossible. Every representation is, inevitably, a construction. Landemore's claim that social scientists can produce a perfect "mirror image" of the people is therefore deeply problematic. Making a representation always involves decisions about which features are meaningful and which features are less meaningful. These decisions cannot be made in a neutral, "scientific" manner and will always be subject to debate.

For Landemore, democracy hinges on the possibility of a "true" or "neutral" representation of the citizenry: decisions are democratic when made by an assembly that is descriptively "identical" to the entire population. So does the impossibility of a "true" or "neutral" representation spell doom for the project of representative democracy? On a more sophisticated reading of democracy, it is rather the other way around. Claude Lefort has argued that democracy begins precisely when one accepts the impossibility of a truly "good" or "correct" representation of the people (Lefort, 1988). For Lefort, recognising the constructed nature of collective representations is crucial. Non-democratic regimes believe that the structure, the components and the very identity of society can be defined once and for all. Democratic regimes operate on the opposite logic: society lacks a definitive self-description. And it is precisely because there is no "pure" or "correct" representation that debate and contestation become legitimate. The fundamental point is that the people, unlike the landscape represented on a map, do not exist prior to their representation. The will of the people, and even the self-image citizens have of themselves as members of this specific people, is constructed through a process of representative claim making (Geenens, 2019). Obviously, this undermines the idea that there can be an "identity" between representatives and represented, and that this identity can serve as a touchstone to legitimate the role or the selection of representatives. It also implies that democratic representation is a more intricate process than Landemore suggests. This leads to a second critique of her conception of representation.

For Landemore, the essence of the representative process happens inside the citizens' assembly, where a small number of citizens engage in a deliberation that is "carefully curated and facilitated" by social scientists so as to ensure the epistemic quality of its outcome (Landemore, 2020, p. 139). Admittedly, she hints at some additional elements that might link the "black box" of the assembly with the wider citizenry. Ordinary citizens have agenda-setting power through citizens' initiatives (*ibid.*, p. 203). And under the heading of "transparency" Landemore explains that all political activities should have "windows": ordinary citizens should be "able to witness, observe, and thus make up their minds about the activities of the actors engaged in the political process" (*ibid.*, p. 143). Unfortunately, these interactions between political debates and the broader citizenry are not fleshed out. Landemore's reader does not learn how they would function in practice and they do not play a crucial role in her normative story, which centres on sortition and rational deliberation within the sortition chamber. On a richer understanding of democratic representation, however, the interaction between the political process and the broader citizenry is essential. If one understands representation as a process that is *interactive* and *constructive*, the back-and-forth between representatives and represented is not a useful add-on, but is the very heart of democratic life.

The interactive and constructive properties of representation are closely tied to the epistemic argument made above. Rhetorically skilled politicians and well-functioning parties build communicative connections with citizens and civil society actors, thereby exposing all citizens to the relevant arguments so that they too—and not only the select few in the assembly—can alter their views. Parliament, in particular, is a crucial focal point: here, the most important considerations are brought together and the core of the conflict is made *visible* (Rummens, 2012). As opposed to rational debates between unknown representatives selected by lot, a vivid clash between well-known, elected politicians lends itself well to transmission through mass media and can thus capture wide attention. Citizens play a bigger role in this process than it might appear. When politicians put forward certain views and claim to speak in the name of those whom they represent—i.e. when they formulate "representative claims" (Saward, 2010)—they are not just mouthing the preferences of their voters but are often proposing new ideas or solutions. These proposals might be actively challenged, but they might also be accepted and hence bring citizens to new views and new positions. Thus, representation is an interactive process, in which the "audience", even if it appears to be passive, is involved to various degrees, for instance because it is to "adjudicate claims" (*ibid.*, p. 56) made on its behalf. It is through these *interactions* that we collectively *construct*, in an often messy way, an ever-evolving understanding of the common good.[2]

Democratic representation is also a *constructive* process in a more fundamental sense. Political debates should not just produce good decisions, as Landemore likes to believe. They are also crucial in constructing and maintaining our collective self-image. Political representation is, first of all, collective self-representation. How a democratic society represents itself on its political stage is constitutive for the self-understanding of that society and its members as a whole. It is through

---

[2]   The constructive role of representation is strongly emphasised in the recent literature on the "constructivist turn" (cf. Disch, van de Sande and Urbinati, 2019) and it is difficult to see how this role can be fulfilled by an assembly of unknown, randomly selected citizens. Bizarrely, Landemore herself cites this constructivist turn and seems to agree with its findings (Landemore, 2020, p. 66).

political discourses that we come to see ourselves as members of one and the same society, and as members of this specific society, with a shared responsibility for its future. This awareness of a common fate is indispensable to create solidarity among citizens. And without civic solidarity it is doubtful whether citizens would be willing to uphold collective decisions and to maintain ties of economic solidarity.

Political parties play a particular role in this process. Landemore herself is undecided about the necessity of parties (she writes that the question of parties reveals the "conceptual limits" of her paradigm; Landemore, 2020, p. 145), but she hopes that they can be replaced by "transitory, fluid, and self-reconfiguring associations of citizens" (*ibid.*, p. 147). Just like today's parties, these would be "bundling platforms" (*ibid.*, p. 148), merging principles and ideas into a coherent long-term vision, yet they would do so without electoral incentives. This seems like a rather unrealistic proposal. Landemore is certainly correct in characterising the work of parties as one of "bundling". Political parties do the hard work of constructing clear ideological positions. And they give permanence to these positions, functioning as "epistemic reservoirs" —even when they are not in power—that can inform and inspire citizens to construct their own position. The opposition between parties also helps to give structure and ideological clarity to public debates: the presence of multiple parties on the political stage shows how opinions and concerns are interwoven with a more encompassing political outlook and how these different outlooks are related or differ. Most fundamentally, the sheer presence of multiple parties, proposing policy packages that would push us toward different futures, constantly reminds us of our collective freedom. The open clash between different ideologies makes it very clear that our future is not fixed or predetermined, by the iron laws of history or by economic necessity. Rather, it is us who, through our political choices, can shape the future of our society. Our self-image as an autonomous society is thus closely tied up with the presence of a political stage where there is an ongoing conflict about our collective decisions.

A third striking lacuna in Landemore's view on representation is the connection with *power*. Landemore seeks to reconstruct the normative core of democracy without making use of the concept of power (the word "power" is even absent in the book's index). But is this possible? In democracy as we know it, procedural rules concerning the allocation and the exercise of power are normatively highly important (Geenens, 2007). The most important of these procedural rules is voting.

The voting mechanism—one person, one vote—is typically valued because it gives citizens an equal slice of influence over the decision-making process. It is responsive to the input of all citizens and weighs their influence equally, thereby creating a moment of mutual recognition: citizens are respected as equal members of a self-governing collectivity rather than as mere objects of legislation. In referendums, the citizens' equal participation in a decision is very direct. In elections, citizens exercise their power by selecting representatives. The power to appoint representatives is an important one and democratic electoral procedures are democratic precisely because they distribute it in a strictly equal manner. In elections, the input of every citizen is recognised as irreplaceable and is given equal weight. Voting cannot substitute for the process of rational justification, but it does provide a unique moment where the political or ideological orientation of every individual is taken into account and is considered equally relevant.

That citizens can select their own representatives follows from their political freedom. Electing politicians is, after all, an act of *authorisation*: one authorises someone else to speak in one's own name. Elections reflect the basic normative given that in a democracy no one is naturally entitled to hold power over others. The only possible source of all decision-making power is the citizens themselves. Hence, they alone can authorise certain co-citizens to exercise it in their place. And there seems to be no reason for distributing this authorising power unequally.

Voting plays a further role in that it helps citizens to hold their representatives *accountable*. It follows from the citizens' political autonomy, and from the very concept of authorisation, that those who are authorised to legislate, administer and govern in our name can be held accountable by us. In parliament, members of government are answerable to the representatives of the people. Again, this is an adversarial and visible process, driven by the dynamics between government and opposition and stimulated by an inquisitive and critical public opinion. This process helps citizens making up their mind in a next round of elections. The result is a strong chain of accountability between citizens and decision-makers, a chain that crucially depends on the mechanism of elections: it is because citizens elect their own representatives that they have power over the decision-making process.

Representatives selected by sortition, in contrast, are problematic from a power perspective. In Landemore's model, citizens have no official channels to steer the decision-making process. Landemore might object that, when the sample is perfect, the proportional distribution of political positions in the assembly mirrors the distribution in the general population, so no steering is needed. In practice, however, assemblies will be composed by social scientists with criteria like age, gender or ethnicity. Unless one operates on the very crude assumption that people who are, in this sense, "like me" will also share my political or ideological views, this assembly will not match the actual distribution of views in the population.[3] In an electoral system, in contrast, the choice between competing parties gives citizens the possibility to consciously steer the collective decision-making process in a specific ideological direction (e.g. liberal, conservative, ecological, …). And the law-giving body literally represents the proportional strength of these different positions in the population.[4] Thus, citizens can push politics in the direction that they, on the basis of their personal interpretation of society's situation, needs and priorities, find most important. In addition to voting, they can engage in public debates, raise awareness, mobilise other citizens, launch petitions, target representatives, join or create civil society associations and even become politicians themselves. Politicians, in turn, have an obvious electoral incentive to take this pressure seriously. In Landemore's model, citizens have no means to formally authorise or control their representatives. Nor is it clear how they could influence the decision-making process in a more informal way, as the representatives are not supposed to be constantly exposed to the pressure of public opinion. It is difficult not to describe this situation as a complete disenfranchisement of the citizens.[5]

---

[3] One could twitch the procedure and introduce political attitudes as the key descriptive marker so as to obtain an assembly that is ideologically representative. This would require asking potential representatives for their views, grouping them in coherent blocks, asking all citizens for their views and composing the assembly accordingly. But then one is reconstructing the electoral process as we know it, albeit in an awkward and paternalistic manner.

[4] Surprisingly, Landemore admits the importance of proportionally representing the citizens' views when she discusses the possibility of a "weighted" forum where different representatives have different "degrees of power", depending on the number of delegated votes they amass (2020, p. 126).

[5] Tom Malleson (2018, p. 407) writes that, in a sortition system, citizens are "disenfranchised from the political process" as they lack the means "to transform their dissent into political power". And he adds that this might push frustrated citizens to extraconstitutional and possibly violent means.

3. Legitimacy and Motivation

In this final section, we draw out the consequences for legitimacy. Landemore herself, in *Open Democracy*, tones down the importance of legitimacy, but she clearly believes that non-elected representatives could make decisions that are as legitimate, or even more legitimate, than those of elected representatives. When she explicitly discusses the notion of legitimacy, she relegates it to the status of an "extrinsic" or "secondary" democratic property (Landemore, 2020, 87).[6] And she interprets this property very narrowly. Legitimacy is required, but it can be obtained in an isolated moment of authorisation. And she sees no reason to apply this demand of authorisation to every individual representative. Instead, she claims that the selection mechanism as a whole (i.e. the lottery) should be authorised by the citizenry in a one-off majority vote. In Landemore's own words: "the democratic legitimacy of mini-publics or self-selected assemblies (or any other political body really) should be traced to a majoritarian vote authorizing the procedure of random selection, as a necessary, but insufficient condition for their overal legitimacy' (*ibid.*, p. 108). The authorising vote is only an "insufficient" condition because, as Landemore adds, the legitimacy of the citizens' assembly will also depend on the merits of its policies and the deliberative quality of the debates. Still, the majority vote seems central for legitimacy. This is surprising because it assumes that legitimacy has a natural connection with a majoritarian procedure in which all those concerned have an equal right to vote.[7]

More fundamentally, it is unclear how a one-time vote could generate permanent, long-term legitimacy for the citizens' assembly, even if that assembly deliberates in a rational way and tries to make excellent decisions. Can democratic legitimacy indeed be guaranteed in a durable

---

6   Landemore distinguishes "legitimacy" from "democraticity" and from the primary democratic principles of "inclusiveness" and "equality" (2020, pp. 87–8). Thus, a decision-making body can be democratic (because it is composed in an egalitarian and inclusive manner) without being legitimate (because the citizens have not authorised it). Inversely, there can be non-democratic decision-making bodies that are legitimate (*ibid.*, p. 108).

7   If a descriptively representative citizen panel is more democratic than a majority vote, one would expect that the agreement of such a panel is needed to legitimate the majority vote, rather than the other way around. Landemore only evades this problem by stating, *ex nihilo*, that "legitimacy" and "democraticity" are independent principles (cf. the previous note).

way without classical representative institutions? We believe it cannot, for various reasons.

Think of the transformative effect of deliberative procedures. The views of representatives often evolve as an effect of contributions made by other representatives. If this would not happen, there would be little point in deliberating. But unless the wider citizenry is mentally plugged into the debate and exposed to the arguments, their views cannot change. In consequence, the gap between the views of the "transformed" citizens and those of the public at large risks becoming very large. Thus, if deliberations are not genuinely public, decisions made by an allotted chamber might not be perceived as an adequate interpretation of the common good (Lafont, 2020, p. 116). Landemore writes that an open democracy will not see too many demonstrations and protests because "the causes for discontent would be nipped in the bud much earlier in the process" (Landemore, 2020, p. 205). But this sounds implausible. It is an essential epistemic shortcoming of sortition that it does not provide the citizens with an opportunity to learn and understand why the decisions made are good decisions. Without this opportunity, citizens might well see decisions as illegitimate directives imposed on them from above by decision-makers they do not know on the basis of considerations they do not share. Absent a proper mediatisation of the deliberative process — something nearly impossible given the lack of dramatic dynamics — the citizens' assembly remains to outsiders a black box, producing singular decisions with which they will often disagree. Thus, the epistemic deficits of sortition will also lead to a legitimacy deficit. Only by participating — even if only mentally — in the argumentative process can citizens be convinced that the eventual decision deserves their recognition and has a plausible claim to rational justifiability.

The procedures that distribute, allocate and control formal political power have an equally important role in legitimating democratic decisions. Voting, by creating a chain of authorisation and accountability between representatives and citizens, promises to the latter that it is they who, ultimately, control collective decisions and hence strengthens their sense of joint authorship. Universal suffrage is valuable precisely because it shows that the political views of every individual citizen are taken seriously. This moment of equal recognition is especially important for the outvoted minority which, by definition, remains unconvinced by the winning arguments and hence will not find in these arguments enough ground to legitimate the decision. The voting procedure offers additional ground here: the equal distribution of power helps dissenters recognise the legitimacy of the winning decision. This situation contrasts sharply with the bleak prospects for popular control in a lottocratic regime.

It can be added that the sheer visibility of representatives, which comes naturally in classical democratic institutions, already generates a sense of recognition: citizens can literally see that their views have been voiced and received a fair hearing. Again, this is especially important for dissenters. Political actors have articulated their position in a well-argued manner in plain view and have been listened to by opposing political actors and by the broader public. This sends a clear message that the minority's ideological outlook is taken seriously by their co-citizens. Moreover, a democratic decision is—at least in principle—never final. Even if a position is outvoted, it does not become illegitimate. The debate can always be reopened and the minority can always try again to convince the majority. A multiparty system offers a clear advantage in this regard: all political positions remain visibly present on the political stage, even the outvoted ones, giving these positions a form of public recognition and signalling that the current majority is only a temporary one.

In sum, we believe that the public staging of conflicts, as realised in classical representative institutions, is crucial for democratic legitimacy. Societal disagreements should be dealt with by staging and channelling them in the political sphere. Politics is not simply about reason but also about emotions and identification. That is why democracy needs a vibrant confrontation of ideas, which makes sure that oppositional voices are heard and recognised, which gives citizens real political choices, and allows them to identify with particular political actors and, through them, with the political process as a whole. And it needs an electoral process, allowing citizens to appoint their own representatives and hold them accountable. In all these ways, electoral representation pulls citizens into the decision-making process and gives them a genuine sense of collective authorship. This is not what lottocracy would bring us. When power is handed over to representatives who have not been authorised by the citizens, whose deliberations are not publicly mediatised and who cannot be held accountable for their decisions, citizens will not just feel that they are being disenfranchised, they *are* being disenfranchised. This might lead to very real motivational problems. Landemore's sortition-based model risks exacerbating depoliticisation and will likely strengthen the feeling that citizens are no longer in control of their own society.

Cristina Lafont and Nadia Urbinati

Defending Democracy Against Lottocracy

Abstract: *The development of citizens' assemblies and other deliberative mini-publics like citizens' juries, deliberative polls, etc. over the past two decades is one of the most exciting democratic innovations. Involving randomly selected citizens in political decision-making is seen by many scholars of politics as the most promising way to overcome the current crisis of democracy. We agree that these institutions have a lot of democratic potential. However, we are worried by the "lottocratic" conceptions of democracy that are guiding proposals for democratic reform using these sortition-based institutions. The most ambitious among these proposals call for dismantling electoral democracies and replacing them with a lottocracy. Our main worry with this new development is not that a lottocracy is going to be established any time soon. Our worry is with what we call the "lotto-cratic mentality" that underlies these conceptions and which is based on deeply undemocratic assumptions. This mentality amounts to a peculiar form of techno-populism, a combination of a technocratic conception of politics and a populist conception of political representation, both of which normalise anti-democratic assumptions by making them appear more democratic than those that sustain electoral democracies. In the first section we focus on the devaluation of political equality and the normalisation of the expectation of blind deference, and in the second section the focus is on the devaluation of political freedom and forms of collective agency (like political parties, social organisations, etc.) in favour of a highly individualised and passive view of political citizenship.*

The development of citizens' assemblies and other deliberative mini-publics like citizens' juries, deliberative polls, etc. over the past two decades is one of the most exciting democratic innovations.[1] The success of the Irish citizens' assemblies which led to the legalisation of same-sex marriage and decriminalisation of abortion, as well as the proliferation of citizens' assemblies for addressing climate change, are getting more and more political actors, social movements, etc. involved in the process of designing and organising them.[2] Involving randomly selected citizens in political decision-making is seen by many as the most promising way to increase citizen participation and democratic control and thus to overcome the current crisis of democracy.

We agree that these institutions have a lot of democratic potential. However, we are worried by the "lottocratic" conceptions of democracy that are guiding proposals for democratic reform using these sortition-based institutions. The most ambitious among these proposals call for dismantling electoral democracies and replacing them with a lottocracy (this would require getting rid of elections, the right to vote, political parties, elected assemblies and replacing them just with assemblies of randomly selected citizens).[3]

Now, our main worry with this new development is not that a lottocracy is going to be established any time soon. Our worry is with what we call the "lottocratic mentality" that underlies these conceptions, and which is based on deeply undemocratic assumptions. Our worry is that the lottocratic mentality is not only spreading among academics and democratic theorists but also among practitioners involved in designing these institutions, along with politicians, social movements and the

---

[1]   For a detailed analysis of the key similarities and differences between these types of deliberative mini-publics see Smith and Setälä (2019, pp. 3–5). On citizens' juries see Crosby and Nethercut (2005); on citizens' assemblies see Fournier, Kolk and Carty (2011) and Warren and Pearse (2008); on Deliberative Polls see Fishkin (2018).

[2]   In the 2000s, citizens' assemblies were launched in British Colombia (2004), Ontario (2006) and the Netherlands (2006) to discuss proposals for electoral reform. They offered a model for subsequent assemblies that have been established with broader mandates such as the recent Irish Citizens' Assembly (2016–18) that issued reports on several topics (some constitutional in nature) or the Citizens Convention for Climate (2019 and 2020) that discussed reducing France's carbon emissions by 40%. For a good overview of this development see Reuchamps *et al.* (forthcoming).

[3]   See e.g. Guerrero (2014), Landemore (2020), Van Reybrouck (2016).

citizenry at large. This mentality amounts to a peculiar form of *techno-populism*, a combination of a technocratic conception of politics and a populist conception of political representation, both of which normalise anti-democratic assumptions by making them appear not just compatible with democratic ideals but even *more* democratic than those that sustain electoral democracies.[4] Our additional worry, of course, is that, to the extent that the lottocratic mentality guides the development and institutionalisation of citizens' assemblies and similar mini-publics, the democratic potential of these institutions would be lost. They will become yet another shortcut that enables political decisions to be made by the few while bypassing the citizenry.[5]

It is because of these worries that we offer an in-depth analysis of the various elements that form the core of this approach in our forthcoming book, *The Lottocratic Mentality.* We don't have the space to provide an overview of all of them here, but we would like to focus on the most important ones. Since the very core of democracy is the ideal of treating each other as free and as equals, focusing on the reinterpretation of political equality and freedom at the core of the lottocratic mentality helps identify the main worries.

In the first section we focus on the devaluation of political equality and the normalisation of the expectation of blind deference, and in the second section the focus is on the devaluation of political freedom and forms of collective agency (like political parties, social organisations, etc.) in favour of a highly individualised and passive view of political citizenship.

1. Lottocratic Technopopulism:
Political Inequality and Blind Deference

As mentioned before, lottocrats see themselves as radical democrats and argue that political inclusion and equality would be better realised if democracies were to use sortition procedures—such as lotteries or random selection among ordinary citizens—instead of electing representatives from political elites. As also mentioned, the most ambitious proposals envision replacing legislative assemblies of elected representatives with assemblies of randomly selected citizens. According to them,

---

[4] We offer an in-depth analysis of these claims in Lafont and Urbinati (forthcoming).

[5] On the anti-democratic shortcuts involved in many current proposals for institutional reform see Lafont (2020).

the big advantage of lottocracy, from a democratic point of view, is that it promotes political equality—something that electoral democracy necessarily fails to do. They argue that in electoral democracies only the elite of elected representatives can exercise political power and the rest of the citizenry is simply excluded. By contrast, in a lottocracy all citizens have equal opportunities to be selected to exercise political power. As Guerrero puts it, selection by lottery reflects the ideal of political equality better than electoral democracy since "anyone might wield political power, and everyone has an equal chance of doing so" (Guerrero, 2014, pp. 168–9).

However, a detailed analysis of the lottocratic conception of political equality reveals two fundamental problems. First, the equalisation of the opportunities to exercise political power entails an extreme levelling down of the political rights and power that citizens in fact exercise in electoral democracies. Second, and even worse, this extreme levelling down is brought about with the aim of equalising asymmetric relationships of power among citizens which are objectionable precisely from the point of view of political equality. Let us briefly show each of the two problems.

The first problem is similar to the standard objection to egalitarianism, namely, that it allows levelling down in order to equalise everyone's situation, even if doing so leaves everyone worse off. The levelling down of actual political power involved in a lottocracy is alarming. Whereas in electoral democracies all citizens have the effective right to make important political decisions by voting in elections on a regular basis, the lottocratic reinterpretation of political equality transforms citizens' "equal right to make political decisions" into "the equal opportunity to be selected" to make political decisions. Keeping in mind that the actual chance of being selected once in one's lifetime is near to zero, the extreme levelling down involved in the reinterpretation of political equality is obvious. If we take a different right as an example, like the right to health, it's easy to see what is so objectionable in the lottocratic interpretation of equality. Following the lottocratic formula, the right of "equal access" to health care, for instance, would be reinterpreted as the right to "equal chances to be selected" to have health care. Securing a lottocratic right to health care would be remarkably cheap, since only a few randomly selected citizens would actually enjoy access to it. This can't plausibly count as a way of providing equal rights to health care to everyone. Political rights are no different. Excluding the bulk of citizens from effective opportunities to exercise decision-making power can hardly count as a "democratic" strengthening of the political rights that citizens currently enjoy in democratic societies. Citizens would lose the effective right to exercise political power by voting in elections in order to have the opportunity to be selected (perhaps once in their lifetime if they are lucky) and to exercise some political power in a particular lottocratic assembly. But this is not the only problem. As we indicated earlier, this extreme reduction of the effective opportunities to exercise political power is done for the sake of establishing asymmetric relationships of power among citizens which are objectionable precisely from the point of view of political equality.

In electoral democracies, citizens elect their representatives based on their different political programmes and policy objectives. It is true that, once elected, representatives have many more opportunities to exercise political power than the rest of the citizenry. However, they do not have unilateral power because the citizenry, in turn, also exercises power over them. Elected representatives are accountable to the citizenry for their political decisions and, if citizens dislike their decisions, they can simply remove them from office in the next election, just by voting for a different political party or for other representatives. The power relationship between the elected representatives and the citizenry is bilateral.

By contrast, in a lottocracy the power relationship between representatives and the citizenry is asymmetric and unilateral. Representatives are randomly selected to make political decisions as they see fit and the rest of the citizenry must blindly defer to their decisions. The power relationship between them, far from being egalitarian, is actually a paradigmatic case of domination: the representatives exercise unilateral power over the represented and the latter must blindly obey their decisions. The situation is very different in electoral democracies, where citizens have the power to select from among the different political parties and programmes available. In so doing, they have the final say in shaping the political space within which representatives will need to operate until the next election. However, citizens exercise this very important power collectively as equals (according to the principle of "one person, one vote"). They exercise this power "omnilaterally" (to adopt the Kantian term). By contrast, in a lottocracy there are no egalitarian power relations. Political decisions are unilaterally taken by the randomly selected representatives as they see fit and the rest of the citizenry simply obeys.

Lottocrats argue that rotation among citizens equalizes the opportunities to be selected to exercise political power for all citizens in the long run. However, the problem is not that the opportunities are unequal. What is objectionable is that what is equalised are the opportunities to exercise the unilateral domination of some citizens over others. Equalising citizens' chances of "ruling" at least once in their lifetimes at the cost of being ruled over for most of their life *is not a plausible interpretation of political equality* any more than equalising the chances of being masters once in their lifetime at the cost of being slaves most of their life would be a plausible interpretation of social equality.

Lottocrats do not see the exclusion of the citizenry as a whole from political decision-making as a form of political inequality due to their peculiar blend of populist and technocratic assumptions. The incompatibility between these assumptions undermines the plausibility of lottocratic technopopulism. But, apart from these internal difficulties, once the populist and the technocratic traits of lottocratic conceptions are identified, then its non-democratic core becomes readily apparent.

Like populists, lottocrats are suspicious of political elites and think that ordinary citizens must take matters into their own hands in order to solve current democratic deficits. Citizens must enter the political system and do the job that the non-responsive political elites and political parties are unable or unwilling to do. Moreover, lottocrats also share the populist view of political representation as "embodiment".[6] Like the leader in traditional populism, the lottocratic assembly is supposed to embody "the people" because its members are *like* them. It is because the assembly "mirrors" the people that non-participants, who are the overwhelming majority of the citizenry, are expected to simply *trust* those few who are randomly selected, and to let them do the thinking and deciding for them. Under a highly problematic assumption of political homogeneity, the citizenry should trust that the recommendations of the assembly will invariably reflect their own interests, values and policy objectives.[7] Because those who are randomly selected are expected to make the same

---

[6] For an in-depth analysis of the lottocratic conception of representation as embodiment, see Lafont (2023). For an analysis of the conception of representation as embodiment in traditional populism, see Urbinati (2019).

[7] Elster, for example, defines democracy as "any kind of effective and formalized control by citizens over leaders or policies" (Elster, 1998, p. 98), without any apparent concern as to *which* citizens are in control.

decisions as the rest of the citizenry, there is no inequality of power or loss of democratic control.

However, there is a catch. Like technocrats, lottocrats are suspicious of simply letting citizens vote. Lottocrats are fearful of ignorant citizens and endorse the epistocratic assumption that political decisions should be made by the knowers—by those who are well informed and who have deliberated about the issues in sufficiently ideal conditions. This is why, instead of having the citizenry make political decisions collectively as equals (through, for example, elections or referenda), they insist that political decisions should be made by a few randomly selected assembly members whose views have been properly "filtered" through a careful deliberative process. Like technocrats, they expect that the (randomly selected) few will make *better* political decisions than the ignorant citizenry.[8]

Unfortunately, lottocrats cannot have it both ways. The populist "mirror" and the technocratic "filter" are mutually incompatible. Either the few participants in the assembly are supposed to make the *same* decisions as the rest of the citizenry because they are *like* them (and this is why citizens don't lose democratic control by blindly deferring to them) or the participants in the assembly are expected to make *better* decisions than the rest of the citizenry because they have become properly informed and have deliberated about them (and *this* is why the citizenry ought to blindly defer to them so that these better outcomes can be achieved). Both claims cannot be simultaneously true. Lottocrats must choose between these technocratic and populist claims. Yet, no matter which option they choose, excluding the bulk of the citizenry from political decision-making is equally anti-democratic in both cases, although for different reasons.

2. The Devaluation of Political Freedom and Forms of Collective Agency

The lottocratic mentality is part of the contemporary discourse on the crisis of democracy. Its *raison d'etre* is a reading that locates the reason for this crisis in the decision-making process or, rather, in the method of selecting those in charge of making decisions. After modifying the selection mechanism so that citizens feel less "under the yoke" of a self-

---

[8] We offer an in-depth analysis of the technocratic conception of politics at the core of the lottocratic mentality in Lafont and Urbinati (forthcoming).

referential, publicity-seeking political class, lottocracy goes on to theorise an alternative form of indirect power, which is called "lottery representation". Its project is to empower the people without restoring direct democracy and without using elections, procedures which it characterises as undemocratic. Its main problem is the form of participation that elections promote, which is competitive and conflictual; its purpose is to rid democratic politics of partisan opinions and replace it with a politics in which disagreements are at best incorrect assessments of objectively collected data within a framework of impartiality. Guerrero and Landemore argue in their works that the lottery combines recorded facts without the contamination of biased evaluations because it is based on "morality" ("common sense") as a condition of evaluative equality that aims at impartiality and belongs to all people (the lottery reflects the fact that all people are "morally legitimised to govern"); and on "knowledge" obtained from statistical representation, in which selected samples of the population speak for themselves, as it were (Guerrero, manuscript 81, p. 205; Landemore, 2020, pp. 86–7).

As we saw in the first section, lottocracy chooses descriptive representation, an impersonal form that mirrors the characteristics of groups or classes without any intentional effort on the part of the elected to advocate for or represent them as best they can. This makes lottocratic representation the opposite of political representation, which problematises the social conditions of citizens and makes the social political by reinterpreting people's needs, claims and perspectives into objects of political contestation and legislative decision-making. Lottocratic representation puts a halt on political judgement and also political pluralism; in fact, by changing the starting points (facts rather than ideas), it depresses party affiliations and voluntary participation of any kind. Facts should speak for themselves. For example: age, job, residence, educational qualification, gender, etc. are "objective" subdivisions from which the drawn samples derive ideas and proposals directly, with dispassionate assessments.[9] So one understands why elections *per se* are seen as the source of the problem, rather than how they are held or obtained. Replacing elections would make it unnecessary for associated citizens to flaunt their opinions and influence decision-making, because this would bring partisanship and

---

[9]   A reductive perspective on political ideology which is not dissimilar to sociological representation.

political representation back into the decision-making framework. Therefore, the link between the non-selected and the allotted citizens must be severed, with the result that democracy comes to be identified only with the selection system and the moment of decision-making.

This mentality is nourished by an historical interpretation, which goes back to ancient democracy in order to prove that only selection by lottery is consistent with democratic equality (anti-elites); that it allows for better (epistemic) and more ethical (anti-corruption/non-partisan) deliberation; and that it produces sociological representation. The main evidentiary arguments are derived from Athenian democracy in the fourth century BCE and depend essentially on Mogens Herman Hansen's *Athenian Democracy in the Age of Demosthenes* (1991) and Bernard Manin's *Principles of Representative Government* (1997). Aristotle is their inspiration because "he focused on the difference between sorting and electing, calling the former democratic and the latter not" (Van Reybrouck, 2016, p. 46).

We do not question the comparative and selective use of history in the debate on political regimes. This is part of a long, honourable tradition that can help us to understand political history. The problem is that when the use of the past becomes ritualised and knowledge gives way to simplifications, the function of historical knowledge takes a back seat and is easy sacrificed if it conflicts with the desired practical purpose. For instance, in stressing the polarisation between lottery (democracy) and elections (aristocracy), today's lottocrats gloss over the fact that lottery was not an exclusively democratic tool in ancient societies—it was also used by aristocrats; second, they tend to elide the fact that lottery was used to choose administrative and judicial personnel, *not* to select the members of the Assembly; third, they don't consider that it did not apply to all citizens but came with important limitations that secured accountability through legal sanction; and fourth, they don't consider how the political use of lotteries was essential to a society that resisted the struggle for power because it feared political conflict and civil war.

In the end, lottocrats' very meaning of democracy comes to be altered, moving from a regime based on the centrality of direct participation of adult citizens in the Assembly to one in which the many are "ruled" by "the few" chosen by chance (Buchstein, 2015, p. 140). Through a critical analysis of the historical argument that supports the lottocratic mentality, in our forthcoming book we question both the identification of democracy solely with lottery and the identification of elections solely with aristocracy. We make the argument that lottery is definable as a democratic system of selection provided that: a) it does not replace voting in the Assembly or the equal power to make laws; b) it is not applied to the selection of individual leaders; c) it is not applied on any basis other than membership of the political community of all citizens (e.g. to create or protect a homogeneous society made up of "perfect men" or invincible warriors as in Plato's kallipolis or as in contemporary despotic China, in which lotteries are widely used); and d) it does not result in selection for a life term or even a long term but in ongoing selections and short time rotation.

This means, by default, that (as ancient Athens also shows) use of the lottery alone does *not* make democracy; what makes democracy is equal political freedom (*isonomia* and *eleutheria*) among the citizens and thus the inclusion in the *demos* of the poor or ordinary people, who enjoy the equal freedom to speak in public and in the Assembly (*isēgoria*), thus to dissent and express their reasons for and against. The nature of a constitution is "determined exclusively by the issue of who has access. [...] If it is only a few, it is an oligarchy; if it is all, it is a democracy, regardless of lottery or election" (Canevaro and Esu, 2018, p. 118). Therefore, while it is true that Aristotle wrote in *Politics* that "it appears to be characteristic of democracies for the magistracies to be sortitive, but of oligarchies that they be elective" (4.1294b7–9), yet he also recognised that there are oligarchic and democratic ways of holding elections, and the democratic way is that "everyone can be elected (without franchise)" whereas it was also possible to use lotteries among the few and this was not listed as a democratic system. The problem with contemporary simplification of the past is that it focuses not on the inclusion (who can participate in candidacy and electing) but solely on the method of selection. In the end, the problem is that lottocrats fail to consider that Athens applied the lottery to select members of judicial and administrative organs; it did not have a bureaucracy with paid staff selected through public and blind examinations based on defined and tested requirements. In effect, as Robert Dahl (1970, pp. 72–3) aptly observed, it was the building of the *state* that decreed the fate of lottery in modern and contemporary societies.

This historical argument for lottocracy is meant to prove that to get rid of a political class without renouncing the indirect system of government, elections must be replaced. Lottocrats do not judge voting and elections from the perspective of political freedom.[10] As mentioned above, they judge them from the perspective of justice as impartiality, governed by equality of probability, which they claim, following Manin, it qualifies democracy. Legitimacy by virtue of impartiality is distinct from legitimacy by election because it is interested in preventing anyone from benefitting disproportionately from a given practice.[11] But elections seek to meet the demands and aspirations of citizens in a competitive environment. This is not to deny that there are shortcomings in the representative fairness of virtually every existing democracy, nor should we claim that all the proposed solutions are satisfactory. Such problems underlie various draft electoral systems (proportional representation versus first-past-the-post; group representation; special minority seats or quotas) and various bills aimed at regulating constituencies, ballot access and control of the distribution of financial resources to parties and campaigns. But the lottocrats are not interested in improving electoral representation and think, like the realist theorists of democracy, that no reform can mitigate the vices of a system that breeds an elite and that consists in discriminating among candidates based on supposed individual qualities.[12]

It is fair to say that the lottocratic mentality belongs to the anti-party tradition and aims for a partyless democracy. The assault on parties and partisanship makes it the late bud of a critical attitude toward democracy whose aspiration is to realise deliberation fully by depoliticising it: "if deliberation is really supposed to rule in public life, then there is no option but to depoliticize public decisions in various ways" (Pettit, 2004, p. 64). Lottocrats are part of this depoliticisation project and point to a paradigmatic change that intends to revise the meaning and practice of politics, from deliberation to decision-making, in a profound manner;

---

[10] According to Charles Beitz (1989, pp. 194–5), a corollary of political justice in elections is as follows: a democratic goal is to establish and preserve equilibrium between potential candidates so that they can compete on a fair basis, while providing voters with a chance to enter the competition, if they so choose, and to make their voices heard.

[11] The logic is the same as that of ruling independent authorities, whose procedures are also based "on the project of destroying individual advantages" (Rosanvallon, 2020, p. 132).

[12] "The basic argument is simple. Voter ignorance undermines meaningful electoral accountability. An absence of meaningful electoral accountability results in capture. And capture results in what might well be described as epistemic disaster" (Guerrero, 2021, p. 163); which meets with the detailed description of the election entrepreneurs in Achen and Bartels (2016, pp. 73–9).

their object of contention is not simply parties but the broader concept of partisanship, which shapes the "political attitude" toward all public issues. Lottocrats view partisanship as political pathology and propose lottery as a cure to restore authority to independent citizens and their genuine "cognitive" diversity. Consistent with the broader phenomenon of anti-partyism, lottocrats reiterate the classic accusation that parties divide the *demos* and are instruments of power elites; in addition, they claim that parties make dialogue into an art of compromise. These strategies are meant to advance partial interests rather than general ones and facilitate the tyrannical propensities of elected majorities. Guerrero's arguments echo Madison's attacks on factions in Federalist 10.

In conclusion, like traditional critics of parties, lottocrats make the case that parties are obstacles to good deliberation; and because lottocrats seek to educate citizens to reject partisan forms of participation, like anti-party theorists, they claim that parties cannot be reformed. Thus, partyless democracy is a moral imperative, not simply a political experiment or a factual occurrence. It is the most consistent answer to what is seen to be the structurally unethical nature of electoral democracy.

The best response to lottocratic anti-partisanship would be the valorisation of parties as expressions of divisions among citizens that help structure deliberation in the public sphere and state institutions through their ability to unite people around projects and ideas, to motivate their interest in politics and participation, nurture their desire to be informed and be involved in political issues far removed from their daily lives, teach respect for political opponents and pluralism, and to practice tolerance. Political parties are indispensable to, and valuable for, democracy.[13] As a tool, they are intermediary political agencies based on the voluntary decisions of the citizens to associate and collectively partici-pate in interpreting problems, devising solutions and imagining effective strategies that influence decision-making. Parties are rooted within society but work within institutions. The function of agenda-setting and articulating political agendas by establishing consistent long-term priori-ties and strategies to achieve policy goals is an essential component of indirect democracy and deliberation that cannot be performed by indi-vidual citizens alone. If the agenda-setting were done by a sorted

---

13   Among the theorists who deem parties essential to democracy we mention at least Hans Kelsen, Elmer E. Schattschneider, Norberto Bobbio and Nancy Rosenblum.

assembly, it would not be possible for citizens excluded from the lot to participate in choosing programmes and priorities; it would make no sense for them to associate to advance proposals, voice their views and try to influence the mini-publics.[14] Lottocracy would be similar to a one-party system: the options would simply be imposed on the society without the citizenry having the opportunity to exercise collective political freedom in choosing one programme over others. Thus, it is wholly unclear how the communication between those who are allotted and those who are outside the sorted assembly can be welcome if accountability is missing (which cannot be overcome by asserting that it is an imposition of "campaign contributors and party leaders"). Parties and elections give agency to all the citizens; sortition does not.

A scholar of classic Athens, Matt Simonton has written recently in a yet unpublished manuscript that:

> While the use of sortition guarantees democratic "breadth", in the sense of ensuring extensive participation by average citizens, election could introduce greater democratic "depth", in the sense of candidates running on agendas that attempted to give voice to the will of the *dêmos*, considered collectively. Election could provide policy direction and ideological coherence in a way that the widespread involvement of random, uncoordinated individual citizens (many of whom might have held no particularly strong feelings about *polis*-wide issues) could not.

This brings us to the last point of contention between lottocrats and electoral democrats, namely representation.

Representation is a construction that creates constituencies and gives direction to groups of citizens but also to the entire community—it unites and pluralises at once. The problem of bringing together a multitude of individual citizens without incorporating them in an organic unison is extremely important for a democracy and pertains to the making and managing of pluralism; elections as a system of selection are an institution that accommodates this problem. The ability of candidates to run on specific platforms gives citizens the opportunity to articulate competing visions of the public good, on which the citizenry bestows public legitimacy through the mechanism of choice. Without elections, the "will of the people" cannot be known *ex ante* and the people would be a multitude of atomised individuals; on the contrary, the "will of the people" is created through the formulation of contending solutions—we might say that the

---

[14] See Sutherland and Kovner (this book).

role that was played by semi-professional speakers, the *rhêtores*, in ancient Athens, is played by parties in our form of democracy.

The threat of lottocracy highlights the strengths and role of parties: they enable pluralism, and in doing so, activate and protect political freedom. This is exactly what would be missed in a lottocracy. The lottocratic mentality represents a dystopia that marks the encounter of two undemocratic imaginaries: partyless democracy as an ideal of good community, and party divisions as identical to corruption and personalised politics. As a dystopia, however, it would fatally end up with more corruption and personalistic relations of power because it defies that which democracy needs the most in order to divide, contain and control power: voluntary political association among free citizens. Parties are the empirical demonstration that in a democracy citizens enjoy political freedom; they are the functioning "value" of representative democracy. Through them, citizens publicly reveal their views on the issues that interest them most and influence the work of the government. Parties are not clandestine factions, nor do they conspire to achieve power; and citizens associate in order to make their views and interests effective and strong enough to guide, condition and control the government of society. At the end of the day, parties reveal the positive side of political conflict as they prove that while citizens associate and identify with some, not the whole, they presume that their fellows do the same. It is fair to say that political parties are the *form* that politics takes in a representative democracy regardless of their empirically specific organisation. In fact, the verb "to participate" means to take part, to join and "take sides" or to occupy a specific place in the political space. To take a side for or against any proposal is an expression of democratic politics and an exercise of political freedom.

In conclusion, we agree with lottocrats that parties have become a factor in the crisis of legitimacy of contemporary democracy. But the solution we propose is diametrically opposed to theirs: first because we think that parties exist because democracy exists, that the two live and decay together; and second because we argue that today's challenge is to revitalise collective agencies and parties rather than sweep them away. Unlike lottocrats, we claim that the decline of parties' moral legitimacy is both a factor in, and a sign of, the decline of the political value of democratic participation. We believe that the best way to respond to anti-partyism is to understand the meaning and defend the ethics of partisanship. Recovering the value of political associations and of collective agency may require new rules and laws (e.g. on party funding and electoral campaigns) and new organisational forms (attentive, for example, to the physical, not just the digital, interaction of members and to the effective authority of party members in the decision-making process and in the making of political agendas and nominations). These decisions are in the hands of the citizens.

Part III

Sortition and Deliberative Assemblies

Alex Kovner and Keith Sutherland

Turn Down the Noise
on Citizens' Assemblies

Abstract: *This chapter argues that current citizens' assemblies (CA) follow a chaotic deliberative model that cannot hope to win legitimacy from the general public. Their use of facilitators and their insistence on generating proposals rather than judging pre-existing proposals are the two primary flaws this chapter identifies. While the authors believe that random selection can play a role in modern democracy, that role must advance the aim of producing policies that are broadly acceptable to the general public. Due to the high volatility inherent in producing policies (as opposed to judging policies create by others), and due to the bias introduced by facilitators, current CAs cannot hope to create such policies.*

While random selection creates a population that is descriptively representative of the general public, this alone does not guarantee that the policy outcomes will represent their preferences. Designers of CAs must ensure that the process followed by the CA will converge with the views of the general public, subject to the limits of statistical uncertainty. Current CA advocates make no attempt to do this. In fact, many advocates of CAs seem to argue for exactly the opposite, requiring the members of CAs to "come together" around a facilitated consensus, often intended to represent the consensus of scientists and other so-called "experts". While this idea may have epistemic merit, it is certainly not democratic, and will inevitably generate the very populist backlash that CA organisers wish to circumvent.

This chapter has no objection to the use of random selection in order to create a descriptively representative assembly. But the real question is, what do you do with such an assembly? Ultimately, CA organisers will have to reverse their philosophical assumptions and accept the possibility that their personal policy preferences may lose if CAs are to gain mainstream legitimacy. This chapter directly echoes that of Gil Delannoi.

The case for the modern use of sortition in politics is based upon the supposed deliberative capacity of ordinary citizens when thrown together into an assembly. But this notion involves a linguistic confusion: "deliberation" in this case referring to every aspect of a process that includes generating policy ideas, advocating for one's own policy ideas, negotiating with other members, analysing the possible effects of policies under consideration and ultimately coming to a final decision about one or more proposals.[1]

The only thing tying these activities together is the assembly itself — as activities, they have very little in common either cognitively or as forms of social action. How is sitting alone in a room analysing different policy proposals considered the same act as negotiating with one's colleagues? We lump these together only because we take it for granted that the modern political assembly is the only democratically legitimate structure for crafting legislation.

The public sphere (in the sense of Habermas, 1992) is a transformational space. People actively engage with each other over matters of policy as well as less weighty topics like fashion and sports. Whether in the coffee shops of eighteenth-century London or on Twitter today, people enter the public sphere to change society by changing the minds of their fellow citizens. Current efforts at sortition mirror the transformational model, assembling randomly chosen citizens in a single place in order to be transformed in their views by hearing expert testimony as well as by the complex social interactions that take place inside the assembly. For example, in her recent State of the Union annual keynote speech (von der Leyen, 2022), the EU Commission President announced a Democracy Defence Act to (among other things) introduce randomly selected citizen panels into European policy-making. In her view citizen panels can contribute to what the European Union has lacked for so long: a Europe-wide public sphere.[2]

But the transformative model has a flaw: it only applies to those who are actually selected. The rest of the population sees the assembly from

---

[1] This composite term involves the conflation of the Germanic *deliberative Stimme* (deliberative voice) and the Latinate de-*liber*-ate, which involves the "weighing" of competing arguments (Sutherland, 2017, pp. 127–44).

[2] Citizen panels are attractive to those seeking a *transnational demos* for the EU, but need to adhere to other demanding standards for descriptive representation (see below).

afar, and many will not see it at all, they will only live with its outcome. Such an assembly can be said to have democratic *inputs*, in that the population of the assembly is (in theory) a statistical portrait-in-miniature of the public, but not democratic *outputs* because the work product of the assembly reflects highly volatile and transformational social processes. Not everyone participates in a citizen panel, and public debate is by no means a rational conversation. The result is that policy proposals from citizen panels can evoke strong opposition. The Conference on the Future of Europe provides a good example (Lemaire, 2022).

Sortition, broadly conceived, is the random selection of people to perform *de jure* roles in government and politics. This can include any branch of government over any length of time, though contemporary uses of sortition focus on the legislative branch. Historical uses of sortition (in ancient Athens and medieval Venice, for example) focused on the executive branch (Dowlen, 2008). The only surviving use of sortition under this broad definition is in the judicial branch, for jury selection.

This chapter will not take issue with any use of sortition under the above definition, but rather with Citizens' Assemblies (CAs) as they are commonly practised now.

1. Contemporary Motivations for Sortition

There has been a lot of recent interest in appointing CAs on a variety of issues over the last decade, particularly in Europe. CAs are meant to be an antidote to the failings of elected assemblies, which are often perceived as elitist and out of touch with the public. In theory, CAs operate much like elected assemblies, though in practice it is necessary to impose some structure in order to carry inexperienced citizens from beginning to end in the short time allotted to them. Some examples include the Ostbelgien model, the Citizens Convention for Climate (France), the Citizens' Assembly of Scotland, the Constitutional Convention (Ireland) and the UK Climate Assembly. These various assemblies operated under different rule sets, but importantly they all follow a "noisy" model of deliberation. They met in both large and small groups, mostly in person (though with some virtual meetings due to COVID) and, most importantly, they came up with their own proposals rather than voting on pre-existing proposals.

The noisy model is by no means the obvious choice. The ancient Athenians did not follow this model in their legislative trials (*nomothetai*), requiring that juries listen in silence to the proposer and five advocates elected by the Assembly to argue against the proposed law (Hansen, 1999,

p. 169). Even in the Assembly, speeches were mostly made by semi-professional *rhetores*, though this was more a matter of social convention, as any citizen could, in principle, address the Assembly (Finley, 1976, p. 24).

The current focus on sortition seems to come from a few different sources. First, the presence of several assemblies devoted to climate change suggests a perception that elected assemblies cannot address this issue due to the power of entrenched interests. While fighting climate change might be a "good" cause, calling CAs to achieve particular policy outcomes calls into question the democratic integrity of the process. Anyone designing a democratic system must accept the possibility that it may generate outcomes that conflict with the personal political views of the designer. Do these climate assemblies meet this test? The enthusiastic advocacy of campaigning group Extinction Rebellion for a Citizens' Assembly on Climate and Ecological Justice would suggest that the designer has a high level of confidence that the policy outcomes will be favourable to its cause (XR, 2022).

A look at the French Citizens Convention for Climate raises concerns. The members were selected via stratified sampling from among people who were phoned at random, but only if they expressed an interest. This introduces self-selection bias. members are not really selected randomly from the general population, but from among the population *with an interest in climate change*. This is very far from the same thing and should be a red flag in an era when conventional polling seems to reflect a lower willingness of conservative voters to participate. This is especially problematic because the convention was called in response to the *gilets jaunes* movement, whose followers are precisely the people we expect to be underrepresented by self-selection bias. Stratified sampling is actually doing us harm here: it is providing the illusion of proper distribution while missing the most critical demographic category.[3]

---

[3] Self-selection would be viewed by statisticians as a highly significant population parameter, which could only be addressed by quasi-mandatory participation in the allotment—stratification being ruled out *ex hypothesi*. The 4% acceptance rate of the initial sortition for the 2004 British Columbia Constitutional Assembly (Goodin, 2008, p. 14) has been shown to be fairly typical—research from the Sortition Foundation coming up with an average response rate of 4–7%. (Sortition Foundation, 2019). How this low response rate is compatible with an organisation's strap line of "delivering legitimacy" is

Secondly, the convention followed a deliberative model that required a considerable amount of structure and guidance. This was done by the Economic, Social and Environmental Council, a quasi-independent body within the French government. This also raises red flags. Whether or not the organisers are independent of the French government isn't really the point here. The question is whether the final output reflects the views of the participants, the organisers or the target population that the sample "describes" (Sutherland and Kovner, 2020).

A second motivation appears to be dealing with issues that are perceived to be intractable under the conventional political process.[4] The Irish Constitutional Convention falls into this category. Again, the selection process involved self-selection bias. However, this convention has a couple of positive features as well. First, its agenda was highly specific. There were six agenda items that mostly revolved around very specific decisions; for example, whether to legalise same-sex marriage. In addition, the deliberation model was far less noisy than that of the French CCC:

Each meeting had three components: presentation by experts of papers which had been circulated in advance; debate between groups advocating on either side of an issue; and roundtable discussions involving facilitators and notetakers (Arnold, 2014).

While the use of facilitators is still a concern, the presentation of expert papers and debates among advocates are closer to the Greek model and introduce fewer of the chaotic social dynamics that call representative legitimacy into question.

A third motivation is a desire to express the views of smaller communities that may feel marginalised by the mainstream political process. The Ostbelgien model (OIDP, 2019) falls into this category. This model has two components: a Citizens' Council, which sets the agenda and prepares

---

another matter. Whilst stratification can deliver an accurate gender balance, self-selection is (arguably) a more politically significant population parameter.

4   A 2009 Deliberative Poll on health care options undertaken in Rome enabled elected officials to argue that the "perceived legitimacy" of the DP results gave them the "cover to do the right thing" (Fishkin, 2009, p. 151). Although sortition advocates claim the mandate of "descriptive" representation, this is not so far removed from the (ascriptive) claim of medieval monarchs that citizens should be bound by the decisions of those chosen (by a variety of balloting mechanisms) to represent them, whatever those decisions may be (Manin, 1997, p. 87).

the second component, which is the Citizens' Panels. These short-term panels consider single topics, then report recommendations to the Eastern Belgian government.

There is more to like in this model than the previous two. For one, it has historical provenance, as it mirrors the successful Athenian model of *nomothetai*, in which the Athenian Assembly did not vote directly for new laws, but instead voted to hold a legislative trial to settle the question. It also mirrors the assembly itself, whose agenda was set by the *Boule* (council of 500).

It also has the advantage of being a permanent feature of Belgian politics, meaning that it is not subject to the charge that its structure is designed to achieve a particular outcome. In addition, its permanence allows it to call a greater number of panels on more specific agenda items, lowering the stakes of each panel while providing a broader array of feedback to the government.

Unfortunately, the Ostbelgien model suffers from some of the same problems as the previous two. Its panels follow a noisy, facilitated model, which, as noted before, introduces a volatility that is not actually present in the general public.

2. Why the CA Model is Flawed

Thus far, we have looked at the main features of three CAs and criticised the problems with them in an informal manner. Now we must formalise these criticisms in a systematic way, rooting them to the ultimate motivation for CAs as we see it. But the motivation for CAs is ultimately the same as the motivation for democracy, so we can make some observations about electoral democracy as well. As we shall see, the pathologies of both sortition and election ultimately can be characterised in common terms.

The main feature we have criticised so far is the "noisy model" that all of our examples demonstrate to some degree. This model has several features:

1. Extensive interaction among the participants, at both small group and plenary levels.
2. The use of facilitators to guide the discussion.
3. The production of open-ended output, as opposed to merely voting on options prepared prior to the assembly.

The motivation for this model seems to be to "empower" the members of the assembly. But is empowering participants really a desirable goal?

Certainly, we want to empower them *to do their jobs*, but simply empowering them for its own sake doesn't necessarily accomplish this goal. This reflects a "ground up" bias demonstrated by many deliberative democrats, reflecting Jon Elster's minimalist definition of democracy as "any kind of effective formalized control by citizens over leaders or policies" (Elster, 1998, p. 98). Note that Elster is not concerned *which* citizens get to be in control; indeed, many sortition advocates appearing to believe that any system that privileges the 99% at the expense of the rich and powerful will suffice.

Hélène Landemore advocates for this position in her recent book, *Open Democracy*. Harking back to the historical antecedents of modern democracy, she says:

> Democracy, in these older, perhaps simpler times, was "open." In theory, any individual qualifying as a member of the political community (admittedly defined in exclusionary ways) could access the center of power and participate in the various stages of decision-making. Citizens could literally walk into the public space to be given a chance to speak and be heard. Once you were counted as a member of the demos, or a citizen, in other words, you were in. (Landemore, 2022, p. 2)

This characterisation of democracy in terms of personal empowerment and inclusion has a great deal of emotional resonance in modern societies, as well it should. But that doesn't mean that it's the proper motivation for sortition. The problem here is that sortition is not direct democracy, and it is not at all clear that the empowerment felt by the member of a CA will transmit to the population at large. Indeed, evidence from the French CCC seems to suggest otherwise. As one major paper put it:

> While succeeding in creating consensus among the citizens who were involved, this co-constructive approach [the methodology used by the CCC organisers], however, failed to generate significant support among the broader public. (Giaudet *et al.*, 2022)

This is a serious problem, since CAs are not called in order to benefit their participants, but rather society as a whole. But if personal empowerment isn't the proper measure, what is?

3. Democratic Outputs

We believe that sortition (and democracy in general) should be measured based upon its outputs, not merely its inputs. What do we mean by that? Our basic criterion is this: on every issue, we want to enact the policy that is acceptable according to the informed view of the greatest number of people.

This is clearly impossible to achieve directly. Most people are not informed on most issues, and never will be. But the rubric does guide us as we try to judge deliberative models. It suggests that, for a given issue, there is one policy that is optimal, and other policies that are less optimal in proportion to their distance from the optimal policy. This optimality is not, however, technocratic in nature; we are not suggesting that such a policy is the best in some scientific or epistemic sense. Rather, it is the best in a normative sense, where our normative ideal is expressed by "acceptability". We don't want to get hung up on this particular characterisation, however. If we replaced "acceptable" with "best", not much would change.

Under the acceptability criterion, politics becomes an exercise in *finding the political centre*. But we do not mean by this phrase what is commonly meant by the political centre. Centrism in contemporary politics is a position on a political axis defined mostly by elites. It is often synonymous with compromise between parties, or with a negotiating style within an elected legislature that emphasises finding common ground among vested interests. That is not what we mean here. Instead, the centre is understood in a statistical sense, as being the policy that minimises some notion of a policy "distance" between the views of citizens and the policy adopted.

While this ideal is not technocratic, there is a substantive component: the informed opinion of the public should factor in rigorous examination of a policy's actual effects. Only when a group of citizens understands the real-world implications of a proposed policy can it express a normative preference.

4. Repeatability

The theoretical existence of an optimal policy gives us a real-world test: (synchronic) repeatability. If a proposed democratic process really tends toward our criterion for democratic outputs, then running the process multiple times should give us results that are close to each other in the policy space (needless to say, democratic mechanisms also need to reflect the fact that preferences change over time).

In 1996, James Fishkin and Robert Lushkin conducted a deliberative poll concerning energy production in the Texas electricity market. Actually, they conducted eight such polls over a short period of time, each using the same methodology. This gives us the test of replication we seek. The results were mixed:

In his report on deliberative polls done for three different local public utilities in Texas, Fishkin is pleased to report that in all three cases the shift in public opinion, pre- to post-deliberation, was in the same direction (Fishkin, 1997, p. 220). But the absolute numbers nonetheless diverged wildly. In one case, half the respondents thought post-deliberation that "investing in conservation" was the "option to pursue first", whereas in another case less than a sixth thought so. In one case, over a third still thought post-deliberation that "renewable energy" should be the top option, whereas in another case less than a sixth thought so. Clearly, these deliberating groups ought not to be regarded as interchangeable. Neither, in consequence, does this evidence inspire confidence in the general theory of "ersatz deliberation", treating smaller deliberative groups as microcosms capable of literally "substituting" for deliberation across the whole community (Goodin, 2003, p. 74).

While the consistent directionality is heartening, the large volatility in magnitude suggests that replication is by no means proven. Also, Fishkin had tested a much easier model. These groups did not come up with any affirmative policy, they were merely asked about how their views on fixed policy questions changed as they participated. This makes the deliberative poll on the quiet end of the noisy deliberation model.

When a group is asked not merely to discuss a set of pre-existing options, but to come up with options of its own, it introduces perhaps the most volatile of all group dynamics: negotiation. Negotiation fundamentally transforms the role of a participant from a consumer of information to a producer. This introduces "confirmation bias", as participants invest themselves psychologically in whatever preference they advocate. These dynamics are explored by Hugo Mercier and Dan Sperber in their "Argumentative Theory of Reason" (Mercier and Sperber, 2017). Examining this theory is beyond the scope of this chapter, but it supports the idea that a negotiating assembly will show a significant increase in volatility.[5]

There is a separate issue with the use of facilitators that is not measurable with the repeatability criterion. Ultimately, we are looking for

---

[5] For an extended discussion of the Argumentative Theory of Reason and its implications for sortition and deliberative democracy, see Sutherland (2017, pp. 181–86).

convergence: the notion that CAs are ultimately approximations to a representational ideal, and if conducted properly will approach this ideal in a statistical sense. The use of facilitators, however, introduces the possibility of bias, i.e. the idea that CAs might converge to an unrepresentative value.

We might trust someone like Fishkin, an academic who is insulated from day-to-day politics and has devoted his career to honest and accurate opinion research. But what happens when CAs start making binding decisions on public policy issues with multiple stakeholders? The position of facilitator will be the first thing to become "politicised" (in the negative sense of bare-knuckle politics). Well-resourced stakeholders[6] will move heaven and earth to exert some influence on the facilitator selection process. And the power of facilitators will grow as the issues involved become more obscure, as participants lean more heavily on the nearest available professional to wade through muddy waters. Even if the facilitator is honest and competent, the existence of a professional guiding the CA can be exploited by demagogues looking to cast doubt on the legitimacy of the process.

5. Sortition from the Top Down

The flaws identified thus far have their source in the bottom-up approach to sortition. Wishing to empower individual members, we let them engage in any activity that seems related to the issue at hand, without reference to issues of repeatability or bias.

If this approach is failing us, why don't we reverse this process? Let's play "King for a Day" and imagine ourselves as the enlightened despot of a realm that we wish to run according to the above "acceptability" criterion. In addition, we wish to be a lazy king, so at no time do we attempt to judge the public mood ourselves, nor do we rely on any chosen advisors to do so. We exercise discretion only over the design of the system.

The first thing we observe is that self-selection is out. The government must serve all its citizens, so the government cannot tolerate citizens opting out for any but the most extreme hardships. This is probably not

---

[6] Most of the online contributions to the Conference for the Future of Europe were from well-organised pressure groups, rather than unengaged citizenry (Youngs, 2022).

possible in the current political climate of western democracies; it would be perceived as too heavy-handed. But we should take inspiration from the Athenians, whose level of citizen participation was orders of magnitude greater than ours and included random selection for executive positions that involved substantial investments of time and energy.[7] Even today, many countries do enforce compulsory voting, though usually with only a small fine for non-compliance.

In this respect we think the language of rights that permeates so much of western political rhetoric serves us ill. Political participation can be viewed as both a right and a duty. Going even further, we should see participation as *neither* a right nor a duty, but rather a system property. Public policy will not converge to the acceptability criterion by itself, it requires guidance to do so, and democratic participation is fundamental to providing that guidance. This marks political participation as different from civil rights, which are rights agreed upon through the democratic process, but which are not part of the machinery of democracy.

The second thing we observe is that the noisy model is out. Convergence in the statistical sense rests on the law of large numbers. But this law in turn only applies when the outputs can be operationalised, such as when people choose from a set of pre-existing options (Pitkin, 1967, pp. 144–45). It also depends on statistical independence between the participants (Surowiecki, 2004, pp. 40–65). Our goal is to get feedback from citizens that reflects the considered views that the public would have if they all participated. But social interactions can cause people's views to align, destroying independence and undermining the credibility of the group's output.

Most of all, we must avoid the temptation to "bring people together". As King, let's say we survey our realm and everywhere find people evenly divided on some issue. We convene an assembly on the issue and find at the end that the members of the assembly are in perfect agreement. What are we to do with this?

Quite simply, we should ignore the result completely. We convened the assembly to benefit the general public, not create a political Disneyland for its participants. If we have followed a noisy model for the CA, we can be reasonably certain that the "coming together" was the result of internal social dynamics that tell us nothing about the general

---

[7]   Even Socrates, no friend of democracy, served for a year on the Athenian *boule*.

public. Whilst this might buttress Habermasian faith in the forceless force of the better argument, it is hard to see that this has anything to do with empowering the *demos* (Habermas, 1981, vol. 1, p. 47).

There is one caveat here. Going back to the acceptability criterion, we wanted the *informed* views of the public. This means that there is one acceptable source of transformation within a sortition body, namely each person educating themselves about the issue under consideration. But every other form of transformation is just a source of error. This suggests a model in which participants deliberate alone,[8] or perhaps in small groups, but without facilitation. They do not produce affirmative policies, but merely consider policies laid out prior to the event. We minimise confirmation bias by eliminating policy creation. From the point of view of statistical independence, we would like participants to deliberate alone, but evidence from the argumentative theory of reason suggests that small groups are best. But these small groups are not negotiating, because there is nothing to negotiate. They are merely helping each other weigh the proposals. How to generate these proposals is a topic we have explored in another paper (Sutherland and Kovner, 2020).

This model will surely bother most contemporary deliberative democrats and sortition advocates, who will see such restrictions as disempowering. But as the King trying to find the centre of our citizenry under the acceptability criterion, that is not our focus. That's not to say we're trying to disempower the participants. We will pay them a decent wage for their service and ensure they have plenty of coffee. But they are there to do a job, nothing more. The participants are acting as public servants, not in their capacity as citizens. The nature of this type of public service is to vote according to one's conscience, and participants should be protected for doing so. But voting according to one's conscience is simply a requirement of this particular job, as opposed to, for instance, serving in the military or working for the parks department.

6. Democratic Diarchy vs. Deliberative Democracy

The model we have laid out here is philosophically fundamentally different from the animating model for most CAs. Current CAs seek to take a

---

[8]   A study of the Bloomfield Track deliberative poll concluded that preference transformation largely took place at the information reading stage, prior to any discussion (Goodin and Niemeyer, 2013, pp. 127–28).

small number of citizens and transform their views, then hope that public awareness about the "openness" of the process will cause the result to be accepted as legitimate. We put openness in scare quotes because it is an illusion, a snow globe version of democracy. The snow globe is quite pretty, but what goes on inside is completely disconnected from the outside world.

Our model seeks to take a snapshot of the public at a particular moment in time. It is similar both to polling and elections in this respect, except that we seek the *informed* views of the public. We readily admit that we are chasing a mythical object: what would the public view be if everyone had the time and inclination to think about an issue? We think this approach gives us a stronger claim to legitimacy in the public eye. Most members of the public will judge a policy's legitimacy by the output (i.e. the content of the policy) rather than by the input. And every aspect of our approach is designed to select the policy that most people would find acceptable if they thought about it. If the sampling procedures are followed carefully, it should make no difference which citizens are selected – the outcome would be the same, subject only to statistical error bounds. Citizens who don't care about a given issue will simply ignore that issue, but citizens who do take the time to examine it are likely to view it as legitimate. The process has been designed from scratch to produce precisely that result.

An immediate consequence of our model is a need to split proposing from deciding, and to use citizen juries (this term is more in keeping with our approach) *only* for deciding. In fact, the three CAs discussed also split proposing and deciding to some degree, but then go on to use a noisy deliberation anyway. This suggests that the split between "democratic diarchists" (us) and "deliberative democrats" is, at its core, a philosophical one. An assembly of random citizens cannot act the same way as an elected legislature, where leaders set the agenda and run the chamber according to rules of order honed over centuries of history in the parliamentary tradition. Deliberative democrats wish to improve upon the debate in parliament with different actors, and they create the agenda and introduce facilitators because they have a predetermined idea of what a good debate should look like.

The problem is that parliamentary debate is not in the public sphere anymore, it is just theatre, as anyone watching prime minister's questions knows.[9] Historically, the public sphere has migrated any number of times. In ancient Athens, it was the *agora* and the *pnyx* — physical spaces where citizens met and exchanged ideas face to face. In early modern Europe, it was the Monarch and their courts. For a brief moment in the Enlightenment era, the public sphere really was (or at least included) the assembly. Sometimes this worked well, as in America, which produced the Declaration of Independence and the Bill of Rights. Sometimes it produced horror, as in the Reign of Terror. Either way, the assembly really was the centre of public life.

That time is no more. The public sphere is now cable television and social media. Modern legislatures just channel partisan interests, with a party's numerical presence serving as a score. That's not to say that nothing happens in elected legislatures, just that the debate and discussion that occurs in them is mostly posturing for the cameras.

Current sortition efforts fail because they try to go back to a time when assemblies were the public sphere. In so doing, they create a political fantasyland that cannot claim legitimacy. But they do respond to a real need. The public sphere of the past had agency. The Athenian assembly could express itself clearly through a show of hands. What the King and his court lacked in democratic credibility they more than made up for in their ability to act decisively. The Enlightenment era assembly, notwithstanding its rancour, had a system of committees that could channel its members' collective energies into policy.

Of course, elected assemblies today have committees, but they are not the public sphere anymore. This schism seems to be behind the dramatic decline in democracy the world over. But creating artificial mini-publics with their own, isolated versions of a public sphere is not the solution. Instead, we must embrace the public sphere we have, warts and all. We must seek to give it agency in the public policy space. We have the tools to do this. Some of these tools involve sortition in the broad sense, i.e. random selection for participation in politically oriented public service. But we must take the right approach. We must not try and transform or "bring people together" around an artificial consensus.

---

9   Bernard Manin's claim that "audience democracy" is a legitimate metamorphosis of representative government has been met with widespread scepticism (Manin, 1997, pp. 218–34).

Jérôme Hergueux

From Social Media to Congress

Towards an Institutional Theory of Direct Democracy through Sortition

Abstract: *The beginning of the twenty-first century has been marked by the rise of (technology-mediated) social networks. Over the past couple of decades, citizens have become accustomed to expressing their views and relating to one another directly in the absence of gatekeepers and expect that their voices will be heard irrespective of social status and legitimacy. Accordingly, in the political realm, we see social media capital (e.g. "followers", "likes"…) emerge against financial, political and cultural capital as one major determinant of electoral outcomes. Our democratic systems, built around the notion of "representation" for the past 250 years, thus have undergone a severe epistemic crisis. Hence the rise of "plebiscitary democracy" (otherwise called "illiberal democracy" or "populism"). In this context, sortition emerges as a high-promise institutional solution to the crisis of representative democracy. Herein the author argues, together with Rousseau, that sortition can represent the organising principle around which Western democratic systems could address their legitimacy crisis by reinventing themselves as <u>direct</u> democracies. Informed by the recent history of large-scale deliberation on social media platforms (e.g. Twitter and Wikipedia), the author shows how deliberation through sortition can more effectively lead to consensus building among citizens (i.e. the formation of the "general will") than existing representative systems, which increasingly generate polarisation and mistrust. However, compared to elected assemblies, the implementation of direct democracy through sortition requires that a re-evaluation of many of our most entrenched assumptions be carried out in terms of (i) the source of political legitimacy and trust in the deliberative system, (ii) its very purpose, (iii) how its decisions are* *evaluated (and sanctioned), (iv) how it avoids social reproduction and (v) how it prevents individualism.*

Information and Communication Technology (ICT) has fundamentally transformed the way we acquire information, express ourselves and interact with one another. To be sure, the most notable aspect of this transformation is the drastic global reduction in communication and coordination costs brought about by the internet, which has enabled citizens to cut intermediaries and dampen the role of institutional gatekeepers in social interactions.[1] We portray ourselves directly over the web, tell our stories and illustrate them with our own pictures and videos. Journalists—as well as other cultural, political and scientific authority figures—no longer have a monopoly on storytelling. Increasingly, citizens with no particular qualifications or legitimacy shape the way we document our environment and build narratives around our world.

To put it bluntly, the internet has killed authority. People speak up as individuals, and demand that their voices be heard irrespective of social status and legitimacy. This technological revolution did not cause the collapse of formal authority. It merely accelerated a process which can be traced back to the Enlightenment. An old internet meme used to say that "on the internet, nobody knows you're a dog". This is a way of saying that because interactions on the early internet were mostly anonymous, discourse could not be judged according to the speaker's credentials (a "philosopher", a "public official", a "priest", a "scientist"...). For the very first time in history, speech therefore had to be evaluated in the absence of social cues—which forced everybody to take everybody seriously (or no one at all). Much has changed since this meme got crafted in 1993, but the attack on formal authority remains. Nowadays, everybody knows you're a dog—you most likely asserted it yourself to begin with—but this is no reason not to listen. Quite the contrary in fact: in today's networked culture, asserting one's individuality can be effectively used as a legitimising tactic against arguments of authority ("I hear what you are trying to say, professor, but *as a dog*...").

---

[1] Over the same time period, gatekeepers of a new kind have emerged: platform algorithms which select, prioritise (and sometimes curate) the content to which users are exposed—and which therefore shape the nature and dynamics of social relationships.

The political consequence for liberal democracies is straightforward. The internet has created a culture that encourages individuals to speak out. As long as you have something to say, it will be better put by yourself than by any representative or intermediary—and the cost of doing so is essentially zero. A dog that barks well enough might attract significant attention. This is the main reason why social media capital (e.g. "followers", "likes"...) sometimes supplants financial, political and cultural capital as the major determinant of electoral outcomes. Simply because direct communication creates *trust*, political campaigns can be run successfully on social media without an articulated programme, and people can be considered worthy of public service without relevant qualifications or experience. From Donald Trump to Jair Bolsonaro, and from Boris Johnson to Rodrigo Duterte, this fundamental logic of "plebiscitary democracy" underpins the rise of populism.

Now more than ever, politics requires a *story*—one that allows affect and trust to grow in the audience. Based on this emotional link, logic gets oriented and careful demonstrations lose much of their power to convince. This is a natural human tendency which has been long studied by psychologists. We listen to the people whom we trust, and we trust those that tell us things to which we can relate. But the current architecture of the web—largely determined by private algorithms that play on human bias to generate traffic—has worked as a powerful catalyst leading to the negation of the relevance of the concept of *truth* in politics. Truth becomes relative. Any search on the web readily delivers hundreds of elements that appear to be inconsistent with the most widely accepted scientific or historic wisdom. Even if no argument is conclusive in its own right, such a large body of suggestive evidence cannot all just be random, you might wonder.[2]

Still, education levels have significantly risen around the world. According to UNESCO, the number of students entering university has been multiplied by almost three since 1995, and while only 20% of the world's population could read and write in 1900, this proportion rose to

---

[2]   In what typically qualifies as a "conspiracy theory" (as opposed to a *demonstrated* plot), the answer to this question is always "yes, it absolutely can". People have a well-known tendency to vastly underestimate the amount of randomness in their environment (which is certainly an adaptable trait from an evolutionary perspective: being "better safe than sorry" and detecting intentions or patterns around us are good ways to prevent potential threats).

86% in 2020. The consequence is clear: people understand enough about politics to realise that politicians can be captured—both financially and, perhaps more importantly, ideologically. They increasingly doubt the ability of their representatives to meet their promises, when they do not question their very willingness to do so. Hence the growing lack of trust that citizens exhibit toward traditional political elites. *The liberal democracies we live in appear as a new form of electoral oligarchy which, ontologically, cannot truthfully represent the best collective interest of the people.* As a result, extreme political candidates—those who we haven't tried yet but who look as sincere as any other—appear to bloom.

At the same time however, people do *not* know enough to efficiently govern themselves. Most of us don't have the time—let alone the grit—to run our daily lives while studying all politically relevant subjects with the depth and breadth required for sensible collective deliberation and decision-making. A great deal of specialisation appears necessary in politics—one which is not so much technical than informational. In other words, politicians need not be experts or scientists, but they must gather and process significant amounts of information before reasonable political trade-offs can be achieved. This leads current liberal democracies to an aporia. While the overwhelming majority of citizens in the rich world now appear qualified to participate in the political decision-making process, very few possess the time and resources necessary to meaningfully do so. Democracy thus remains representative despite citizens' growing discontent and mistrust, and institutional solutions are sought to ventilate representation with direct citizen feedback: *democracy needs to breathe.*

At the national level, such institutional solutions include the referendum based on popular initiative. However, interesting political questions rarely present themselves in binary "yes" or "no" form. Further, respondents have a well-known tendency to answer questions other than the one actually asked (e.g. "do I trust the government?", "do I like the president?"). At the local level, cooperatives are formed and participatory city budgets are voted. However, many of our most pressing political problems are global ones (e.g. environmental protection, global taxation, rising inequality, the reform of the welfare state...). Besides, indistinctly calling upon voluntary citizen participation actually *reinforces* social inequalities since, as we already noted, there are few who possess the time and resources needed to meaningfully contribute to the public debate.

How can representative democracy breathe, then, if nationwide referenda are of limited political relevance and if local democracy, when it does not reproduce pre-existing social inequalities, cannot address the most critical political problems of our times? In this context, *sortition* emerges as a high-promise institutional solution to the crisis of representative democracy. The idea is to use the tools of statistics to select—or "sort"—a *representative sample* of the population (in terms of, say, regional location, age or income level). Members of the recruited collective are then assigned some relevant political problem to solve. Importantly, they are given the time and resources needed to deliberate based on state-of-the-art analyses provided by scientists, legal scholars and other topical experts. Over the past decade, sorted assemblies of this kind have, for instance, deliberated around constitutional reforms in Ireland and Iceland. In France, they broke new grounds on highly sensitive political issues, such as tackling climate change and implementing legal reforms to enable active assisted dying.

Perhaps surprisingly, individuals participating in the above *citizens' assembly* experiments have proved quite successful at building a large consensus *while* converging towards ambitious political reforms. However, sorted assemblies remained confined to a consultancy role, and their recommendations have been regularly overturned by elected officials who, ultimately, are the ones held "politically accountable". Thus, in such an institutional form, sortition is unlikely to achieve anything more politically than to put an oxygen mask on our existing institutions. And perhaps this is for good reasons: a few stimulating citizens' assembly experiments cannot erase two-and-a-half centuries of democratic experience built around elective representation overnight. The idea that the road to Congress goes through elections runs deep.

From the perspective of the history of legal thought and institutions, however, the concept of sortition is fundamentally subversive. Historically, electoral democracy has evolved according to two underlying principles: (i) in a large modern democracy, direct citizen participation in political deliberation is practically impossible, and (ii) while most citizens do not possess the knowledge required to usefully contribute to the public debate (because of, e.g., a lack of instruction) they certainly know who is best suited for public office in their local community. Hence, elective democracy emerges as the most effective way—in fact, the only viable way—to collectively govern ourselves. Direct democracy sometimes remains an ideal type, but one that mostly does not yield itself to workable institutional arrangements.

Such reasoning lies at the heart of the liberal philosophy of the Enlightenment. Western philosophers and legal scholars from the eighteenth century onward readily identified the strong disconnect between the ideal type of direct democracy (a *"true" democracy*) and the practice of representative democracy (an *elective oligarchy*). As Montesquieu put it in *The Spirit of Law* (book II, chapter 2), "suffrage through drawing lots is in the nature of democracy; suffrage through choice (i.e. voting) is in the nature of oligarchy." Over the years, however, legal theory has erased this unpleasant disconnect thanks to the development of a legal fiction around the notion of *general will*. For the reasons outlined above, the general will in modern democracies is expressed through the law, i.e. a majority vote of the people's elected representatives.

This statement of identity between the majority vote of an elected legislative body and the "general will" appears heroic. But this legal fiction is necessary for us to be able to unambiguously characterise our legal system as a "democracy". Instead, Montesquieu may have qualified it as an "aristocratic republic", one where the sense of *moderation* of those in power seems to be fading away in conjunction with of the rise of social media. This legal fiction according to which the elective systems speak *for* the people lies so much at the heart of modern political thinking that it is largely entrenched into constitutional legal theory. To be sure, this legal fiction appeared as early as in the Declaration of the Rights of Man and of the Citizen, written in 1789 during the French Revolution (emphasis added): "The law is the expression of the general will. All citizens have the right to contribute personally, *or through their representatives*, to its formation."

What is all the more remarkable is that the French revolutionaries were deeply inspired by the work of Rousseau, who conceptualised and popularised the notion of general will. However, as Rousseau coined it— less than 30 years before the French Revolution!—the notion of general will *negated* the possibility of representative sovereignty, as this would contravene the sovereignty of the people as well as the moral equality of the citizens (Douglass, 2016). Hence the sharp distinction between a *democracy*, where the general will is expressed through the deliberations of the citizens' assembly (a task which cannot be delegated) and an *elective oligarchy*. In this respect, the French revolutionaries remained elitists. They did not seek to establish a democracy in the sense of Montesquieu or Rousseau (i.e. the self-government of the people), but eventually sought to move from one oligarchy system, based on nobility titles, to another, based on elections. As Rousseau puts it (emphasis added):

> The Sovereign can well say: I now want what this or that man does, or at least what they say they want; but it cannot say: what that man wants tomorrow, I will want it still… *Will does not lend itself to representation*: it simply is as such, or it is not; there is no middle-ground. *The people's deputies are therefore not and cannot be their representatives; they merely are their agents*; they cannot conclude anything definitively. Any law that the People itself did not ratify is null; it is not a law. (*Of the Social Contract*, Book II, chapter 1)

Why, then, does sortition stand out as such a subversive legal concept in the modern history of political thought? The argument is most powerfully expressed through the lens of mathematical statistics: assembling a *representative* sample of the population means that, on average and under similar circumstances, *this subset of the population will deliberate and behave just like the underlying population of citizens* from which it is drawn. From a legal perspective, this implies that sortition allows the population, however large or scattered, to represent itself *directly*. In other words, it is not necessary for the entire population of citizens to deliberate in order for the general will to emerge—only some carefully selected sample is necessary. The stated identity between the deliberations of the citizens' assembly and the sovereign remains, of course, a legal fiction, *but one that becomes grounded in reality*. Why, then, would democracy still resort to *elected* representatives to form the legislative body, when this increasingly represents a strain on the legal fiction that legitimises our institutions? As we noted above, education levels in rich democratic states have moved far beyond what they were even a century ago. Any citizen may be virtually assumed to be fully able to understand and participate in political deliberations. If such was not the case, why would we bother to assemble consultative citizens' assemblies to begin with, if not out of sheer political hypocrisy?

The major blocker, I argue, comes in two flavours: one conceptual, the other institutional. First, at a conceptual level, one needs to be convinced that collective deliberation within a population of citizens who differ so widely in terms of private interests and personal backgrounds can indeed produce meaningful results. One may even point to the beginning of this text as providing good reasons for caution: Twitter politics is certainly mastered by educated people who do *not* demonstrate any ability or willingness to converge on anything constructive. Quite to the contrary, political issues discussed on Twitter typically generate *divergence* and *polarisation* (Yardi and Boyd, 2010; Conover *et al.*, 2011; Garimella and Weber, 2017). Binary positions emerge, individuals "choose sides" for one narrative or the other, and "informational bubbles" thus form. In a sense, Twitter offers us a poor example of "popular" political deliberation aimed at creating consensus, one worse than the standard practice of elected representatives in parliament.

Thankfully, technology does not have deterministic political consequences, and Twitter cannot be used as a valid thought experiment for distributed public political deliberation. The reason for that is simply that *Twitter does not have any publicly stated goal.* It does have a few rules (e.g. pornographic content is not allowed) but no *principles* or *procedures* aimed at guiding the conversation towards some shared common objective. If anything, Twitter encourages us to "move fast, feel free to be ourselves, and have fun" (https.about.twitter.com, retrieved November 2022). In the background, Twitter effectively functions as a *market for assertions.* Attractive assertions are typically emotionally loaded, appeal to (binary) identity and push for simple (if not simplistic) worldviews. Those produce "Likes" and "Followers"—which converts into significant social (and, hence, political) capital for superstar users, and increased attention (i.e. more advertisement money) for platform owners—but also a highly polarised and quite unproductive political space for people to "have a free and safe space to talk" (https.about.twitter.com, retrieved November 2022).

Contrast the Twitter situation with that of Wikipedia. Both platforms are wide open to public contributions (Wikipedia even more so as it allows anonymous contributions) and both draw upon a highly diverse (and often contradictory) set of individual perspectives on politically controversial issues. By contrast, however, contributing to political entries on Wikipedia effectively generates a process of *ideological convergence* among participants (Greenstein, Gu and Zhu, 2021). Because Wikipedia has a clearly stated purpose—to organise the sum of all human knowledge in the format of a free encyclopaedia—contributors with extreme or polarised viewpoints cannot break out in segregated social spaces without leaving the community altogether. The common purpose binds people together, and leads to the refinement of principles according to which *all* voices share in the right to contribute to consensus building. "Neutrality" on Wikipedia, for instance, does not mean that one has to remain "objective" or "neutral" in their contributions (the attempt would probably prove futile). It merely means that when some statement qualifies as "human knowledge" — and what counts as "knowledge" is also subject to precise developments — then it *belongs* to the conversation in due proportion of the body of evidence that supports it. This principle therefore has the property of shifting many heated conversations from the question of "who's right?", to the question of "how do we articulate these conflicting statements into a coherent whole?". In other words, neutrality is never a precondition for individual participation. Quite to the contrary, it is the expected *result* of the conversational process as designed. As a consequence, Wikipedia articles grow *better* whenever the confrontation of ideas becomes harsher, or there is simply some undisputable *truth* (Giles, 2005; Greenstein and Zhu, 2018).

The reality is that the Twitter space is quite unrepresentative of what the recent history of information technology use teaches us in terms of people's ability to deliberate collectively. In January 2012, a collective deliberation on English Wikipedia involving thousands of participants successfully concluded that the Stop Online Piracy Act (SOPA), a bill project recently put forth by Congress, was threatening free speech and online innovation.[3] Participants converged towards a strong yet costly political stance: for the only time in its history, Wikipedia, whose very purpose is to provide the world with free knowledge, went black for 24 hours, on January 18–19. All searches rendered a black screen that read "Imagine a World without Free Knowledge", with the only redirects pointing to the pages describing the bill. This political intervention certainly contributed to the demise of the bill project. But effective collective deliberation is not unique to Wikipedia. Rather, it underpins the whole history of the internet. The basic infrastructure and organisation of the web as we use it every day is largely built around open standards and software. Those are produced collaboratively through open deliberation and consensus building without us even noticing, together with a large number of popular programming languages (Python), operating systems (Android, Linux), web browsers (Firefox) and video games (counterstrike). Similar to Wikipedia, when it comes to producing software, the common purpose is clearly stated. Contributions may come from any angle, as long as they serve this purpose and abide by a few procedural rules.

---

[3] See: https://en.wikipedia.org/wiki/Stop_Online_Piracy_Act

Of course, one may resist the idea that the success of collective deliberation for the development of software or encyclopaedic content tells us anything about the prospects for successful legal deliberation. Have a closer look. Larry Lessig, a professor of Law at Harvard, famously argued that "code is law" (see Lessig, 2009). This means that, similar to the law, computer code functions according to its own internal logic which, when it gets enacted, creates *facts* that need to be accounted for. One could quite literally reverse the latter proposition and argue that "law is code" — both technically and epistemologically. The assimilation comes from the fact that the law is essentially a large, organised *information system* which runs according to its own logic to serve a specific purpose — that of expressing the general will. In practice, large-scale public deliberation has proven highly successful at producing information systems of this kind, even benefiting from a competitive advantage over other modes of production driven by, e.g., governments or private firms (Benkler, 2002; Hergueux, 2023). At a conceptual level, the recent history of technology-mediated collective deliberation therefore provides no grounded reason to doubt the ability of the citizens to deliberate effectively on legal matters. The law is, in essence, yet another information system organised around a clear common purpose, no less than that of a software program or encyclopaedia. Rousseau may concur (emphasis added):

> If a people, *furnished with adequate information*, held its deliberations, the citizens having no further communication with one another, *the general will would always result from the grand total of the small differences*, and the deliberation would always be good. (*Of the Social Contract*, Book II, chapter 3)

But:

> How can a blind multitude which often does not know what it wants because it rarely knows what is good for it, execute by itself an enterprise so great, so difficult as a system of legislation? The people themselves always want the good, but by themselves do not always see it. *The general will is always right, but the judgment which guides it is not always enlightened. This judgment must be made to see objects as they are*, sometimes as they ought to appear to it, *to show the general will the good road that it seeks, protect it from the seduction of particular wills*, to bring together time and place before its eyes, to balance the attraction of present, palpable advantages with the danger of distant and hidden evils. Individuals see the good that they reject; the public wants the good that it does not see. All equally need guides. It is necessary to obligate individuals to conform their wills to their reason; it is necessary to teach the public to recognize what it wants. *Then*

from public enlightenment results the union of understanding and will in the social body, and from that the perfect harmony of parties, and finally the greatest force of the whole. (*Of the Social Contract*, Book II, chapter 6)

Based on this assumption that the law, as with any other information system, can be produced effectively through collective deliberation, the relevant question becomes that of the *institutions* and *procedures* which may enable such deliberation through "adequate" information acquisition. This is a complex design problem, the discussion of which goes beyond the scope of this text. Instead, in what follows, I identify five higher-level institutional properties of the social contract implied by direct democracy through sortition. By systematically contrasting those institutional properties with those traditionally attached to our elective systems, I seek to stress that the transition to direct democracy through sortition requires a deep re-evaluation of the philosophical underpinnings of our political institutions. Namely, I discuss in turn the specific institutional properties of the citizens' assembly in terms of (i) *public trust* and *legitimacy*, (ii) *purpose*, (iii) *evaluation* and *sanction*, (iv) *social reproduction* and (v) *individualism*.

First is the issue of public trust. In an electoral democracy, trust is typically built *before* the election. Historically, citizens put trust in their representatives based on the programme they presented and discussed during carefully institutionalised political moments: that of electoral campaigns. We have seen how the rise of social media has been concurrent with—and, to a large extent, fuelled by—the collapse of public trust in political speech expressed in the form of articulated worldviews and programmes. Instead, we see political trust increasingly built around one's *story*—a simplified narrative based on affect and identity which creates a *personal bond* that largely shields the relationship from factual evidence and reasoning.

Still, from an institutional theory perspective, it remains relevant to ask: why would people trust the citizens' assembly, and from where it would it receive its political legitimacy? In other words, what is the source of trust and legitimacy for an assembly whose members are anonymous *a priori*, and chosen through random sampling in the absence of any pre-existing programme or commitment? The answer to this question is that *trust and legitimacy must reside not with the elected representatives, but with the sampling procedure*. One can resort to reliable statistical tools to assemble a representative sample of any population, but this requires that we define the *criteria* according to which this population is to be sampled. In other words, *we need to define the social criteria which we consider relevant for representing the "diversity" of the people in the citizens' assembly.* This is an eminently political question—one that needs to be debated openly. In the French legal system, relevant criteria may for instance include a person's *age group, geographic location* or *income level.* In different legal traditions (e.g. in the US) other criteria might be introduced and discussed, such as *race* or *religion.* In any event, public trust in political sortition requires that those criteria be (i) made very explicit and (ii) deemed legitimate by the people (and so discussed and adopted though a procedure that is itself considered legitimate). Political sortition implies that the people do not trust nor legitimise the assembly based on individual campaigns and elections, but because it set the general principles according to which it was called upon, and which ensure its "representativity".

Another institutional question of interest is that of the *role* or *purpose* of the citizens' assembly thus gathered. Historically, elective democracy has produced the law through an institutionalised process of confrontation between political movements organised around ideologies (i.e. an all-encompassing, more or less neatly articulated view of the social world which organises it around some set of "facts" and ideas). Individual candidates seek affiliation and define their programme in accordance with their preferred political organisation, and hence receive support to run their electoral campaigns. As a result, *the main role or purpose of elected parliament members is to represent and defend the electoral interests of their political group or movement.* This may come at the expense of what group members themselves believe to be in the best interest of the people, but the theory is that elections discipline the system by allowing citizens to regularly redefine the balance of power between existing groups in the assembly. In practice, however, the political wandering and inefficiencies generated by political groups defending their electoral interests at the expense of the common good appear increasingly unbearable to many citizens—many of whom decide to vote with their feet, or turn to alternative political offers (e.g. plebiscitary democracy or "populism"). Again, Rousseau had long identified this relative disconnect between the interests necessarily defended by political groups or "factions" and the pursuit of the general will (continued from the citation on p. 9, emphasis added):

> But given the formation of factions, *partial associations at the expense of the large association, the will of each of these associations becomes general in relation to its members and particular in relation to the State.* It can then be said that

there are no longer as many voters as men, but only as many as there are associations. The differences become less numerous and produce a result less general. Finally, when one of these associations is so large that it prevails over the others, you no longer have as a result a sum of little differences, but one decisive difference; then there is no longer a general will, and the opinion that prevails is only a particular opinion. (*Of the Social Contract*, Book II, chapter 3)

Direct democracy through sortition crucially differs from the elective model in that parliament members, because they are randomly selected, can neither commit to any course of action nor signal their political orientation *ex ante*. In other words, sortition renders political affiliation irrelevant to the assembly's deliberation process. Accordingly, *the sole role or purpose of individual members of the citizens' assembly is to represent themselves.* As in Wikipedia and other instances of collective deliberation, participants are expected to bring their diverse backgrounds and experiences with them, together with their preconceptions, beliefs and biased views. But the principle that governs legislation-building here is not the institutionalised confrontation of political groups and movements. Rather, *it is an institutionalised exercise in collective deliberation aimed at building consensus around the fabric of the law.* As a consequence, individual members of the citizens' assembly are *not* required to affiliate with some articulated vision of the general will *ex ante* in order to defend it *ex post* against that of political competitors. Instead, *the general will is admittedly undefined at the start of the deliberation,* and only emerges through the procedures and institutions that enable collective deliberation. Quite remarkably, it is precisely the *absence* of explicit political assignation to an "ideology", "movement", "group" or "party" which, in this system, provides parliament members with the ability to converge freely as the deliberative process unfolds.

Third is the important question of who would evaluate (and sanction) the decisions of the citizens' assembly. As we've discussed above, under elective democracy, electoral campaigns play a crucial role in disciplining political movements, so that the conception of the general will that they propose cannot diverge "too much" from citizens' *naïve* preconceptions about the common good. Whenever the disconnect becomes too strong, parliament members may pre-emptively seek affiliation with another group and/or voters will sanction the group in question by reducing its relative political influence in the assembly. By contrast, under sortition, selected members of the citizens' assembly are appointed for one term, after which they return to civil life. While the quality of their decisions can certainly be assessed by the people, such assessment can therefore not translate into political sanctions.[4] How, then, can we ensure that members of the citizens' assembly have the incentives to behave in the people's best interest?

The answer to this question is that *direct democracy through sortition does not require a political disciplining device*. Because citizens determine the relevant sampling criteria that guide the constitution of the assembly so that it may truthfully represent the underlying social "diversity" of the people, there is a perfect identity of interests between the sorted sample (the "small" society) and the people (the "big" society from which the former is drawn). In agreement with Rousseau, the "grand total of the small differences" within society — if revealed through the right collective deliberation procedures — *always* produces the general will. In other words, under political sortition, *the general will cannot err*, and disciplining mechanisms are not necessary.[5] By contrast, as Rousseau notes, the people's representatives in an elective democracy can only be its *agents*, meaning that their interests are never perfectly aligned: "The people's deputies are therefore not and cannot be their representatives; they merely are their agents" (*Of the Social Contract*, Book II, chapter 1). This is why elections are so instrumental to discipline this political system and align the private incentives of the agents (i.e. "defending the electoral interest of their political group") as much as possible with that of its principal (i.e. "seeking the general will").

Fourth is the issue of oligarchy and social reproduction. In this respect, our above developments should make a strong case for political sortition

---

4   Unless, of course, the member in question violates the internal rules, procedures and principles that govern the collective deliberations of the assembly or breaks the law itself, in which case they may be dismissed through some internal procedures (and/or face the judiciary).

5   One difficulty remains, however: under political sortition, the general will is assumed to be unknown *ex ante*. The citizens' assembly (or the people from whom this assembly is drawn) can only discover it through an adequate process of information acquisition and deliberation. This implies that the general will as expressed by the citizens' assembly may, at times, contradict people's naïve worldviews and intuitions. The general will still does not err (and so it does not require a political disciplining device), but the public simply fails to recognise it. Dedicated procedures and institutions should be crafted to ensure that the general will is communicated in an accessible way to the people. This is yet another complex institutional design problem that we do not discuss in this text.

against electoral democracy. The people itself defines the factors that meaningfully reflect its inner social diversity, and the citizens' assembly is called upon so as to precisely reflect said diversity. But is this enough to spell the end of oligarchy and social reproduction among the people's representatives? Not necessarily, as one additional institutional caveat needs to be avoided: the individuals randomly selected to form the citizens' assembly need to be provided with the resources — i.e. time and money — needed to focus on their task. *Members need to be financially compensated, freed from their civil jobs, and ensured that they may return to practising said job after the end of their term* (if they so wish). Otherwise, individual levels of engagement with the citizens' assembly will be determined according to personal wealth, available free time and job security, all of which would contribute to the perpetuation of an oligarchy which, because it concentrates the resources necessary to effectively contribute to the collective deliberation process, will exert disproportionate influence on its result, thus biasing the expression of the general will.

Last is the question of individualism. As we have seen, the sole role or purpose of the individual members of the citizens' assembly is to represent themselves. This may suggest an atomistic or individualistic view of society whereby the goal of each member would be to defend their own private interest — necessarily at the expense of the collective. *Such an interpretation, however, reduces the general will — the search for a unique legal expression of the common good — to the arithmetic addition of individual wills, each looking for their private interest.* Indeed, political sortition does not seek to represent the underlying social diversity of the people in the citizens' assembly so that members would individually defend the competing private interests that result from this diversity. Such reasoning, whereby members of the assembly represent themselves in the sense of a "micro political movement" (one without any predefined worldview or doctrine), is a misplaced extension of the legal theory of political representation.

Instead, sortition seeks to faithfully represent social diversity within the citizens' assembly as so many different perspectives and takes — rooted in individual background and experience — on the general will. *The formation of the general will therefore does not proceed through the confrontation of those individual perspectives in a zero-sum game (the "individualistic" interpretation), but through their articulation around a common objective: that of the greater good of the community.* It follows that, to the contrary of to elective democracy which works through the confrontation of segregated political groups, *members of the citizens' assembly need to consider themselves as a single body, one that shares a unique goal despite individual differences.* As Rousseau puts it:

> As long as several men assembled together consider themselves as a single body, they have only one will which is directed towards their common preservation and general well-being. Then, all the animating forces of the state are vigorous and simple, and its principles are clear and luminous; it has no incompatible or conflicting interests; *the common good makes itself so manifestly evident that only common sense is needed to discern it.* (*Of the Social Contract*, Book IV, chapter 1)

When Rousseau published *Of the Social Contract* in 1762, he could not anticipate the developments of mathematical statistics and the advent of random sampling methods. Accordingly, he assumed that direct democracy may only be practised in small states (e.g. free cities), where the population was limited enough to allow *all* citizens to share equally in the collective deliberation around the fabric of the law—a necessary condition for the emergence of the *general will*. Irrespective of the size of the underlying population, however, *political sortition enables direct democracy* by gathering a limited but *representative* sample of citizens to deliberate around the common good. This achieves the same result, yet more efficiently, as it only requires a small but carefully selected subset of the population to invest in acquiring the information and expertise necessary to deliberate on legal matters.

What Rousseau did anticipate, however, is that *given the right guiding principles, procedures and institutions*, deliberation could indeed converge to some largely shared consensus, even within a highly diverse crowd with apparently conflicting worldviews, interests and opinions. Far from Twitter politics which effectively produces divergence and polarisation, Wikipedia, open-source software and other successful technology-mediated deliberation efforts conducted at a large-scale hint at what such principles, procedures and institutions might look like. It falls on us to learn the right institutional lessons from those (and other) experiments and to seek to apply them to collective political deliberation in the context of the citizens' assembly. To be sure, electoral democracy needs to breathe. But does this mean that Congress as we've known it for the past couple of centuries needs an oxygen mask, or simply to die a natural death?

Keith Sutherland and Alex Kovner

Superminority
Sortition and the
Democratic Diarchy

Abstract: *This chapter argues that the recent enthusiasm for "citizens' assemblies" ignores key aspects of statistical theory. The sample sizes used by the public opinion polling industry and classical-era Athenian councils and juries are often an order of magnitude larger than modern sortition bodies. Most citizens' assemblies are effectively composed of volunteers – acceptance rates are generally in the order of 4–7% – and this leads to the over-representation of activists. In addition, the speech acts of individual participants are not subject to the law of large numbers. Stratified sampling can only ensure a statistical match on a very limited range of population parameters, and the use of moderators would not be acceptable in a body with statutory powers, on account of the* quis custodiet ipsos custodes? *problem.*

We make a limited case for sortition, involving large decision juries with quasi-mandatory participation. Policy proposals, however, should be left in the hands of elected politicians, and the chapter proposes a "superminority principle" to ensure a broader range of proposals that better match the diversity of the electorate. This is the modern analogue of the diarchy at the heart of the classical Athenian demokratia *and also addresses Madison's concern that "a body of men are unfit to be judges and parties at the same time" (Federalist, 10, p. 8).*

1. Introduction

The last few years have witnessed a burgeoning interest in sortition-based citizens' assemblies. In many cases citizens' assemblies have followed the template of existing legislatures, but with members selected by lot, rather than by preference election. Like elected bodies, citizens' assemblies have been charged with initiating proposals and determining the outcome of the assembly deliberation by voting. This chapter argues that sortition is *only* suitable for the latter function and also agrees with James Madison's critique of the conflation of the proposing and judgement (disposing) roles in elected legislatures, which can undermine their democratic (and epistemic) legitimacy as:

> [a] body of men are unfit to be both judges and parties at the same time [...] Yet the parties are, and must be, themselves the judges; and the most numerous party, or, in other words, the most powerful faction must be expected to prevail. (Federalist, 10, p. 8)

The democratic case for the aggregate judgement of a large randomly selected assembly that "describes" its target population statistically is straightforward and depends on the law of large numbers. However, while a descriptively-mandated representative "must *vote* as a majority of his [virtual] constituents would",

> [a]ny activities other than voting are less easy to deal with. Is he really literally to deliberate as if he were several hundred thousand people? To bargain that way? To speak that way? And if not that way, then how? (Pitkin, 1967, pp. 144–45)

Taking our cue from Robert Dahl's *Democracy and Its Critics*:

> The process for making binding decisions includes at least two analytically distinguishable stages: [1] setting the agenda and [2] deciding the outcome. (Dahl, 1989, p. 107)

Political representatives are not just lobby fodder, they also have to formulate policy options, and the law of large numbers does not apply to the speech acts of a tiny group of randomly selected citizens, only to its final vote (Sutherland, 2017, pp. 322–32). This would suggest a distinction between "proposers" and "disposers" (deciders), with the remit of randomly selected bodies limited to the latter. Indeed, this was the case with fourth-century Athenian legislative juries (*nomothetai*), who "deliberated" in silence before voting on the outcome of the debate between the proposers and five defenders of the existing law, elected by the assembly (Hansen, 1999, p. 169). We suggest a modern analogue of Athenian practice, focusing on the role of the proposing body. Taking on board Dahl's further requirement:

> The demos must have the exclusive opportunity to decide how matters are to be placed on the agenda of matters that are to be decided by means of the democratic process. (Dahl, 1989, p. 113)

If so, then there is no alternative to competitive elections between political parties (*pace* the view of most sortition advocates and many deliberative democrats).

This is true of proposing but not disposing because proposing is an extreme bottleneck in any legislative structure. Of course, any citizens can exercise their free speech rights to make an *informal* proposal, using the myriad resources of civil society. But a *formal* proposal (i.e. one that is subject to deliberation and final vote in some legislature, or perhaps a referendum) can only happen at most a few hundred times a year. Even that number includes many minor technical fixes and updates to major laws. Most legislatures in practice only introduce a few dozen significant proposals in any given year (the political analogue of Bateman's limiting factor in reproductive biology).

The rate limitation on proposing, together with the steep learning curve associated with crafting actual legislation (as opposed to merely making vague policy suggestions), means that proposing must be delegated. For any delegation of this kind to respect *isegoria*, or the equal speech rights of all citizens, the ability to participate in the precious few proposing opportunities must be proportionate to public support; hence the need for elections in anything other than a tiny direct democracy such as classical-era Athens.[1]

The success of citizens' assemblies in Europe seems to contradict this conclusion. However, the French Citizen's Convention on Climate (CCC) was by no means an assembly in the vein of the US Congress or British Parliament. For one, it had only one agenda item:

> The Citizen's Convention on Climate, an unprecedented democratic experiment in France, aims to give citizens a voice to accelerate the fight against climate change. Its mandate is to define a series of measures that will allow to achieve a reduction of at least 40% in greenhouse gas emissions by 2030 (compared to 1990) in a spirit of social justice.
>
> Decided on by the President of the Republic, the Convention brings together 150 people, all drawn by lot; it represents the diversity of French society.
>
> These citizens will learn about, debate and prepare draft laws on all issues relating to ways to combat climate change. The plenary sessions will be streamed on this site.

---

[1]   The Athenian *demokratia* involved a hybrid of two forms of equality — equal speech (*isegoria*) and equal political rights (*isonomia*) (Hansen, 1999, pp. 81–85). We argue here that sortition is only of relevance to the latter.

> The President of the Republic has committed to submitting these legislative and regulatory proposals "without a filter" either to a referendum, to a vote in Parliament or to direct implementation.
> (https://www.conventioncitoyennepourleclimat.fr/en/)

The members of the assembly were then divided into "thematic groups", which considered different aspects of the problem. The themes for these groups were defined by the organisers of the assembly, not its members. In fact, the schedule and manner in which assembly members considered all of its issues were highly circumscribed, from the questions asked to the facts and witnesses admitted. Without external structure, the CCC would have failed completely.

Perhaps a better way to think of the CCC is as a jury, not an assembly, whose purpose was to render a verdict on various aspects of the technocratic consensus. Given that the facilitators of the conference were heavily involved in creating the technocratic consensus, we might ask if the purpose of the conference was to let the people decide, or to coax the people into making "right" decisions.

What is needed to combat such paternalism is an adversarial engagement of different ideological viewpoints. Bernard Manin, whose 1987 paper helped kick-start the modern deliberative democracy movement, has more recently advocated "debate" as opposed to deliberation aimed at consensus:

> Debate format—in which speakers address an audience that merely listens to them—is a more promising set-up for exposure to conflicting positions than interactive personal engagement amongst holders of opposing views, as people tend to avoid face-to-face disagreement.[2] [... S]peakers should be primarily policy experts, group leaders, moral authorities. Politicians may be involved too, but on the condition that their participation is decoupled from electoral campaigns. (Manin, 2005, pp. 18–19)

In a court case, the "debaters" would be lawyers from opposing sides. But for the CCC, the structure came from a single source: the French Economic, Social and Environmental Council (ESEC). Perhaps it did a good job from a substantive point of view, but from a Dahlian procedural perspective, a single technocratic source is unacceptable. What's needed, then, is a way to accomplish this task pluralistically.

---

[2]   Solomon Asch's conformity experiments have led to a wealth of experimental evidence on the effect of information cascades in social psychology (M. Potter, Appendix II, in Pope, 2023, p. 190).

2. Superminority

We argue the case for narrower mandates and increased pluralism. The best path forward is to call citizen bodies more frequently, with narrower mandates, and external structure determined by ideologically diverse elements from within the existing political order.

The traditional legislative assembly has (depending on the prevailing electoral rule) the virtue of being a reasonable portrait in miniature of a country's ideological diversity, at least to a first approximation. And yet any diversity it has gets destroyed by the need to achieve consensus. In practice, consensus means 50%+1, so groups that fall below that threshold are effectively discarded, unless they can form alliances to get above that magic number. Why is this the case? It doesn't have to be this way; there is a simple method for expressing the diversity of a chamber to a far greater degree.

We call this the "superminority" method; it simply involves lowering the threshold of acceptance to get more than one output. Want two outputs? Set the threshold at ⅓+1. Want three outputs? Set it at ¼+1. Want 99 outputs? Set is at 100+1. We call these a superminority of *n*; i.e. a superminority of 2, 3 and 99 in these examples. (We anticipate that the number of political parties will closely approximate the output rule.) Notice that a majority becomes a superminority of one, indicating its monolithic and destructive nature. The superminority method must always be paired with a downstream decision-making process, such as a citizen jury.

For example, let's say we have a 100-person legislature that wants to deal with climate change, similarly to the CCC. They would decide how many options they want to send to the jury, let's say three for this example. In order to get three separate proposals, you need three separate groups in the legislature to write their own proposal. The lowest threshold to get three groups is 26 of the 100 members. Any number between 26 and 33 will work, but the lower number gives members more flexibility to figure out who to work with. Any number 34 and above produces two or fewer groups, and 25 and below means you can get more than three groups.

The people in the legislature then decide who to team up with to write a proposal. In this example, a business-oriented group might try to write a modest proposal that doesn't change much, a more environmental group would write a very aggressive proposal, and a labour group might write a proposal with a lot of infrastructure spending. The three proposals would go to a citizen jury. Each member of the citizen jury would have time and resources to learn about the proposals. Then each member would rank all three proposals in order of preference, and a winner would be determined by aggregation.

Superminority can also be used to make other citizens' assemblies fairer. Let's return to the CCC for a moment. Instead of a single set of managers, we would go to the French National Assembly and have them appoint three sets of managers, using a superminority of 3. Each set of managers would organise the CCC for one third of the allotted time. Even better, we can use the superminority principle to produce multiple final bills, and simply call the assembly as a true jury to consider and vote on these proposals.

A common objection to this is that the assembly members must be "empowered", but is this the appropriate standard? From the perspective of democratic theory, it is the public at large that should be empowered through the participants. It is perfectly acceptable to place restrictions on the assembly if those restrictions make the final result more representative of the overall population (Kovner and Sutherland, 2022).

The CCC certainly made a lot of recommendations, 149 in all. But given the paternalistic, expert-driven source of so much of their information, this number is misleading. The ideological spectrum that contributed to these recommendations was quite narrow. Whether intended or not, the dynamic of the assembly was a small number of carefully selected experts guiding a larger number of volunteers (the selection process involved both an expression of interest and random selection). That the participants were volunteers is important. Consider Amandine Roggeman, who described accepting her invitation this way:

> "I first thought the text message was a joke," Roggeman said. "But I felt strongly about the climate. I also felt privileged to be randomly picked from the entire population. Above all, I was curious." (Phainikar, 2021)

The fact that she "felt strongly about the climate" marks her as different from the average citizen, and it is highly likely that someone who did not feel the same way would not have volunteered. Self-selection would be viewed by statisticians as a highly significant population parameter, which could only be addressed by quasi-mandatory participation in the allotment. The 4% acceptance rate of the initial sortition for the 2004 British Columbia Constitutional Assembly (Goodin, 2008, p. 14) has been shown to be fairly typical—research from the Sortition Foundation indicating an average response rate of 4–7% (Sortition Foundation, 2019). How this low response rate is compatible with the organisation's strap line "delivering legitimacy" is another matter. Whilst stratification can deliver an accurate gender balance, self-selection is (arguably) a more politically significant population parameter.

> Wherever sortition is employed, it must be rigorous and compulsory. The reason lies in the nature of random sampling. Unless the sample is taken from the whole population and unless the procedure is absolutely random there will be error. Error is rapidly magnified. It cannot therefore operate with volunteers or with improvised means (Pope, 2023, p. 167)

The picture of the CCC assembly should be clear now. It was made up of a demographically diverse group that was nonetheless selected for their interest in the issue and guided by members of the cognitive elite. It should come as no surprise that the result was mostly well-known proposals from climate activists. This might be an epistemically good result, but it certainly isn't a democratic one (Kovner and Sutherland, 2022).

Instead, the democratic goal must be to make sure that any proposals considered come from sources that approximate the ideological spectrum of the country, especially given that the CCC was established as a government response to the *gilets jaunes* movement—a populist protest that was sparked off by high levels of fuel taxation. With this criterion in mind, the superminority structure can handle any proposal, whether laws or appointment of government officers—though always in conjunction with a citizen jury. Just have the elected assembly produce some number of alternatives (never less than 3) and then have the citizen jury choose from among them. But what does this change do to the assembly chamber itself?[3]

3. Pathologies of Traditional Assemblies

First, we need to explore some of the procedural pathologies that plague traditional legislative assemblies. Most such assemblies are unstructured, at least at the constitutional level. Instead, they have procedural rules that are built up over time to regulate day-to-day business. But, for the most part, assemblies simply operate by majority rule, with the agenda set by a single leader or a small leadership group.

The fact that the agenda is set by a small leadership group leads to our first pathology: *issue conflation*. If the ruling coalition wins 60% of the

---

[3]   It should be noted that altering the decision threshold is a relatively minor change, but the effect on political outcomes would be considerable.

vote, one might expect it to generate 60% of the agenda, but that is not the case. Instead, the ruling coalition sets the entire agenda. Any legislature will wish to consider several issues during a given legislative session, and for the sake of transparency as well as coherence of the law, one would expect each agenda item to be a "unit"; that is, to be a comprehensible whole. Instead, most bills (particularly important ones) contain a wide array of unrelated provisions, either to attract particular votes, or because an influential member wishes to squeeze a favourite policy into a bill that is likely to pass.

From the perspective of parliamentary leaders, what is the optimal way to organise the agenda? Obviously, they should optimise the passing of their most valued provisions however they can, and this rarely leads to coherent and easy to understand bills. It also means that backbench assembly members often must vote on huge bills with unrelated provisions, some of which they may favour, others not.

A second pathology of traditional assemblies is **obstructive bias**, or the tendency of small factions within the assembly to wield disproportionate power by threatening to obstruct or sabotage important legislation. In parliamentary systems, this often takes the form of a small group within the ruling coalition threatening to bring down the government unless they are granted some concession. This illustrates a basic fact: consensus-based assemblies favour those who have the least concern for the public good, and the greatest willingness to inflict pain on political adversaries, regardless of the consequences to the general public.

A third pathology is a bias towards **non-specificity** in one's public proposals. Non-specificity carries a significant advantage because one can earn votes (in a general election, in an elected chamber or in a sortition body) on imaginary grounds. As proposals become specific, the space of imaginary reasons to vote for or against shrinks.

Non-specificity bias benefits opposition parties more than incumbents, as opposition parties can claim any benefit to their policy proposals without having to back them up. Their policy proposals can be quite vague, as well, which can lead to political volatility when an opposition party (or a faction within the governing party) assumes power and has no idea how to govern.

4. Sortition as a Solution to Political Pathologies

What would happen if we simply replaced elected members with allotted ones? None of the pathologies mentioned above would go away, as none of them are the direct result of elections. Nevertheless, might we expect that using ordinary citizens would reduce these pathologies due to the lack of electoral pressures? Possibly, but they certainly wouldn't go away. Even an allotted chamber will have members who are more willing to use hardball tactics than others (and all members will be subject to pressure from external lobbyists, without the protection of party discipline). In addition, there is a downside to using ordinary citizens. A traditional assembly lacks agency—it's just a bunch of people with nothing in common who've been thrown into a room together. The agency of the chamber comes from its organisation into a ruling coalition and an opposition. We can expect the same from a sortition assembly. Factionalism has its roots in the unstructured nature of the assembly as much as reflecting any fissures within society—Madison's hope that the "enlarged republic" would provide a cure for factions being dashed almost as soon as the US Constitution was ratified.

It is worth remarking that most sortition theorists do not advocate replacing elected assemblies with allotted ones in a one-for-one swap;[4] instead, they advocate single-issue assemblies. We believe this is because it is obvious that the wholesale approach would fail miserably. None of the pathologies would go away, and a bunch of inexperienced politicians (for politicians they would be, once selected) would be thrown into the unenviable position of having to craft a functional legislature from nothing.

Instead, the focus is on citizens' assemblies that are almost the opposite of traditional assemblies. They are single-issue instead of general, they are structured from the outside and they are facilitated by professionals who are not members of the assembly.[5] In a sense, it does solve our pathologies, however. There is no issue conflation because there is only one issue. There may be some obstruction bias, but the fact that the schedule and structure of its activities are determined externally means this can be minimised. And finally, non-specificity bias is reduced because the external structure eliminates the need for a formal ruling coalition and opposition.

---

[4] Exceptions include O'Leary (2006), Callenbach and Philips (2008), Barnett and Carty (2008), Sutherland (2008), van Reybrouck (2016) and Hennig (2017).

[5] The three decades of experiments from Stanford's Deliberative Democracy Lab also fall into the single-issue category (cdd.stanford.edu).

All of this sounds good until we look at the price we are paying. The external structure is imposed by the entity that organises the assembly. In the case of the CCC, the ESEC was touted as being "independent" of the French government. So what? The question isn't whether an assembly is independent of the government, but whether it is democratically representative. In order to be democratic, we must loosen the grip of the organising entity. But as soon as we do that, we are right back where we were before, with the three pathologies. In addition, we have the agency problem as well. The party system, for all its flaws, does solve the agency problem.

It seems then that citizens' assemblies along the lines recommended by sortition advocates are either undemocratic or suffer from all the pathologies of elected chambers. Elected chambers, at least, are usually populated by experienced politicians capable of navigating those pathologies. In a sense, the organisers have separated proposing from deciding, but in order to preserve the superficial appearance of a more traditional legislative chamber, they have chained themselves to a model in which the proposals the assembly considers, and the structures and facilitation they use, come from a single source. This is a fatal flaw.

Now let's look at how superminority handles these pathologies. The agenda of the legislature would be set using the superminority method itself (Kovner, 2020). The first task of any legislative session would be to set the agenda. A jury would get a small number of options and make its preferred choice. This minimises issue conflation because each party is in competition with the others as judged by the citizen jury, and the jury is unlikely to choose an agenda that is an incoherent mess.

Superminority eliminates obstruction bias completely. The consensus-based approach favours those who act in bad faith, by allowing them to shut down the process while blaming their adversaries. The superminority method eliminates this tactic. Once an agenda item is adopted, multiple options *will be* produced, those options *will be* advanced to a jury and a winner *will be* chosen. There is no obstruction.

Finally, non-specificity bias is all but eliminated. Let's say we use the superminority method to get five options. The threshold to advance a proposal is approximately 17%. With five proposals, that means 85% of the chamber's members are needed to advance proposals, and the other 15% should be able to join one of the five groups, because, with smaller groups, ideological alignment gets much easier. And non-specificity won't do, because each proposal could become law. Could members deliberately make vague policy proposals, knowing they will lose with the jury? Perhaps, but then they develop a public record of losing. Even more embarrassing would be to fail to join a proposing group on a regular basis.

Superminority thus provides a structural solution to these pathologies. We say that this process is "procedurally complete" because it is guaranteed to produce a binding agenda, and each item on that agenda is guaranteed to reach a final vote with a jury. With procedural completeness in place, members must now internalise political conflict. Screaming that the other side is negotiating in bad faith is out: there are no negotiations among groups. There are negotiations within groups, but these take place under the threat that one's political opponents will win, with no possibility of obstructing them. Each group can only write their own bill and submit it by the deadline. In that sense, the different groups in the chamber need not interact at all. That's a good thing. Direct interaction of politicians does not require good faith, it *assumes* good faith. In so doing, it gives a massive advantage to bad-faith actors, who have no stake in the public good and are usually quite skilled at embarrassing their opponents.

Elected representatives will now be judged mostly on whether their viewpoint wins with the jury, just as prosecutors are (or should be) judged by success with traditional juries. The best legislators will internalise the policy preferences of the general public as expressed by citizen juries, an outcome anticipated by James Harrington's 1656 constitutional proposal, with his analogy of two girls dividing a cake equally:

> Two of them have a cake yet undivided, which was given between them: that each of them therefore might have that which is due, "Divide", says one to the other, "and I will choose; or let me divide, and you shall choose." If this be but once agreed upon, it is enough; for the divident, dividing unequally, loses, in regard that the other takes the better half. Wherefore she divides equally, and so both have right. (Harrington, 1992, p. 22)

Political parties that fail to internalise the preferences of the public will face extinction and be replaced by ones that do. Perhaps we can have our cake and eat it after all.

Vincent Aerts

The Use of Sortition in the Reconfiguration of Democracy by Neoliberal Governance

A Neutralizing but Risky Operation: The Case of the Citizens' Climate Convention in France

Abstract: *Sortition is often described as a tool of direct democracy. In France, numerous writers defended the democratic essence of sortition, they were followed by a social movement aiming for a radicalisation of democracy. However, sortition is only a tool and the context of its use matters. In this chapter, I would like to explore the possibility of the recuperation of sortition by a neoliberalism government that is facing a social movement aiming for a radicalisation of democracy. Building on the work of Wendy Brown and Grégoire Chamayou, I explore the use of sortition by Emmanuel Macron's French government in 2019 in its organisation of the Citizens' Climate Convention.*

I suggest that the reconceptualisation of democracy by governance explained by Wendy Brown may justify a neoliberal use of sortition to gain democratic legitimacy. The concept of governance reconceptualises democracy with ideas of inclusion, participation and decentralisation of state. The CCC was first promised decision-making power, but Emmanuel Macron went back on his word and vetoed some proposals. Citizens were then reduced to a stakeholder role without real decision-making power. I suggest then that sortition was used for its neutralising virtue, aiming to evacuate the conflict and promote consensus.

During the Yellow Vest movement, political conflict was important, and the French president proposed the organisation of a citizens' assembly during the Grand Debate organised in response to the Yellow Vest movement. I suggest that the use of sortition directly responds to this conflictual context and tries to escape from it by using a participatory mechanism to solve the conflictual issues problem.

For several decades, sortition has been making a comeback in the public debate. In the French-speaking world specifically, several authors, voluntarily or not (Viktorovitch, 2021), have been set up as thinkers on sortition for different social movements advocating radical or direct democracy.

Thus, Jacques Rancière, following the effervescence of citizen deliberation experiences around the question of the 2005 referendum on the European draft constitution, defended the democratic character of sortition. Indeed, he saw in this procedure the very essence of democracy, described fundamentally as an anarchic "government" founded on nothing else than the absence of any title to govern" (Rancière, 2005, p. 48).

Other major writers, such as Bernard Manin, have been the object of interpretations and political recuperations by writers and movements (Hayat, 2019) defending the use of sortition in politics as a central demand of a renewed democracy project (Chollet and Manin, 2019). David Van Reybrouck's book, *Contre les Elections* (*Against Elections*) (2014), occupies a central place in the Francophone debate on the renewal of sortition. These three writers are part of a larger constellation of writers who recall the democratic character of sortition and who would be notably mobilised in France from the winter of 2018–2019 within the Yellow Vests movement.

Sortition clearly appears to be an important demand for movements advocating a radicalisation of democracy. However, sortition remains only a tool, and although it is philosophically democratic as some people suggest (Montesquieu, 1748), its use does not mechanically lead to a democratisation of the representative system.

The question of the political context therefore seems to be a determining factor in the uses and consequences of sortition in practice. For several years now, France has been governed by policies that can be linked to neoliberalism (Burland, Popelard and Rzepski, 2021), advocating a specific form of governance and redefining not only the processes for governing but also our conceptions of democracy (Brown, 2015). This question about the contingency of sortition experiences leads us to a main question: could sortition be recuperated by the opponents of its first defenders to make it an argument for democratic legitimisation?

To answer this question, I will look at Wendy Brown's work (2015) on how the neoliberal revolution sought to develop the reconfiguration of democracy through governance. I will then discuss the idea of the decentralisation of the state in governance and the relegation of actors to the "stakeholder" role (Chamayou, 2018). Finally, I will discuss the neutralising virtue of the sortition in its role of evacuating conflict and replacing it with the search for consensus (Cervera-Marzal and Dubigeon, 2013). I will apply these theoretical elements to a concrete case in France: the Citizens' Climate Convention organised at the initiative of French President Emmanuel Macron in 2019 (CCC, 2019).

1. Governance: A Redefinition of Democracy?

In order to understand the potential use of sortition by neoliberal governments, it is important to look at their conceptions of politics and democracy. This vision can be summarised by the vague and now common concept of "governance". First of all, it should be recalled that governance and neoliberalism were not particularly connected in the thinking of the great neoliberal authors such as Friedrich Hayek or Milton Friedman. Over time, however, governance has become "neoliberalism's primary administrative form, the political modality through which it creates environments, structures constraints and incentives, and hence conducts subjects" (Brown, 2015, p. 122).

Like many concepts used in political science, governance, a notion that probably comes from the business world, does not have a clear definition that has been agreed upon. Nevertheless, certain elements are commonly shared in the literature on the subject. Thus, governance refers to "a mode of managing complex businesses in which vertical hierarchy gives way to a more horizontal, even egalitarian arrangement" (Ryfman, 2007, p. 289). In the field of policy-making, governance has been synonymous with "governing without government", with the state stepping back from the development of public policy to play the role of mediator between different actors called to the table (Rhodes, 1997).

In terms of political philosophy, the idea of governance, and the decentralisation of the state that it promotes, no longer considers the representative government as the holder of national sovereignty entrusted to it through election by universal suffrage but sees it as a mediator between the various stakeholders.

Governance replaces the opposition between public and private, between sovereignty and the market, with the advocation of collaborative and complementary relationships: a certain division of political labour in which everyone participates in the areas in which they are most competent (Salamon, 2000, p. 1624). The decentralisation of the state allows for the implementation of delegation and decentralisation processes "synonymous with democratization in the sense of inaugurating a 'new politics' of participation, partnership and inclusion" in the elaboration of public policies (Meehan, 2003, p. 7).

Following this new vision of politics that advocates inclusion and participation of citizens and civil society, sortition may be seen as a process for including the population in governance. But will it appear as such in reality?

2. The Citizen's Climate Convention, a Randomly Selected Assembly with Decision-Making Power...

This use of sortition by neoliberal governments advocating new governance can be illustrated by the Citizens' Climate Convention (CCC). Proposed on 25th April 2019 by French President Emmanuel Macron (Elysée, 2019), this randomly drawn assembly was to be made up of 150 citizens and would be tasked with drafting proposals with the aim of "reducing greenhouse gas emissions by at least 40% by 2030, in a spirit of social justice" (CCC, 2019). For this new governance experiment, presented as unprecedented, the President formally promised that the measures defined "will be submitted without filter either to a referendum or to a vote in Parliament, or will be implemented by regulation" (Elysée, 2019). Supported by a governance committee, the CCC's work was spread over seven sessions between October 2019 and June 2020. At the end of these sessions, the citizens drawn by lot presented their final report composed of 149 proposals intended to form the future Climate Law (CCC, 2020). These proposals and the experience as a whole seem to have been well received and enjoyed great legitimacy, especially in the academic world (Guérineau de Lamérie, 2020).

Following their final report, the President received the 150 citizens drawn by lot from the Citizens' Climate Convention. He gave a speech during which he went back on his commitment to translate the proposals of the CCC into policy by vetoing three proposals. Thus, the 110km/h limit on highways and the 4% tax on dividends were rejected, while the wish to modify the preamble of the Constitution was also rejected (France Info, 2020a). This veto appears to be contrary to the commitment of 25th April 2019, but it had already been announced by the President during his meeting with the actors of the Citizens' Convention in January 2020. During this meeting, he had already gone back on to his commitment to transposition "[…] without taking this either to a referendum, or to a vote in the Parliament or to an act of regulation […]" since he announced "[…] in a scenario involving an individual, who could be me, I say to you 'I do not agree' […]" (Elysée, 2020).

A competition of narratives then began as to the fate of the Citizens' Climate Convention's proposals. By refusing three proposals, even though he had promised to submit them without a filter, Emmanuel Macron also foresaw changes to several other proposals. Feeling that the President's commitments would not be kept directly, some of the 150 citizens formed an association (Daoulas, 2020) in order to "continue to carry our measures" and avoid "nine months of work being thrown away" (Baïetto, 2020). Since then, on one hand, the government has been using a double narrative consisting of gradually diminishing the original commitment of the President (France Info, 2020b) while defending the claim that most of the measures of the CCC had been established (Gallo, 2022). On the other hand, the participants in the Convention have severely judged the government's action in not keeping its word (Le Monde, AFP, 2021), giving rise to a feeling of "disappointment, a lack of confidence and also a lack of coherence on the part of the government", particularly "with regard to the measures that have not been established, that have been partly set up or that have been watered down" (Veysset, 2021).

Likewise, many environmentalist associations question the presidential narrative and criticise the lack of implementation of the proposals by the government (Extinction Rebellion, 2021). Thus, in February 2021, the environmentalist media *Reporterre* considered that only 10% of the proposals had been taken up "without filter" as promised by the President in April 2019 (D'Allens, Bœuf and Dang, 2021). At the end of 2022, these two narratives were still clashing both in the media and politically. In September 2022 Olivier Véran, then Minister Delegate for Democratic Renewal and Government Spokesperson, stated that 85% of the proposals had been "retained and applied", an assertion invalidated by the Ministry of Ecological Transition. Activists such as Cyril Dion, one of Citizens' Climate Convention's idea's initiators, and politicians such as Clémence

Guetté, deputy of the Nupes (New Popular Ecological and Social Union), denounced this misleading discourse, the latter relying on a study in the newspaper *Le Monde* (Garric *et al.*, 2021) that reported figures similar to those of *Reporterre* (Gallo, 2022).

In summary, and without taking a position on these debates around the calculation of implemented measures, we can see that this experiment, which was presented as unprecedented and able to give direct democratic power to an assembly of citizens drawn by lot by allowing them to "define measures that will be submitted without a filter", has swiftly turned into a list of non-binding proposals for the French government, who can pick whatever proposals they please to build a new Climate Law, while trying to claim a certain democratic legitimacy from this experiment in sortition.

From this, we can link this use of sortition to a certain conception of democracy carried by neoliberal governance. As mentioned above, governance can be a proposal that resonates with a democratic discourse that "inaugurates a 'new politics' of participation, partnership and inclusion" in public policy-making (Meehan, 2003, p. 7). In fact, by separating a participatory and inclusive experience such as a randomly selected citizens' assembly from the real decision-making power it was promised, the discourse of democratic governance has been misused, as Wendy Brown argues:

> What has happened here? Inclusion and participation as indices of democracy have been separated off from the powers and the unbounded field of deliberation that would make them meaningful as terms of shared rule. Put another way, while inclusion and participation are certainly important elements of democracy, to be more than empty signifiers, they must be accompanied by modest control over setting parameters and constraints and by the capacity to decide fundamental values and directions. Absent these, they cannot be said to be democratic any more than providing a death row inmate with choices about the method of execution offers the inmate freedom. Rather, this is the language of democracy used against the demos. (Brown, 2015, p. 128)

By ultimately denying a real role in decision-making, governance has rendered a democratic instrument such as the lottery meaningless:

> Thus, governance fundamentally reconceptualizes democracy as distinct or divorced from politics and economics: democracy becomes purely procedural and is detached from the powers that would give it substance and meaning as a form of rule. Democracy defined as inclusion, participation, partnership, and teamwork in problem solving is also absent all concern with justice and the designation of purposes, along with pluralistic

> struggles over these things. As power vanishes and ends become givens in the way problems are specified, democracy becomes divested of politics, defined either as the handling of power or as struggle over common fundamentals or goals. Thus, democracy reformulated by governance means that participants are integrated into the process of benchmarking, consensus building, policy making, and implementation. Civic participation is reduced to buy-in. (*ibid.*, p. 128)

By reducing sortition to a procedure, without granting it decision-making power, the Citizens' Climate Convention and many experiments before it "contribute to demonstrating the deliberative capacities of ordinary citizens, [but] have only exceptionally contributed to increasing their power in decision making" (Talpin, 2019). The Citizens' Climate Convention promised to go beyond a deliberative mini-public without power, sometimes imagining a deepening of democracy through inclusion and participation, but in fact, like most other mini-publics, it did not have the impact hoped for, "issuing recommendations that mostly go unheeded" (Papadopoulos and Warin, 2007; Blondiaux, 2008).

Thus, sortition, which was imagined as an essentially democratic instrument (Manin, 1996), becomes part of neoliberal governance by allowing governments to "adopt a form of 'selective listening'", choosing the proposals that seem most relevant to them while ultimately retaining the power to decide (Sintomer and Talpin, 2011; Font, Pasadas Del Amo and Smith, 2016). This idea was confirmed at the Citizens' Climate Convention when Emmanuel Macron announced a referendum on a bill to enshrine environmental preservation in the Constitution (Cuny-Le Callet, 2021). By taking one of the CCC's 149 proposals and putting it to a popular vote, the President could claim to be a voice in defence of these drawn citizens, but this "form of 'consultative' democracy, currently using sortition, was in this sense only a legitimization of representative government as it exists" (Cervera-Marzal and Dubigeon, 2013, p. 167). Finally, this referendum project was abandoned in July 2021, due to a lack of agreement with the right wing in the Senate (Paillou and Revault d'Allonnes, 2021).

The participatory mechanism within governance resulted in the full power for government to choose *à la carte* from the CCC's proposals. This allows us to question the idea of "decentralisation of the state" acting as a mediator between different stakeholders, which is advocated by the discourse on governance. In the context of this sortition experiment, the state's power seemed to present itself as a simple transmitter of proposals towards a referendum, a legislative vote or a direct regulatory implementation. A certain decentralisation of the government was thus advocated in order to leave the necessary room for manœuvre by granting the decision-making power to the 150 citizens drawn at random from the Citizens' Climate Convention.

This narrative proved to be misleading, however, as while a certain effacement of the state was advocated in the discourse, we may observe that it is still the government that has the last word and the real decision-making power. This discourse of decentralisation of the state with the aim of democratic governance can be traced back to the discourse on "stake-holders" developed in the 1970s by business theorists preparing the neo-liberal turn (Chamayou, 2018). Thus, in order to escape the criticism of civil society towards the company, which is sometimes considered as an authoritarian private government, a discourse on the non-existence of the company and on the stakeholders has emerged (*ibid.*).

In this context, in order to conceal and make more acceptable the absolute power held by shareholders in private firms, some actors explained that in reality the firm was a "nexus of power" (Loevinger, 1961, p. 357; Quicherat and Daveluy, 1871, p. 753), an interweaving of power relations between different stakeholders and not a hierarchical body dominated by capitalists. This mobilisation of the "nexus of power" then made it possible to defend the idea that the firm was a collective construction in which each actor, whether a capitalist or not, had a say. There was therefore no longer shareholder sovereignty within the firm, but only relations between different stakeholders, including the firm's consumers and its employees (Rhenman, 1968, p. 25). By putting the notion of stakeholders at the centre of the explanation, the shareholders were trying to hide their real power and counteract the criticisms pointing to a lack of democracy in the firm:

> The notion of stakeholders is an amphibious concept, appearing alternately as an ethical notion and as a strategic category. It is this ambivalence that makes it so interesting for management, in that it allows it to play both ways. But this duplicity also leads to important conceptual tensions. While on the ethical side, stakeholders appear as subjects to whom management has obligations, on the strategic side, they are thought of as objects which must be controlled. On the one hand, respecting them, on the other, keeping them in check; on the one hand, recognizing them, on the other, identifying them. (Chamayou, 2018, p. 147)

This conception of stakeholders directly echoes the use of sortition within the reconfiguration of democracy through governance. While some might argue that an assembly drawn by lot, through its mode of selection, would constitute an embodiment of popular sovereignty (Rancière, 2005), the government intends to give an important place to this assembly as a stakeholder. However, by reducing citizens to one voice around the table, governance reduces the *demos* to one of many actors, including businesses and NGOs.

This conception of democracy through governance makes it possible to include citizens without granting them real decision-making power, which remains the monopoly of the government. By combining the reconfiguration of democracy through governance and the conception of "stakeholders", the French government has been able to try to make people forget that sortition and the citizens who participate in the democratic process have no real decision-making power, which always remains with the government. This use of sortition, illustrated by the episode of the Citizens' Climate Convention, brings us back to the neutralising virtue of the lottery that I will now discuss.

3. Avoiding Conflict to Promote Consensus: The Neutralising Virtue of Sortition

Sortition as an instrument has been described by Montesquieu as inherently democratic (Van Reybrouck, 2014). However, in addition to this democratic possibility, sortition also has a certain neutralising virtue, allowing governments to use it to reduce conflict in politics (Cervera-Marzal and Dubigeon, 2013). Thus, according to Manuel Cervera-Marzal and Yohann Dubigeon, "The neutralizing virtue of sortition resides in the fact that by entrusting the choice to chance, it leads to a neutral designation of the rulers, since, contrary to the election, no will, no interest and no human passion are involved in the process" (*ibid.*, p. 158). This neutralising virtue, by integrating itself into the discourse on governance, allows for a use of sortition that depoliticises and seeks to evacuate the agonistic dimension of politics, replacing it with a search for consensus and thus erasing the differences in worldviews and interests between the different actors (Mouffe, 2016). By taking up our analyses on governance and the reduction of the assembly of citizens drawn by lot to a "stakeholder", sortition can be envisaged as an important tool of conflict mediation:

> Thus, while governance analytically describes decentered and devolved power, as a policy term, governance aims to substitute consensus-oriented policy formation and implementation for the overt exercise of authority and power through law and policing. It is a short step from this reorientation of democracy into problem solving and consensus to a set of

additional replacements fundamental to the meaning and operation of governance today: "stakeholders" replace interest groups or classes, "guidelines" replace law, "facilitation" replaces regulation, "standards" and "codes of conduct" disseminated by a range of agencies and institutions replace overt policing and other forms of coercion. (Brown, 2015, p. 129)

By reducing a part of the *demos*, called an assembly endowed with a quality of population representativeness, to a simple stakeholder in the decision-making process, governance depoliticises politics and tries to erase any conflict in politics:

I have already hinted that the emphasis placed on problem solving and consensus by the concept of governance downplays to the point of disavowing structural stratifications in economy and society that could produce different political stakes and positions, as well as normative conflicts over the good. (*ibid.*, p. 129)

This use of sortition to neutralise conflict can be clearly illustrated by the origins of the Citizens' Climate Convention. Although it may be interesting to note that the proposal for a citizens' convention was already present in Emmanuel Macron's programme during the 2017 presidential campaign, imagining then to "Build a new European project with citizens' conventions" (Lui Président, 2022). Thus, the idea of citizens' assembly was not born with the Citizens' Climate Convention. However, the creation of the CCC did not directly respond to the implementation of an electoral promise made in 2017, it was caused by a specific context in France.

Indeed, when the French president announced the organisation of this experiment of drawing lots in April 2019, he did so during the Great National Debate organised following the Yellow Vests movement (Macron, 2019). For several months, every Saturday, citizens dressed in their yellow road safety vests occupied roundabouts. Initially, the mobilisation was aimed at the withdrawal of the carbon tax, which would then see an increase in the price of fuel to finance the ecological transition (Vie publique, 2021). This social movement was thus rising against a conception judged unequal of the ecological fight which wanted to make the middle and popular classes pay the price of the transition.

From this demand for justice in the fight against global warming, the movement quickly opened to other proposals and notably defended numerous proposals aiming at radicalisation of democracy (Bedock, Bonin, Liochon and Schnatterer, 2020), strongly criticising representative democracy (Grunberg, 2019). The movement, initially underestimated by the government, had grown, forcing the president to react with the convening of this Grand Débat National. It was during this debate that Emmanuel Macron tried a political gamble with the Citizens' Climate Convention (Daoulas, 2020), a device "imagined by the Gilets citoyens' collective, a coalition bringing together activists of participatory democracy, ecologists, local elected officials and Yellow Vest" (Guérineau de Lamérie, 2020). By proposing this randomly drawn assembly, the President was responding to the Gilets Jaunes by offering them a mechanism of direct democracy to find solutions concerning the trigger for the social movement, the energy transition and justice in the fight against global warming.

This proposal for a Citizens' Climate Convention thus comes in a political context of great tension and thus it is allowed to escape from this conflictual state "by diverting attention from the Yellow Vests movement" (Courant, 2020). This use of sortition is not new, as it appears "sometimes as a weapon in the hand of elected officials to cut the grass under the feet of associations or more radical social movements" (Talpin, 2019; Barbier, Bedu and Buclet, 2009).

Thus, the French government was acting like many clients of political deliberation experiments who particularly "seek in deliberation a strategy for managing the conflicts they face when potential or tangible resistance to austerity policy measures emerge from social reorganization, state spending cuts, and urban renewal" (Lee and Romano, 2013).

Moreover, this deliberative assembly was organised without directly including the citizens forming the social movement at the base of these demands for climatic, social and democratic justice but preferring "citizens without quality, most often without associative or partisan affiliation". In doing so, the French president hoped to "build up a docile public" (Blondiaux, 2008) with the aim of "depoliticizing sortition, making it an instrument, a procedure, exportable at the cost of losing its political radicality" (Talpin, 2019, p. 462), this last point being the clear objective of the manœuvre. Likewise, the evacuation of conflict and the search for consensus was notably considered to invite "experts and interest groups, [which] although diverse, were not organized to create contradictory viewpoints. Thus, none of the debates among the participants showed the conflict between the opponents and the supporters of growth or of the reduction of working time" (Courant, 2020, p. 62).

All this summarises concretely what happened in the case that interests us in this chapter. Seeing the potential of political conflict carried by the Yellow Vests, the recourse to an assembly of citizens drawn by lot to answer an eminently political question in the form of a problem to be solved made it possible to replace the agonistic dimension of politics with consensus-oriented towards the resolution of the problem and thus to take full advantage of the neutralising virtue of sortition.

> As William Walters notes, the embrace, if not the very idea of governance in politics emerges from a postideological claim—"the end of history"—to be pragmatic and solutions oriented; it features dialogue, inclusion, and consensus, rather than power, conflict, or opposition. Governance aims to supersede the antagonisms and partisanship of realpolitik and democracy alike; the press toward consensus-driven managerial solutions to problems has as its opposite partisan maneuvering or brokering of policy, interest-group pluralism, and of course, class conflict and struggle. (Brown, 2015, p. 130)

To return to our first argument about the absence of decision-making power, the French president has acted like other liberal regimes before him that "practice an essentially apolitical use of sortition in the sense that they instrumentalize it to evacuate conflict (neutralizing function) and dissociate it entirely from the question of the power, or at least the marginal power, of sortition" (Cervera-Marzal and Dubigeon, 2013, p. 167).

This attempt to depoliticise politics through this misuse of the lottery had clear consequences in the discourse of the French government around the Citizen's Climate Convention with, for example, the interview in March 2021 of the Minister of Ecological Transition, Barabra Pompili, who blamed the fact that "part of the citizens [are] in a political approach" (France Info, 2021).

Thus, this episode of the Citizens' Climate Convention clearly illustrates the neutralising virtue of sortition mobilised by neoliberal governments that try to evacuate conflict and the agonistic dimension of politics in order to replace them with a consensus politics oriented towards problem-solving rather than towards the definition and opposition of several societal projects.

4. Conclusion

Neoliberal governance reconceptualises democracy (Brown, 2015). By promoting a discourse claiming greater participation and inclusion in the context of a decentralisation of the state, governance seems to give a place to various devices that favour them. Sortition being one of them, it logically finds its place in this new democratic architecture shaped by neoliberal governments. Drawing citizens by lot for their quality of representativeness of the population, ensuring the inclusion of all social groups, and then allowing them to discuss issues during several sessions in order to respond to concrete problems seems to be an experiment that is now finding its place in this new conception of democracy.

By inviting citizens to the negotiating table, thus reducing them to "stakeholders" (Chamayou, 2018), governance allows for a reduction of conflict by focusing discussions on consensus building. In this sense, neoliberal governments try to use the neutralising virtue of sortition (Cervera-Marzal and Dubigeon, 2013) and escape the agnostic dimension of politics (Mouffe, 2016). In my opinion, the Citizens' Climate Convention is a relevant illustration of this use of sortition in the framework of the neoliberal reconfiguration of democracy through governance. In the context of great political conflict related to the Yellow Vests crisis, calling a randomly drawn assembly to solve the problem appeared to be a way to evacuate the conflict.

This participation and inclusion, to which a decision-making power was promised, finally sees this promise evaporate and its most ambitious proposals are swept aside, reminding us that in the decentralisation of the state advocated by governance, as in the company, the stakeholders remain only that, and the chief, shareholder or president, remains the final decision-maker. This misuse of sortition, while initially providing a certain democratic legitimacy, may be seen as a double-edged sword. When the objective is to avoid conflict, it does not remove all the radicality of political visions. Thus, the search for consensus in the resolution of problem has produced "almost revolutionary proposals, whereas parliamentarians have been unable to put masterful proposals on the table" (Guérineau de Lamérie, 2020). The neutralising virtue of sortition does not always neutralise all political radicalism.

Then, when the project is to deny or evade its democratic virtue, it ends up being noticed. Indeed, when promises are not kept, manipulation soon becomes apparent and sortition in this context turns out to be a masquerade playing a counter-productive role. Citizens no longer believe in it and, instead of granting democratic legitimacy through sortition, they become more and more distrustful, "often feeling deceived or instrumentalized" (Talpin, 2019; Funes, Talpin and Rull, 2014). In short, governance allows the use of sortition to neutralise conflict and to regain democratic legitimacy, but this operation is not without risk and, when citizens understand that sortition is not the democracy they were promised, and after having tasted a democratic experience that has remained a dead letter with political decision-makers, they are suspicious.

Jessy Bailly

Randomly Selected European Citizens' Panels

Could Random Selection Be Detrimental to Deliberation?

Abstract: *The Conference on the Future of Europe (COFOE), described as a genuine "democratic innovation" by its designers, combines diverse but connected mechanisms (participatory digital platform, deliberative democracy through European Citizens' Panels and then through plenary sessions with political representatives). The process, which ran from May 2021 to May 2022, consisted first in the organisation of four transnational, thematic panels of sortitioned citizens from the 27 Member States. These citizens then voiced their recommendations to representatives of the Eurocracy, who debated them in plenary sessions with citizen representatives from the thematic panels. In the case of the European Citizens' panels, which is the focus under scrutiny, the citizens were selected according to classic selection criteria to ensure a representative sample (age, sex rather than gender, professions, nationalities). However, this sought-after representativeness did not lead to citizen diversity in terms of attitudes towards the European Union. Consistent with the overall purpose of the book, this chapter documents a bias regarding the practice of sortition in politics. The main argument of the chapter is to question the effects of the sociological representativeness of citizens' panels (or assemblies) on the diversity of deliberation.*

1. Introduction

Sortition in politics is a growing field of research in political science. Some virtues have been pinpointed by several scholars (Curato *et al.*, 2017; Landemore, 2013; Zakaras, 2010, for instance) to deal with the crisis of representative democracy. Other scholarship has pointed out some drawbacks (Pourtois, 2016; Umbers, 2018). One study from Jacquet, Niessen and Reuchamps (2020) examines the diverse reception of sortition by Belgian Members of Parliament. Some of the latter consider the expansion of deliberative assemblies as a threat to their representative legitimacy (see also Geurtz and Van de Wijdeven, 2010; Vandamme, 2021). Other studies have highlighted the generalisation of the lottery in politics (Talpin mentions the "sortition industry", 2019). The spread of sortition has led some scholars to consider the normalisation (and de-radicalisation) of this mode of political selection, historically associated with a left-wing imaginary and not with liberal democracy (Cervera-Marzal and Dubigeon, 2013).

In this chapter, I focus on a deliberative experiment based on sortition at the level of the European Union (EU). While the EU staff is often seen as driven by an elite of Eurocrats (Georgagakis and Rowell, 2014), or technocrats with no direct electoral legitimacy (Díez Medrano, 2005), some top-level EU institutions decided to lead a major political experiment, the Conference on the Future of Europe (COFOE), using sortition.

I will explain how and why some EU staff used sortition, in a very innovative citizen mechanism at the EU level, starting from the beginning of the citizen participation policy of the EU. I will then show how, compared to previous experiments in deliberative and participatory democracy studied at the EU level (Aldrin and Hubé, 2011; Boussaguet and Dehousse, 2007; Damay and Delmotte, 2018; Wojcik, 2011), the COFOE could be considered unique.

The broader aim of the COFOE was to recreate social ties at the European level between Member States and citizens after the traumatic effect of Brexit on European elites. To this end, in the first moments of the COFOE's establishment, in 2021, the official discourse of COFOE's organisers emphasised:

> We need to make European democracy more responsive, more resilient. There are three pillars inside the COFOE: the multilingual digital platform, which is the entry point for citizens, regional authorities and organizations; the citizens' panels and the plenaries. We want to capture the critical voices.[1]

---

[1] Toma Sutic, Member of the Cabinet of the Vice President for Democracy and Demography, during an event organised by the Association of European Regions Bureau Debate, "The Future of Democracy in the Hands of Regions", 12th May 2021.

> This conference is not about communication, it's not a people's fair where
> we explain the EU to the citizens, but we open up for the citizens' propo-
> sals [...]. we should draw lots of Eurosceptics, not just supporters of
> Europe, we want a cross-section of the EU's population.[2]

Such a perspective should remind us of a far more dated EU doctrine of
communication. The 1987 European Parliament (EP) resolution on European information policy highlighted that an effective EU communication
policy must attract the attention of those who had shown little interest in
the European project. The COFOE organisers operationalised it through
sortition so as to select citizens to debate broad issues on the "future of
Europe". Such a mini-public experience was thought likely to attract the
attention of the maxi-public and to provoke a wider public debate that
would have curbed the secessionist aspirations of some parts of EU
populations.

For actors advocating deliberation on a European scale (Renkamp and
Vergne, 2020; Huesmann, Renkamp and Petzol, 2022), as for some
scholars (see Landemore, 2013), sortition is defined as a standard of legitimacy of deliberative democracy. It would foster both the constitution of a
sociologically representative ("descriptive representation", Pitkin, 1967)
sample of citizens in relation to the population and the diversity of
opinions from the citizens gathered.

The diversity of opinions, thought as a corollary to the diversity of
citizen profiles, should lead to conflicting exchanges (Ester, Fung and Lee,
2015; Maia *et al.*, 2021) which are considered as a valuable condition for
deliberation (Michels and De Graaf, 2017; Talpin, 2007); the latter being
understood as:

> [...] a way to complete the information and to specify the preferences of
> individuals. It helps them to discover certain aspects (both in terms of the
> solutions offered and their objectives) that they had not considered before
> [...]. But deliberation is not only a discovery process, the discussants do not
> only state various and conflicting points of views, they also discuss issues.
> They strive to persuade each other of the correctness of their point of view
> [...]. However, unlike demonstration, argumentation does not lead to a
> necessary conclusion that the listener cannot not admit. An argumentative
> conclusion is not a necessary proposition, the listener is ultimately free to
> agree or disagree. (Author's own traduction from Manin, 1985, pp. 84–85)

---

2   Guy Verhofstadt, during an event organised by the Portuguese Presidency of
    the EU Council on the Conference on the future of Europe, 17th June 2021.

For example, Michels and De Graaf (2017), when advising deliberative practitioners, argue that:

> Make sure there is room for criticism to be voiced. This means that you should also be open to opponents or dissidents and not only than to your followers. Do not exclude them, even if they may slow the initiative down (inclusion and legitimacy) [...]. The lack of diversity and inclusion is a[n] [...] issue that needs more attention from researchers studying citizen participation and democratic innovations. Even in mini-publics which aim to attract a diverse group of participants, biases are likely to remain due to self-selection.

In this chapter, I contribute to the debate. Specifically, I question this supposed causal link between random selection (supposed to guarantee "inclusiveness", Smith, 2009)[3] and diversity of opinions. Provocatively, I hypothesise such random selection/inclusiveness of a citizen panel could, under certain conditions, be detrimental to the "quality" of deliberations among sortitioned citizens.

I rely on a direct observation of the COFOE that took place between May 2021 and May 2022 to verify the hypothesis. I participated as an observer at the Conference on the Future of Europe in two European citizens' panels, one on "EU democracy, values, rights, rule of law, security", and the other on "Stronger economy, social justice, jobs, education, culture, sport, digital transformation". Firstly, a survey was distributed to 31 citizens on three occasions (September 2021, November 2021, December 2021/March 2022). They were interviewed about the different aspects, including their previous relationships towards European integration before their COFOE attendance, and whether they considered each of three sessions they attended positively or negatively.

Total population	Gender	Age	Nationality
31 citizens	22 men; 9 women	From 20s to over 70s	7 Spanish; 5 French; 4 German; 2 Belgian; 2 Bulgarian; 2 Austrian; 2 Finnish; 1 Romanian; 1 Danish; 1 Dutch; 1 Maltese; 1 Greek; 1 Irish; 1 Hungarian

Table 1: The surveyed population.

This sample is not representative of the 400 citizens who participated in the two panels under observation (comprising 200 citizens per panel).

---

[3] He defines "inclusiveness" as "equal *probability* of being selected to participate" for sortitioned citizens (2009, p. 79).

However, they were diverse enough in terms of nationality, age, profession to question the ambition of the COFOE organisers to gather different social perspectives from citizens on the EU.

In addition to observing the European citizens' panels and the questionnaire, I observed online events during COFOE, where a range of associative actors or institutions organised events within the framework of COFOE alongside the citizens' panels and plenary sessions. Finally, after the COFOE, I was asked by EU institutions to give my opinion during feedback meetings with other observers. Rather than being "conseiller du Prince", these meetings were an opportunity to pursue my fieldwork, to see the discussions and debates of experts on the COFOE experience, and on sortition.

The remainder of the chapter is structured as follows: in the second section, I give an overview of the COFOE and emphasise the importance of the terms and conditions of the sortition that was practised there. I then study the effects of sortition on deliberation through the observation of the citizens' speeches during the European Citizens' Panels and the surveys. The last section highlights why the sortition was problematic in terms of the original purpose of the COFOE organisers.

2. The Conference on the Future of Europe: An Overview

The COFOE is not the first EU-wide experiment with sortition (Tomorrow's Europe/2007 or the European Citizens' Panel/2018). On the basis that the European institutions had had time to perfect their knowledge of participatory and deliberative procedures since the first citizens' conferences studied by Boussaguet and Dehousse (2009), the three EU legislative institutions — the EP, the Council of the EU and the European Commission (EC) — agreed for the first time that such a conference should be established and should be partly based on sortition. Moreover, the three EU institutions initially suggested that citizen inputs would not be solely consultative. Without specifying the precise modalities for the follow-up of citizens' demands, the ambiguity and the uncertainty about the future of the citizen recommendations is palpable.[4]

---

4   There is some doubt as to whether the EC and the EP intend to turn the experiment into a constituent moment.

The COFOE was born out of several factors. While the idea of citizen participation in the EU goes back to at least the 1980s, the new citizen-based agenda of the EU, i.e. the organisation of experiments in citizen participation at EU level, started in the early 2000s, particularly with the European Commission's Plan D for Democracy, Dialogue and Debate. Unsuccessfully challenging what has been described as a deficit of democratic legitimacy in the EU, through the parliamentarisation of the Union, or the involvement of stakeholders in decision-making, a new doctrine of involving ordinary citizens was put in place. During the first part of the 2010s, the citizen agenda of the EU had slowed down. Then, Brexit opened the way to a whole series of reflections on scenarios for the future of Europe, notably those launched by Jean-Claude Juncker. The aim was to recreate the social link between European citizens in Europe. Among these scenarios, the principle of a conference on the future of Europe with citizen participation emerged. Such a scenario was proposed by several consultancies in deliberative democracy such as Missions Publiques and the Bertelsmann Stiftung; by think tanks present at European level, for example the European Policy Centre; and by academics such as political scientists and jurists of the European University Institute. This external lobbying was followed by internal lobbying from EU institutional actors promoting European citizens' assemblies within the institutions. This internal lobbying took place with the arrival of pro-deliberation officials at the head of the Commission's Directorate-General (DG) for Communication, and also with Emmanuel Macron's involvement in the European scene following his election as President of the French Republic in 2017. Indeed, shortly after his election, between 2018 and 2019, he launched an initiative entitled the European Citizens' Consultations. He also wrote a "letter to European Citizens" just before the 2019 European elections, in which he stated "let's set up [...] a Conference for Europe to propose all the changes our political project needs, with an open mind, even to amending the treaties. This conference will need to engage with citizens' panels". Moreover, according to rumours circulated by the COFOE organisers, Macron would have conditioned his support for Ursula Von Der Leyen as President of the Commission in 2019 on, among other things, a Conference on the Future of Europe. Furthermore, France is said to have tried to influence first Germany and then Portugal, which at that time held the rotating EU Council presidency, over the implementation of the conference (interviews with two members of Missions Publiques on 13th July 2022 and 16th August 2022). Finally, at the European Parliament

(EP) level, several German activists for citizen participation had privileged links with German MEPs belonging to the Spinelli Group, who convinced other members of the Group, including Guy Verhofstadt.

The COFOE was officially launched on 9th May 2021. From the outset, the official objectives of the Conference were rather vague. The idea was to randomly select citizens from the 27 Member States to deliberate and express recommendations in four thematic panels (comprising 200 citizens per panel); to rethink the "future of Europe" — stronger economy, social justice, jobs, education, culture, sport, digital transformation (panel 1); EU democracy, values and rights, the rule of law and security (panel 2); climate and health (panel 3); foreign policy and migration (panel 4). Here is what one can find on the three official principles of the COFOE as defined by the three legislative institutions:

> The Conference on the Future of Europe will open a new space for debate with citizens to address Europe's challenges and priorities [...]. The Conference is based on inclusiveness, openness and transparency. (European Parliament, Council and European Commission, 2021)

Each panel met three times: in sessions where citizens made thematic recommendations in subgroup discussions facilitated by professional facilitators. Thereafter, there were plenary sessions. These included MEPs, national MPs, members of the Council and of the EC, trade unions and European civil society representatives, as well as citizen ambassadors.[5] In this chapter, I will mainly focus on the panel part. Within the three panel sessions, citizens mainly participated in small (more thematically specific) discussion groups, where they elaborated the recommendations. These were then presented to the 200 citizens of each panel for validation. I personally observed two panels (the one on economy, social justice; and the one on democratic reforms). Within each panel, I observed a subgroup on "sustainable economy" (panel 1) and a group on "strengthening citizen participation" (panel 2).

After giving an overview of the COFOE process, let us give some elements on the modalities of the sortition process. In the literature, sortition is often considered as providing better descriptive representation of the wider population than traditional elected assemblies, especially in terms of age, gender, ethnicity, education and income (Zakaras, 2010). For

---

[5]   Citizen ambassadors were randomly selected on a voluntary basis, among sortitioned citizens from the citizens' panels.

the COFOE, the 800 citizens were selected by a consortium of entities, chaired by Kantar Belgium. I had access to two contracts between the EC Directorate-General of Communication and Kantar, a company specialising in opinion surveys. The latter was offered €300,000 and €399,000 for selecting the four citizens' panels, according to the following modalities:

> The COFOE should reflect Europe's diversity [...]. These panels should be representative of the sociological diversity of the European Union population. We would therefore like to invite a randomly selected group of citizens covering geographical origin, socio-economic background, education, gender and age to give the outcome of the discussions a higher credibility.[6]

The Commission asked Kantar to select 800 people for the four panels, with 200 reserve citizens (50 per panel). At first sight, the random selection corresponds to the representativeness of European citizens in terms of nationalities (in relation to the population of the Member States), gender, urban/rural area, occupations and education level. However, the sample was not fully representative. There was an over-representation of young people — one third of the 800 — but attracting young people, usually considered a very strategic audience for the EU decade, was seen as a goal of the COFOE organisers. There is therefore a deliberate distortion of strict representativeness (what Warren and Pearse call "near-random selection", 2008, p. 6).

Moreover, in the contracts the Commission highlighted:

> In all previous events such as Citizens' Dialogues, the Commission has relied on Representations and Europe Direct Information Centres to invite participants. The result, research suggests, is that the participants have in general been pro-European and have had higher education than what would have been the result of a random selection.

Thus, the Commission had internalised the principle that drawing lots is a guarantee of what is defined by practitioners and academics as the democratic quality of a deliberative experience. With COFOE, it intended to organise experiences of citizen participation that were different from those it used to organise. Traditional "citizen" EU events tended to be considered by some EU staff as communication exercises rather than

---

[6] European Commission, Specific contracts on sortition with Kantar Belgium, 2020 & 2021.

genuine deliberative dialogues and interactions between citizens and European representatives.[7]

Now let's analyse the impact of the sortition, the content of the deliberations of the sortitioned citizens.

3. Is Random Selection a Sufficient Condition for Deliberation?

Considering the literature on deliberation as mentioned, the virtues of sortition lie in the possibility of constituting a diverse sample of citizens to debate on a subject. The assumption is that the co-presence of sociologically different individuals will lead these individuals to debate and deliberate, expressing a plurality of views. This is in line with Guy Verhofstadt and the Commission's concerns I mentioned above. In their view, the COFOE should invite citizens who are sceptical about European integration to the table. In the Rules of Procedure document that framed the COFOE, it is stated: "European citizens from all walks of life and from all corners of the Union will be able to participate" (Conference of the Future of Europe, 2021, p. 1). Attracting different points of view on European integration then remains a condition for the legitimacy of the experiment. Let's see if this argument works in the context of the COFOE.

When I observed two citizens' panels (one on economy, the other on democracy) for 72 hours, I systematically took notes on the citizens' discussions which alternated between thematic subgroups and citizen plenaries with two hundred people per panel. Through this collection of data, I questioned the interactive dynamics of exchange between citizens. I mainly asked whether the discussions reflected a diversity of views: different gradients of support or rejection for the EU. To put it differently, had the citizens different views on the legitimacy of the EU that they could bring to bear on any given area of discussion?

In the citizens' panels, one might have expected citizen opinions to be diverse. The issues on which citizens were invited to deliberate were broad. My data comes from two citizens' panels on: "a stronger economy, social justice and jobs/Education, culture, youth and sport/Digital transformation" (panel 1), and on: "Democracy, values and rights, the rule of law and security" (panel 2). One might spontaneously think that such

---

[7]   Interview with a former Deputy Director of Coordination, Planning, Impact, Outreach Strategy, Committee of Regions/DG Communication, 18th July 2022.

framing would encourage the citizens to express themselves freely. More-over, a diversity of expressions is to be expected, especially as the litera-ture on citizens' opinions of the EU shows that, even if most citizens are ambivalent about the EU (Dakowska and Hubé, 2011), there are Euro-philes, Eurosceptics and finally those who are indifferent (Van Ingelgom, 2014), i.e. they have no preconceived opinions on European issues.

However, careful observation of several discussion groups showed that highly critical opinions on the EU were in the minority.[8] In my research design, I first sought to assess interactivity (in the sense of Pedrini and Bächtiger, 2010) which could be defined as whether citizens discuss and respond to each other (in the subgroups I attended). Then I questioned whether there were contradictory exchanges, or indeed a diversity of opinions. It can be assumed that the more interactive the discussions are, the more likely they are to be conflictual.

On the one hand, in terms of interactivity, the dialogical or monol-ogical character of the discussions was assessed. Turning to citizens' opinions, from the survey I performed, a third of the citizens said the discussions between citizens in the first session were of good quality. Conversely, 1 out of every 3 citizens judged them to be poor. For the second session, the critical relationship to the quality of the deliberations was reversed. Eleven out of 31 citizens considered the quality of the discussions to be negative. Only 4 out of 31 citizens praised the quality of the second session in terms of the citizens' contributions. For the third session, the situation is even more diverse since only two citizens expressed criticism. The perceived quality of the discussions thus improved. Let us take a closer look at some of the citizens' considerations which are not necessarily representative, but different enough to be meaningful. First, let us look at two optimistic comments.

> Austrian citizen, first session, panel 1: At some point I felt like a politician in Parliament. Our discussions were really productive.

> Spanish citizen, second session, panel 1: Debates have been very intense [...] but very satisfying, because you learn and become sympathetic to the different countries that are part of the EU [...]; it was very enriching.

---

[8] If my observations are admittedly limited to the citizen groups I studied, discussions with fellow researchers who observed other subgroups' discussions in European citizens' panels corroborated my observations and analyses. Therefore, the following results are relatively representative of the full range of dynamics related to citizen contributions.

Like other surveyed citizens, the Austrian citizen assessed the quality of
the discussions in terms of their productivity. The Spanish citizen shared
a similar relationship with the experiment, as he valued learning from the
situation in other countries. There were also critical comments.

> Dutch citizen, first session, panel 2: The session consisted of sequences of
> monologues which sometimes related to what somebody else said, and
> sometimes did not.

> German citizen, first session, panel 2: More background knowledge and
> preparation of the participants would have facilitated this.

> French citizen, second session, panel 1: We need more exchanges and con-
> flict of ideas and thoughts; for the moment we take turns. I really think that
> citizens need to debate more directly to bring out the various problems of
> their daily lives.

> French citizen, third session, panel 2: It was sometimes a bit long,
> especially when you were stuck on a particular word for hours.

Although negative reports from the citizens on the quality of the
discussions were in the minority, they are important for shedding light on
the way in which the citizen talks were conducted.

Indeed, the monological nature of the discussions expressed by the
Dutch citizen can be explained in so far as the first of the sessions of each
panel dealt with a period of deliberation training. The aim was to put the
randomly selected citizens, who were not used to taking part in this type
of exercise, at ease by giving them minimal guidelines so that they could
express themselves relatively freely on the major themes.

During the next two sessions of the European citizens' panels, the
citizens refined their recommendations in small discussion groups and
went into greater depth from one session to the next. However, the French
citizen nevertheless recalled that during the subsequent sessions (2 and 3)
there had been few real debates and little conflict in the citizens'
discussions. Indeed, in each subgroup discussion, about ten citizens of
several nationalities deliberated. They spoke in their native language,
while the others benefitted from simultaneous translations. There was
also a facilitator who took notes of what was said in an Excel table which
was visible to all. In this way, citizens could check whether or not what
they said had been correctly transcribed. Since the translation was not
always ideal, the citizens spent a considerable amount of time
commenting on the translations, to the detriment of discussions on the
substance of the talks.

Furthermore, the observations revealed that the discussions were always animated by the facilitator. This confirms the predominant role of facilitators in deliberative processes (Coleman and Moss, 2012). There was a paucity of moments of direct exchange between citizens. In other words, there was little interaction without mediation from the facilitator, which made the exchanges more artificial because they were less direct and spontaneous. I could not quantify the proportion of mediated and unmediated interactions. While in terms of direct interactivity, talks were limited, this does not mean that citizens did not interact, even in the presence of the facilitator. Apart from the first session, the discussions were not monological, but dialogical.

On the other hand, I questioned how the interactivity targeting of argumentative conflict in citizens' speaking was investigated. I was not able to quantify the proportion of conflictual and consensual exchanges, but the latter were in the majority, and, in 32 hours of observation, I found about twenty conflicting exchanges, which is not very many. Despite the interactivity of the discussions, there were few conflictual dynamics.

Let us give one typical example of the citizen talks I have attended:

Facilitator: Now we need to discuss one previous recommendation you made, namely: "we hope that the EU will reopen discussions on a constitution for Europe. Citizens must be involved."

German female citizen, 20s: I think it is essential to have a constitution because it has been said, there are different treaties, and it is difficult for citizens to know what is in the treaties. A constitution makes it easier to understand, in a document, it brings citizens and politicians closer together, promoting transparency.

German male citizen, 60s: I think we need a constitution. We can identify with a constitution, with values. I think it will depend on the priorities of citizens on freedom of movement. For the details, we would have to discuss them in terms of Human Rights and democracy.

Facilitator: I will then add to the recommendation [the constitution has to be changed] that it is necessary to include citizens in the decision-making process.[9]

In this example, none of the citizens who were debating on the proposal about the European Constitution opposed it. They did not mention the double referendum rejection of 2005 (in France and the Netherlands). In

---

[9] Citizens' panel on democracy, subgroup "strengthening citizen participation", 12th December 2021, Florence, Italy.

addition, none of them pointed to the more contemporary problems raised by Germany, Hungary or Poland, when national institutions felt that certain provisions of the EU Treaty ran counter to national constitutional principles.

Although few in number, I observed conflicting dynamics, for instance: citizens talking about whether to tax companies that did not fit with corporate social responsibility criteria, or whether to subsidise those that did. Another example of a conflict of vision was whether public authorities—not necessarily European ones—should impose a civic education course in schools. However, the few contradictory discussions were rarely about European public action.[10] Conversely, citizens criticised the lack of harmonisation in the sectoral policies between Member States, but rarely European public action as such. So far, there had been little criticism of the principle of European integration and the way it was implemented. However, the aim of the COFOE organisers was to invite critical voices towards the EU to the discussion table.

As there was little conflict in the observed discussions, I returned to my questionnaires. I asked 31 citizens from both panels about their relationship to the EU prior to their participation in the experiment in September 2021. Most considered, for example: "I obviously have a basic knowledge of the EU as a citizen and I try to keep up to date with EU issues, but it's also not my very first priorities, so I have general information from news and from school" (Hungary male citizen, in his 20s); "I can't say I knew much about how the work goes in European Union before coming to the panel" (Bulgarian female citizen, 30s); "Before the panels, all I knew about the EU was what was broadcast on the news, now I do follow the European Parliament channel, but not before" (Spanish female citizen, in her 50s).

The citizens interviewed were mostly indifferent to the EU. They had common ordinary representations of the EU (Díez Medrano, 2005). However, their participation in the citizens' panels made them more aware of the need to coordinate European policies. This refers to one of the classic effects, expected both by the European institutions involved in the

---

10   I only noted a conversation in which several citizens under-criticised the fact that the European Commission would like to legislate on education policies, whereas this is a competence of the Member States. For these few citizens, the competence should remain national. But this type of position is quite rare, at least in the citizen conversations observed.

organisation of deliberative experiments and by the citizens participating in this type of experiment at a European level (Aldrin and Hubé, 2011; Damay and Delmotte 2018). It was confirmed by citizens' answers to my survey:

> Belgian female citizen, 70s: Citizens' European Union is not a utopia.

> Greek female citizen, 20s: Many people are really invested in the EU, and they believe in the idea of a united Europe.

> Irish male citizen, 30s: I guess what struck me about the European Union during this panel was the rich diversity of nations and cultures represented. The EU covers a wide range of different people who speak different languages and have different lifestyles. The EU's motto "Unity through Diversity" really sums up the essence of the EU in one sentence.

> German male citizen, 20s: Many citizens from different countries share the same values & goals on the EU. Young and old share opinions. In fact, I discovered how similar we are.

> Spanish male, 40s: In general, there was a homogeneous idea of what Europe should be.

Participation in the COFOE fostered the identification of a large majority of citizens with the EU (Bruter, 2005, speaks of civic identity, p. 163) and it enabled them to feel more European (Bruter speaks of cultural identity, *ibid.*). Notwithstanding, some citizens contended there was little diversity in the views expressed in the talks. At least five of the 31 citizens interviewed insisted on this aspect, like this German citizen in her 30s: "One should pay attention to a greater diversity of people and not only people who are pro-Europe. There should be a greater selection of different people, different social classes and also religions." It is significant to note that the "social class" criterion had to be respected through occupation. However, no ethnic and/or religious criteria were considered. Moreover, officially, the selected citizens were not "pro-Europe", in so far as the aim was to involve citizens who did not have a predefined opinion on European issues (either negative or positive).

Thus, most of the citizens observed were initially indifferent to the EU. The majority tended to become pro-European in the course of the experiment. While they did not have strictly the same views on European integration at the outset, citizens generally did not reflect on the place the EU should have in a given policy area. In other words, the mobility of citizens' opinions (Lezaun and Soneyrd, 2007) was rather limited to a shift from indifference to sympathy for European integration. In addition, the COFOE's official and broad framing encouraged them to think about how the EU could do more and better. Few citizens expressed the view that the EU should not always intervene. However, contrary to the opinion of the COFOE citizens, it is reasonable to assume that a significant number of citizens in the EU Member States share the idea that some decisions should be taken at a decision-making level closer to the citizens than the European level, according to the very principle of subsidiarity.

The lack of diversity of opinion in the citizens' discussions led to the fact that citizens were not able to deliberate in the sense of Manin (1985), Talpin (2007) and Michels and De Graaf (2017). The diversity/conflict and interactivity criteria of the citizen discussions show that the spectrum of opinions was relatively undiversified. This is directly related to the modalities and practice of the sortition, which I will develop in order to re-interrogate more broadly the criterion of descriptive representation (representativeness) of the randomly selected samples in terms of their deliberative potential.

4. Self-Selection Bias, Weak Deliberation? Revisiting the Criterion of Random Selection

So far, in the context of COFOE's citizens' panels, I have insisted on the fact that the relative descriptive representation of the sample of citizens has not, paradoxically, led to the expression of varied opinions, contrary to what one might have expected. It leads to one of the biases of the sortition which, despite its representativeness, can be detrimental to the plurality and quality of the deliberations.

This bias is due to self-selection (Smith, 2009, pp. 80 and 107). Indeed, although the sortitioned citizens fit with a sociological diversity, they have all agreed to participate in the experiment. Unlike in the case of trial juries (*jurys d'assise*) in France, participation was not compulsory. To that extent, an exhaustive descriptive representation is hard to achieve. Why would citizens initially critical of the EU agree to participate in such an experiment driven by the European institutions? Moreover, people who have less oral proficiency and who feel uncomfortable with politics would have tended to refuse the invitation. That argument is corroborated by the study of Isernia, Fishkin, Steienr and Di Mauro (2014). The latter compared the profiles of those who agreed to participate in the Europolis with those who declined. While this is a deliberative survey, the authors nevertheless found a gap between the two populations:

Participants in the EuroPolis experiment are slightly better educated and from higher social classes than non-participants (which simply accentuates a difference that is present in the standard survey samples, especially if they were conducted by telephone). They are also more supportive of immigration and European integration and more likely to vote in European elections. (p. 127)

These authors do not say that the citizens selected by Europolis were totally Europhile and federalist before participating. They were relatively indifferent to the EU, but ready to value European integration. This is the case for the members of the COFOE citizens' panel. If they had been anti-EU, they would have refused to participate in a deliberative experiment directly organised by the European institutions. Out of my sample of 31 citizens, only one was sceptical. However, the self-selection bias probably favoured the selection of citizens who agreed to participate in the experiment because they did not have *a priori* negative views on European integration.

These elements echo an older debate about who should participate in citizens' conferences, citizens' juries or in any experimental mini-publics. Should sortitioned citizens have pre-constituted opinions (Testart, Piasecki and Morvan, 2013)? Although some deliberation practitioners do not support this proposition, it could be argued that the selection of a body of citizens who are totally indifferent and uninformed about a subject can lead, under certain conditions, to them conforming to the demands that are legitimately expected of them by the organisers.

If, in principle, the selection of indifferent citizens on a given subject does not necessarily lead to the expression of consensual opinions, why is this not the case with the COFOE? This can be explained by considering other criteria, for example the process of training citizens. Enforced by interactions with experts selected not by the citizens directly but by the organisers, this process was relatively weak. The experts gave their opinions and knowledge lessons to the citizens.[11] However, there was very little contradiction between them, with each expert affirming the need for further European integration (or harmonisation of national policies). There were no experts who were sceptical or genuinely critical of EU interventions, to give nuance to the citizens.[12]

As a result, citizens sometimes took up claims about the EU that did not emanate directly from their concerns. This was the case, for example,

---

[11] This was the case in the first and second sessions of the citizens' panels.
[12] Other ways of framing citizens' proposals were observed, such as the brochure distributed to citizens at the beginning of the first session.

when citizens' groups argued that the EP should have the legislative initiative, or that transnational European parliamentary elections should be organised. On closer inspection, these proposals had long been on the agenda of the federalist Members of the EP who sat in the EP Committee on Constitutional Affairs. Therefore, the selection of indifferent citizens, in the absence of a formative process with contradictory opinions (exposure to contradictory being valued by Manin, 1985) reduce the potentiality and quality of deliberations among citizens.

Moreover, one non-consensual solution to this problem was mentioned by the French political scientist Yves Sintomer during a feedback meeting of the COFOE observers I attended:

> Yves Sintomer: [...] Those who are in favour of the EU are more likely to agree to participate than those who reject the EU. Moreover, minorities have not been sufficiently taken into account. An affirmative action process would help [...]

> Dominik Hierlermann (Bertelsmann Stiftung): This is a big debate in political science, the descriptive representativity. There will always be criticism of representativeness. It is less important to be fully representative, since complete representativity is impossible [...]

> Deputy Head of Unit for the Commission's Citizens' Dialogues: The issue of selection was discussed. Some of you have criticised the selection process. But if we look at the criteria of selection, there were well respected. With some small exceptions but compared to other examples, it was quite good. We had issues with Kantar, but it was overall relatively good [...]

> Alberto Alemanno (Law Professor, HEC): Five criteria were mentioned (age, gender, educational background, nationalities, urban/rural). But there is no criterion on the attitude of citizens on the EU. What is meant by "attitude"? No automaticity between pro-EU attitude and self-selection; open to EU does not mean Europhile. For me, attitude is not a criterion to be retained.[13]

The debate here is interesting, even if not new:[14] it is better to say it is a never-ending controversy. Yves Sintomer would have liked to introduce an additional criterion to the ones usually used in sortition processes: the

---

[13] COFOE follow-up with experts organised by the Common Secretariat of the COFOE, 10th June 2022, Brussels.

[14] In an EU citizen conference's evaluation performed by Boussaguet and Dehousse, the latter questioned the criterion of "attitudes" for the selection of citizens, and the "ideological balances of the panel (political and religious beliefs, attitudes towards the issue of the conference, etc.)" (Boussaguet and Dehousse, 2008, p. 10).

attitude of citizens towards the EU. Therefore, there should be the same proportions of sceptical, indifferent and pro-European citizens as in the real population of Europeans. Hierlermann and Alemanno, on the other hand, were opposed to this. Alemanno went so far as to say that, beyond the difficulty of quantifying these attitudes, it was not desirable. He contradicted the link made by Sintomer between pro-EU stance and self-selection. I agree with Alemanno that such link is not automatic. But it is nevertheless a likely phenomenon, confirmed both by my observations and by surveys delivered to citizens. Nevertheless, I must admit that it is difficult to obtain a representative sample on the criterion of citizens' attitudes towards the EU. All the more so as many citizens have ambivalent reports, both positive and negative, on European integration (Dakowska and Hubé, 2011). While Sintomer spoke of positive discrimination for a better representation of minorities in any sample, for future European citizens' assemblies the EU institutions could evaluate the attitudes of citizens by asking them to position themselves on a scale of 1 to 10 on their support to the EU. In order to reach representative profiles, these questions could even be broken down into different areas of public action (monetary policy, environment, health, taxation, etc.).

Beyond this likely self-selection bias, concrete examples were observed and showed there were problems in the selection of the samples. Indeed, some French citizens were selected from a consumer platform. It means that although they were not necessarily used to talking politics, they were used to being solicited as consumers and therefore had a disposition to speak in public. Other examples relate more to sortitioned Italian citizens. Several participants confirmed they had been selected after one of their peers initially selected had declined the invitation. The selectors then asked the person who declined to recommend an individual with the same social and professional characteristics. These few examples illustrate the need to guard against self-selection effects when constituting a representative sample.

Thus, referring to the COFOE organisers' ambition to attract "European citizens from all walks of life and corners of the Union will be able to participate" (Conference of the Future of Europe, 2021, p. 1), there is a significant gap between the target audience and the real audience (Gourgues, 2013, p. 91).

5. Conclusions

So far, I have questioned and discussed that the causal link between the random selection supposed to guarantee inclusiveness (Smith, 2009) does not automatically lead to situations of pluralities of opinions and conflicts of representations in discussions between citizens. The COFOE organisers used the principle of sortition to obtain descriptive representation of the citizens invited to the discussion. The principle of random selection was supposed to guarantee the quality and legitimacy of a deliberative experience (Courant, 2021). However, it did not guarantee one of the criteria valued by democratic theories of deliberation: the diversity of political positions and the register of conflict and contradiction. Indeed, the COFOE sortitioned citizens were certainly socially diverse, but they all found themselves in a position of relative indecision and indifference towards the European Union (Van Ingelgom, 2014).

To explain this discrepancy between descriptive representation and low diversity of opinions, I highlight one of the unconsidered biases of sortition in politics: the self-selection bias, which explains why the more sceptical and critical attitudes towards European integration (European Commission, 2021), initially targeted by the institutional promoters of the scheme, are largely under-represented.

Archibald Gustin

Conclusion
From Against Elections
to Against Sortition?

Abstract: *This book sets out to be a continuation of, or even an opposition to, David Van Reybrouck's book* Against Elections. *Indeed, this book, together with Bernard Manin's* Principles of Representative Government *(even if Bernard Manin himself did not see his work as an ode to the lottery) embodies perfectly the way that the "sortition industry" promotes the inclusion of the sortition mechanism in democratic political systems. The literature on sortition sometimes lacks nuance and often fails to bring a balanced account of the democratic potential of the political use of lottery into the debate. This motivated several contributors to this book to start a collective reflection on sortition which would neither be in favour of nor against the implementation of lottery-drawn assemblies in Western democratic political systems.*

As a conclusion to this book, this contribution has a threefold goal and, therefore, a three-step structure. Firstly, the author sums up the arguments in favour of sortition as presented in the academic debates to this day in order to give the reader some insights on how the literature is currently structured (From "against elections"...). Secondly, this conclusion synthesises the views of the critics of the institutionalisation of sortition for political purposes formulated in the perspective of this collective reflection (...To against sortition). To this end, the author shows how the contributions presented in this book highlight the limits of sortition in respect to its capacity to achieve political equality, inclusion and representation. Furthermore, the author also reintroduces both the theoretical and institutional proposals made in this book. Finally, the conclusion proposes three ways of furthering research on sortition.

This book sets out to be a continuation of, or even an opposition to, David Van Reybrouck's book *Against Elections*. Indeed, this book, together with

Bernard Manin's *Principles of Representative Government*—and even if Manin himself did not see his work as an ode to the lottery (Hayat, 2019) —embodies perfectly the "sortition industry" (Talpin, 2019) promoting the inclusion of the sortition mechanism in democratic political systems. As Rummens and Geenens coined it in this book, we are currently witnessing the rise of a lottocratic paradigm, which suggests that drawn assemblies should not merely provide input for the political process but should indeed be empowered to make the political decision themselves.

According to us, the literature on sortition sometimes lacks nuance, and does not often present a balanced account of the democratic potential of the political use of lottery. This motivated us to start a collective reflection on sortition which would neither be in favour of nor against the implementation of drawn assemblies in Western democratic political systems. Rather, after several decades of theoretical, empirical and political work on sortition, we concluded that the literature on sortition was now mature enough to face a first wave of formal academic criticism, which would allow us better to grasp the advantages and the limits not only of the lottery process, but also of elections.

This conclusion has a threefold goal and, therefore, a three-step structure. Firstly, we sum up the arguments in favour of sortition as presented in the academic debates to this day. This is in order to give the reader some insights of how the literature is currently structured (*From "against elections"*...). Secondly, this conclusion makes the synthesis of the critics of the institutionalisation of sortition for political purposes formulated in the perspective of this collective reflection (...*To against sortition*). To this end, we show how the contributions presented in this book highlight the limits of sortition in terms of its capacity to achieve political equality, inclusion and representation. Furthermore, we also reintroduce both the theoretical and institutional proposals made in this book. Finally, the conclusion proposes three ways of furthering research on sortition.

1. From "Against Elections"...

The author who best formulated a theory of the aristocratic dimension of the election is undoubtedly the French political scientist B. Manin. In his seminal work *Principles of Representative Government*, he defines the representative regime based on the elective procedure as a democratic aristocracy. This definition of the election is to be understood through two considerations. On the one hand, according to Manin, the egalitarian and democratic character of the election is undeniable "provided that all citizens have the right to vote and that no legal condition limits eligibility" (Manin, 2012, p. 191).

On the other hand, however, election also has an aristocratic side in the sense that it necessarily leads to the selection of individuals who are perceived as superior, which the French political scientist describes as the "principle of distinction" (*ibid.*, pp. 125–73). Indeed, the election as a selection mechanism is based on a discrimination between the electorate and its elected representatives, the latter having at its disposal certain distinctive features deemed favourable and politically relevant. This means that the election results in the designation as rulers of members of a political elite that enjoys a level of educational and financial capital, or even a level of communication capital, higher than that of the average citizen.

For its part, a lottery appears to be the democratic method of selecting leaders *par excellence*, since this procedure offers all citizens an equal probability of access to political office (*ibid.*, p. 58). In the context of a lottery, the principle of distinction is inoperative, as the distinguishing characteristics of candidates for political office do not influence a random selection process. The lottery therefore better reflects egalitarian ideals, "since anyone can exercise political power and everyone has an equal chance to do so" (Guerrero, 2014, p. 169) — provided, of course, that no eligibility criteria apply within the population as the basis from which the random selection is employed.

However, the egalitarian virtues of the lottery are not the only ones argued by the proponents of random selection in the face of the monopoly of the elective procedure in contemporary political systems. Indeed, some authors have argued that the main virtue of the lottery should not be located in its egalitarian aspect but rather in its neutralising dimension (Dowlen, 2008; Stone, 2009; 2011). In this sense, the main quality of sortition would be that the lottery is a decision-making procedure whose results do not require any justification, thus neutralising illegitimate (but also legitimate) arguments that may motivate a decision and thus anaesthetising political conflicts.

Thus, Peter Stone refers to the "sanitizing effects" of the lottery as the immunity of this selection method to the influence of reasons, whether good or bad (Stone, 2009, pp. 375–97). Oliver Dowlen follows the same line when he describes the random procedure as an a-rational procedure in which the human faculty of reason does not intervene, along with other human faculties such as passion, instinct or emotion (Dowlen, 2008). Lottery would therefore be neither rational nor irrational and would in fact aim to create a "blind break" in the decision-making process, during which no human factor would intervene. From this perspective, the main purpose of sortition would be to prevent bad justifications from being used in the decision-making process in cases where the mobilisation of good reasons would be impossible because they have already been used or because the context of uncertainty characterising the decision-making process does not allow access to the information necessary to distinguish between those reasons that are considered legitimate (Stone, 2011, pp. 19–44).

Consequently, the main advantage of the use of sortition in politics would not be its achievement of greater political equality, but the possibility it offers of not having to justify the selection of rulers. As Manuel Cervera-Marzal and Yohan Dubigeon point out, it would neutralise two phenomena (Cervera-Marzal and Dubigeon, 2013, p. 174). On the one hand, the use of lottery would neutralise the selection process, since people are nominated independently of the reasons given for their selection. On the other hand, the use of lots would also neutralise the results of the selection process: no candidate can feel aggrieved by his or her non-selection, as lots are deemed to be impartial. As a result, the lottery has a limiting effect on competition between elites (Delannoi, Dowlen and Stone, 2013, pp. 15–16).

In contrast to the election, the lottery seems to offer more guarantees in terms of political equality and the neutralisation of political disputes. However, this is not all. The legitimacy of lottery also differs from that on which the elective procedure is based: "Elective hegemony gives the illusion that representation through authorisation is the only legitimate one, but lottery is based on representation through identification" (Courant, 2017, p. 19). Indeed, proponents of increased use of the lottery in politics have concentrated their efforts on demonstrating how this procedure would lead to the formation of assemblies with which citizens could more easily identify because they would better reflect the real diversity of the population than elected bodies.

Lottery would indeed allow the reproduction of a representative statistical sample of society, in which all opinions, all strata and all classes of society would be represented. "A sample of a thousand people chosen at random provides a microcosm of the population, with a margin of error of a few percent" (Sintomer, 2011a, p. 132). Compared to the considerable gap between the realities prevailing within elective systems and this ideal of similarity, random selection practices seem to offer a different perspective. Through its egalitarian and neutralising effects, the use of lottery brings about a revolution in the figures of power (Lefort, 2001), getting rid of those of the particratic elite and the media expert to begin the reign of the "anybody" (Cervera-Marzal and Dubigeon, 2013, p. 168). The elimination of the principle of distinction then allows power over all to be assumed by "everyone", i.e. interchangeable individuals using "common sense" (Sintomer, 2011a, p. 196).

The person selected by lot, unlike the elected representative, cannot claim any legitimacy based on an apparent superiority. The representative character of the link between the person selected by lot and the population he or she is supposed to represent is based on three distinct but not unrelated elements (Courant, 2017, pp. 21–23). Firstly, those drawn can claim to represent the population by virtue of their proximity and similarity to the population. Secondly, because of the absence of accountability to any electorate and because of this relationship of similarity, the selected persons enjoy horizontal legitimacy. In contrast, elective and nominative procedures are vertical, as they often include recognition of the person or persons responsible for the appointment. Thirdly, since the members of a randomly selected assembly owe their appointment only to the vagaries of lottery, they enjoy a legitimacy of humility and cannot claim any superiority over the non-selected (Goodwin, 2005, p. 99).

Ultimately, it is by virtue of this similarity between the profile of those drawn and that of the population represented that a drawn assembly would prove legitimate. Because the drawn assembly is deemed to be faithful to the statistical distribution of political characteristics in the population, it is supposed to reflect the way the population as a whole thinks. The legitimacy of the randomly selected assembly would therefore lie in the fact that, in the words of Robert A. Dahl, "the judgment of a minipopulus would 'represent' the judgment of the demos. Its verdict would be the verdict of the demos itself, if the demos were able to draw on the best available information to make a decision" (Dahl, 2008, p. 340).

However, taking advantage of the best available information to decide does not only imply the prior consultation of this information before voting, as it also requires the discussion of this information. As such, the idea of increased use of the lottery in politics is fully in line with the deliberative theory of democracy (Talpin, 2019, pp. 453–73), a theory that has dominated contemporary democratic theory for the past thirty years, as evidenced, among other things, by the proliferation of mini-publics, assemblies of citizens drawn by lot who "deliberate on a given political issue in order to formulate recommendations on that issue" (Vrydagh *et al.*, 2020, p. 5).

Deliberative democracy defines democratic government as "an association whose affairs are governed by the public deliberation of its members" (Cohen, 2005, p. 342), the notion of deliberation should be understood as "communication that induces reflection on preferences, values and interests in a non-coercive manner" (Dryzek, 2002, p. 76). The deliberative theory of democracy does not rely solely on the aggregation of given and pre-established preferences, as is done in opinion polls or voting procedures that are not followed by a discussion. In a deliberative democratic framework, it is rather a question of bringing these different opinions into dialogue, so that they are not formed in an exclusively monological manner and can evolve through their debate (Held, 2005, p. 233). Following this logic, the political decision taken to good effect is then "the result of general deliberation, not the expression of the general will" (Manin, 1985, p. 82).

Since deliberation is closely associated with the idea of democracy, proponents of deliberative theory have sought to define criteria for deter-mining the ideal deliberative procedure (Cohen, 2005, pp. 347–48).[1] One of these criteria is that of equality, as the deliberative process should be inclusive, with everyone having the opportunity to put an issue on the agenda, to participate in the formation of a collective will, and then to transform this will into a political decision (Warren, 2017). The ideal of equality is in fact closely linked to the criterion of inclusion in so far as a decision is democratic when those affected by it are able to influence it (Goodin, 2007). It is in this perspective of inclusion in democratic delibera-tions that the renewed attraction for the drawing of lots and its ability to form sociologically more diverse and representative assemblies of the population than the elective procedure should be interpreted.

The advantage of sortition is therefore that it strengthens the egali-tarian and inclusive dimension of democratic deliberation. However, this is not all. As the discussion of decisions is supposed to lead to better decisions than a procedure without communication, deliberation also has

---

1   For a fuller account of the deliberative principles and their development, see Bächtiger *et al.* (2018).

an important epistemic value (Estlund and Landemore, 2018). Indeed, political deliberation would induce a pooling of knowledge and information and would also bring out the process of reasoning about that knowledge and information. This would make it possible, for example, to reveal collusion between positions taken and particular interests, bringing to the fore phenomena of partiality (Held, 2005, pp. 237–38), thus allowing everyone to become more aware of the pros and cons of any decision. In this context, the benefit of greater inclusion in a deliberative assembly would be more cognitive diversity in the assembly, which would ultimately lead to better policy decisions (Landemore, 2013).

The increased diversity inherent in a selection by lot system is therefore beneficial, from a deliberative point of view, because of the capacity of this system to reinforce the inclusive character of a deliberation, but also because of its epistemic potential. In addition to this contribution of diversity, four other factors that are inherent in random selection would favour the quality of the deliberative process (Vandamme, 2018).

Firstly, unlike elected representatives, those drawn by lot have not had to make any campaign promises and are not necessarily linked to a political party. They therefore enjoy more independence of judgement than elected representatives and are therefore deemed to be more open to the arguments of others. Secondly, randomly selected individuals are said to be humbler than their elected counterparts, making them more eager for expert information and advice and for evidence from the field. Thirdly, however, this humility makes the randomly selected individuals more vulnerable to the influence of the experts responsible for providing them with information, so more attention must be paid to the selection of experts. This would make the expertise more objective, or at least more diverse. Fourthly, the drawing of lots would allow for a broader time perspective than election. To these four elements, we can also add that many proponents of the use of the lottery point out that the desire to be re-elected and party discipline restrict deliberation in elected assemblies whereas a body drawn by lot would probably approach public problems with greater openness and seek to discover creative solutions that transcend traditional cleavages (Gastil and Wright, 2018, p. 307).

Finally, in this section, we have highlighted the four main political qualities of sortition. First, by eliminating the principle of distinction inherent in the elective procedure, the drawing of lots is more egalitarian. Secondly, the drawing of lots also has neutralising virtues since, being an a-rational procedure, it anaesthetises possible ideological or human conflicts preceding a decision. Thirdly, through sampling techniques, drawing lots makes it possible to achieve a better (descriptive) representation of the population. Finally, the diversity inherent in assemblies drawn by lot also makes it possible to strengthen the quality of the deliberations of these assemblies. In the second section of this conclusion, we now summarise the book's criticism of the lottery.

2. ...To Against Sortition

According to supporters of sortition, lottery would be more egalitarian than elections, thanks to the fact that anyone could be designated to become a member of a drawn assembly. In this respect, Dominique Leydet wondered if this political equality, understood as an equal probability of participation, was not sometimes confused with equality of participation (Leydet, 2019). Indeed, as Clarisse Van Belleghem pointed out in this book, deliberative assemblies using sortition are often presented as a means of citizen empowerment, when only a very limited number of citizens take part in the discussion (chapter in this book). The egalitarian and inclusive properties of random selection, which give each citizen an equal chance to take part in the political debate, should not therefore be confused with equal participation.

The fact that, on one side, elections would be intrinsically aristocratic, while lottery would guarantee equal opportunities and secure descriptive representation is also something that Annabelle Lever and Chiara Destri tried to argue in their chapter in this book. For, according to them, "mathematically equal opportunities to be selected for office will not produce substantively equal opportunities to serve" (chapter in this book). In fact, randomly selected assemblies are often too small to ensure that all relevant ascriptive features of the population at large are duly reflected in any one assembly. Moreover, in so far as citizens can and do refuse to serve in office, pure randomisation ends up selecting assemblies skewed towards those social groups that are more likely to be politically interested and active.

This has important normative consequences. Often preferred to elections, an aristocratic procedure designating only a particular kind of elite, the equalitarian virtues of sortition now appear more limited. In fact, as Didier Mineur wondered, "why should a system which gives everyone an equal chance to partake to power, but no effective participation at all to those who aren't favoured by lot, be considered as being more egalitarian than the one which gives everyone a real say, albeit restrained, in the decision-making?" (chapter in this book).

As the first part of this conclusion however sustained, the equalitarian quality of sortition is not its only one. For example, Van Belleghem identifies three argumentative registers on deliberative drawn assemblies: epistemic properties, inclusion and representation (chapter in this book). The epistemic properties of deliberative assemblies are related to the quality of deliberation. Indeed, according to her, two main arguments are generally put forward in order to argue that the use of sortition as a mode of designating participants would improve the quality of deliberation: on the one hand, the lottery would have the advantage of designating citizens who are more politically disinterested and less corruptible than those designated by our traditional elective system (impartiality argument). On the other hand, random recruitment would lead to a greater epistemic diversity within deliberative assemblies (cognitive diversity argument).

Nevertheless, as Van Belleghem pointed out, those arguments only refer to the enhancement of the quality of the discussion, and they do not guarantee that drawn assemblies are inclusive and egalitarian: "to do so, it would be necessary to guarantee that all social perspectives can be considered and heard in the deliberation process. However, in the literature on deliberative assemblies, we can find an argument that seeks to value these experiments as being capable of expressing, on a small scale and in a regulated framework, the expectations of the citizens" (chapter in this book). According to her, therefore, there is a shift in the argumentation, which no longer focuses on the epistemic qualities of the sortition but valorises the panels as being intrinsically inclusive and representative.

It is, however, not always clear within the literature on randomly drawn citizens' assemblies what inclusion and representation mean and what are their real implications. Indeed, Van Belleghem concluded her analysis by underlying the polysemy of concepts such as inclusiveness and representativeness, which can be valued for different reasons. Finally, Van Belleghem also observed most proposals on deliberative assemblies tend to claim the possibility of representing the political interests of citizens through a descriptive representation based on socio-economic categories. However, the main problem with that view is that sortition only represents the persons represented in a symbolic and theoretical way, and that there is no way of affirming that the representative will act in the interest of the persons he or she represents. In conclusion, according to Van Belleghem, "sortition thus allows for some form of representation, but it is not strictly speaking a political representation" (chapter in this book).

Following this line, Stefan Rummens and Raf Geenens are also sceptical, in their contribution, of what is regarded as the descriptive representation of drawn assemblies (chapter in this book). Indeed, according to them, such representations offer only a partial under-standing of representation. More specifically they have argued that an electoral system is normatively superior to a sortition-based system, and this on three dimensions: the epistemic dimension, the power dimension, and the motivational dimension. According to Rummens and Geenens, this is due to the fact that the electoral mechanism provides visibility to the decision-making process in a way that allows for a form of interactive representation and hence for a collective process of opinion and will formation. Sortition, in contrast, is characterised by a poor form of descriptive representation in which the mini-public remains a black box that is mostly disconnected from the wider citizenry.

Didier Mineur was also critical of the way the representativeness of drawn assemblies is usually understood (chapter in this book). First is the fact that the descriptive nature of lottocratic representation is based on the statistical representation of some social categories (age, gender, ethnic group) while the individuals concerned have no control over which category is defined as relevant for the lottery process. In other words, in randomly selected assemblies, "while society considered as a whole is represented, because it is reproduced in miniature, individuals as such are not" (chapter in this book). Secondly, the assumption of democratic legitimacy in respect to the decisions made by a sample of persons drawn by lots is not grounded on any presupposition about how individuals might act but in terms of who they are. However, as Van Belleghem also points out (chapter in this book), individuals might not act in such terms. In conclusion, the lottery, despite the appearance of giving the power back to ordinary citizens, presupposes a kind of "epistocracy", since the experts of survey techniques are the only ones to know how any assembly of representatives chosen by lot is to be established.

The issue of democratic representation is not only a theoretical one. Jessy Bailly, for example, addressed in this book the case of the Con-ference on the Future of Europe (COFOE) (chapter in this book). Created after the Brexit vote in order to establish more links between the European elites and the European citizens, the COFOE is the first drawn assembly that brings together the European Parliament, the European Council and the European Commission. While the panel was claimed to be inclusive thanks to its sample representativeness — it was supposed to include Europhiles as well as Eurosceptics — highly critical opinions of the EU were in a minority since most participants were indifferent to European issues. Moreover, because participation was not compulsory, the selection of the COFOE members was biased. In conclusion, "the representativeness of the sample did not guarantee one of the criteria valued by democratic theories of deliberation: the diversity of political positions and the register of contradiction" (chapter in this book).

Another crucial element regarding sortition is that, contrary to elections, it does not provide any accountability mechanism (however, see Vandamme, 2018, pp. 881–83). Although, of course, the accountability system of the elective political system, which is essentially based on the ability to re-elect or not re-elect the rulers, is not always perfect (Courant, 2017, p. 13), Jérôme Hergueux argues in his chpater to this book that, in drawn assemblies, "trust and legitimacy must reside not with the elected representatives, but with the sampling procedure" (chapter in this book). This is also explained by the fact that the drawn assembly is supposed to accurately reflect the interests of the population represented. However, as we just highlighted, this is not always the case. Indeed, sortition requires that someone defines one of several *criteria* according to which this population is to be sampled. Moreover, sortition makes it possible to annihilate the mechanisms of social selection and reproduction only to the extent that "members are financially compensated, freed from their civil jobs and ensured that they may return to practising said job after the end of their term" (chapter in this book).

If drawn assemblies are often seen as a return to a more direct form of democracy, randomly selected panels can also be hijacked in the name of democracy to serve particular political purposes. In his chapter in this book, for instance, Vincent Aerts shows how the lottery can be seen as a process designed to include the population in "governance", a philosophical and political concept involving a neoliberal vision of politics aimed at defining the role of the state, not as a subject of national sovereignty, but as a mediator between stakeholders (chapter in this book). Taking the example of the Citizens' Climate Convention (CCC) established under the leadership of Emmanuel Macron, Aerts shows that while the latter had committed itself to following all of the CCC's proposals, few of these policies were actually implemented. Therefore, according to Aerts, sortition, which was imagined as an essentially democratic instrument, becomes part of neoliberal governance by allowing governments to adopt a form of "selective listening", choosing the proposals that seem most relevant to them while ultimately retaining the power to decide.

At this point, we have demonstrated how egalitarianism, inclusiveness and representativeness—three elements at the core of the argument in favour of the political use of sortition—relied sometimes on unclear argumentative structures. But following Hugo Bonin's example, we can go even further in the criticism of analyses that try to identify the qualities of the lottery process (Bonin, 2017; Lopez-Rabatel and Sintomer, 2019, pp. 20–27; Delannoi, 2010, p. 10; Sintomer, 2011a, p. 193). Indeed, analysing a number of works on the use of election and lot in politics, this author notes that most of these studies aim to attribute intrinsic qualities to these procedures by attempting to define their "nature": on the one hand, the essence of election would be both democratic and aristocratic, while, on the other hand, sortition would be egalitarian and neutralising by nature.

However, for Bonin, who contests the essentialist dimension of these arguments, the effects of these designation procedures can only be understood by considering the whole institutional system in which they are embedded. The random method can indeed lead to an unequal result, for example if it is not combined with very short terms of office or equal access to the deliberations. In other words, contradicting Montesquieu, the drawing of lots would not be "in the nature of democracy" (Montesquieu, 1973, p. 17), nor would elections be the essence of aristocracy. Consequently, Bonin prefers to speak of the potentialities of appointment procedures rather than of the essence or nature of the lottery and stresses the need to carry out an empirical study of the different leadership selection arrangements in order to highlight their advantages and disadvantages.

This is also what Oliver Dowlen meant when he stated in this book "that any assessment of the political value of random recruitment is context dependent, is purpose dependent, and, above all, is design dependent", and that we should avoid therefore simple binaries regarding the use of sortition (chapter in this book). In this context, in his chapter in this book based on a design-process approach, Dowlen proposed three design principles for the consideration of random political recruitment, whose aim is to propose a roadmap to try to determine whether the inclusion of the lottery in a particular political context is relevant or not.

First, if we are seeking to decide whether or not lottery should be used in any specific context, the judgement should be based on the qualities of sortition of the lottery as a decision-making process. In Dowlen's sense, those qualities are that it offers a blind break during the decision-making process. However, according to him, the lottery process is not a-rational in its entirety, since it consists of a number of rationally defined and designed elements that channel or control the actions of the blind break. Secondly, from a design perspective, we should consider the design features that might accompany lottery selection. Thirdly, one ought to seriously look at the way random recruitment can work with other constitutional measures, and to be careful with how the lottery scheme might relate to other procedures. In the end, Dowlen proposes to see the various institutional designs as ranges of "different *problem-solving* applications, or proposed applications operating in a range of different contexts" (chapter in this book), which should guide our contingent decisions to implement sortition in a particular political system.

In a different but similar perspective, Alex Kovner and Keith Sutherland propose a guide for a more adequate frame of the political merits of sortition (chapter in this book). According to them, most contemporary drawn assemblies embody the "noisy model" of deliberation, which is based on extensive interaction among the participants, at both small group and plenary levels; the use of facilitators to guide the discussion; and the production of open-ended output, as opposed to merely voting on options prepared prior to the assembly. Although the motivation for this model seems to be to "empower" the members of the assembly, Kovner and Sutherland believe that sortition should be measured based upon its outputs, not merely its inputs. As a consequence, according to them, the basic criterion used to decide whether we should implement sortition or not in a political system ought to be that we should chose the mechanism that is the most likely to enact the policy that is acceptable according to the informed view of the greatest number of people.

Instead of the "noisy model" Kovner and Sutherland argue that drawn assemblies should be in charge of voting proposals only, and not of initiating proposals (chapter in this book). Indeed, for Kovner and Sutherland, the problem of deliberative assemblies is not so much the method of selection as the voting. The two authors therefore propose a two-stage system. In the first stage, an elected assembly would be responsible for making proposals according to the superminority method.

The superminority method involves lowering the threshold of acceptance to get more than one output (in their proposals, three). This would help to solve the problem of the real diversity of the assemblies' debates such as the one raised by Bailly regarding the COFOE (chapter in this book). In the second stage, a randomly selected jury would then be in charge of voting on these proposals.

In conclusion, the contributions in this book helped to identify the limitations of the theoretical case for the lottery by working around three concepts, namely those of equality, inclusion and representation. These analyses, both theoretical and empirical, also contributed to the formulation of an institutional guide to provide a list of questions to be answered when considering the establishment of deliberative assemblies by lot. However, as with any analysis, the contributions in this book also have some shortcomings. The last section of this conclusion therefore attempts to suggest three ways in which the issue of drawing lots can be further explored in the future. Those inputs regard the relation between deliberative theory and sortition, accounts of power and political and institutional engineering.

3. Conclusion

As our reflections on inclusiveness, equality, epistemic diversity and representativeness witness it, central to the discussion on sortition is deliberative democracy.[2] This is not surprising, given that the centrality of deliberative theory in discussions about democracy is now well established.[3] As a consequence, the argument for lottery is almost always an argument for deliberative theory. In the future, therefore, an interesting question would be to go a bit further not only by asking what the advantages of random selections from a deliberative point of view might be, but also by addressing the question of what sortition might bring to other aspects of democracy. Sortition is indeed not only about representation and deliberation. Or, in other words, politics is not only

---

[2] Sortition is also at the heart of many participatory approaches and theories. On the distinction between participatory and deliberative democracy, see Bouvier (2007).

[3] John Dryzek argues that deliberative democracy is the most active area of political theory as a whole, not just democratic theory (Dryzek, 2007, p. 327), with Stephen Elstub and Peter McLaverty going so far as to speak of the zeitgeist of political theory (Elstub and McLaverty, 2014, p. 1).

Habermasian. For example, analysing the public policies actually favoured by the mini-publics, and underlining their impacts on the criteria of equality, central to the democratic tradition, would be a good starting point to initiate a new wave of research on sortition.

The second issue that would need to be highlighted is the relation between sortition and conflict. Very often, the way in which sortition is considered lacks any reflection about conflict and the effects of power on politics. As the contributions of Dowlen and others invite us to be careful with general evaluation of selection mechanisms (chapter in this book), it might be exaggerated to state that lottery is in essence a-political (chapter in this book). However, it is pretty clear that political theory on sortition is focused on some specific aspects of the democratic phenomenon while therefore neglecting others, such as inequalities, domination and power imbalance. A symbol of this absence is the weak mobilisation of these concepts in this book. As a consequence, we claim that further research on sortition should better investigate the relation between sortition and important notions such as conflict and power, which, according to me, have been overlooked so far.[4]

Finally, another thing that contemporary political theory about sortition is crucially lacking is a reflection on the balance of power within constitutional democracies. Since its invention, representative governments have always been thought of as a balance between the legislative, the judicial and the executive power (Manin, 2012). If deliberative theory mainly focuses on the legislative and is sometimes inspired by judicial bodies, no reflection has been made on the executive, and particularly, on what the relation between the executive power and drawn assemblies would look like. Moreover, as Pierre-Étienne Vandamme argued in his thought on a democracy without elections (chapter in this book), political parties play an important role in democracy. In Belgium, for example, it is the political parties, and not the parliament, that appoint ministers. One should therefore be more careful, in the future, both with the role of political parties in lottocratic design and with the consequences of intro-

---

[4]   In this sense, a good way to start such a reflection would be to engage more thoroughly with the works of political theorists such as Iris M. Young and Chantal Mouffe, who have both addressed important critics to the deliberative theory of democracy—critics who remain unanswered by deliberative theorists nowadays (see Young, 2000; Mouffe, 2005).

ducing sortition in a political system on the balance of power between the three branches of constitutional power.

Bibliography

Abbas, N. & Sintomer, Y. (2021) Les trois imaginaires contemporains du tirage au sort en politique: démocratie délibérative, démocratie antipolitique ou démocratie radicale?, *Raisons politiques*, **82** (2), pp. 33–54.

Abizadeh, A. (2021) Representation, bicameralism, political equality, and sortition: Reconstituting the second chamber as a randomly selected assembly, *Perspectives on Politics*, **19** (3), pp. 791–806.

Achen, C. & Bartels, L. (2016/2017) *Democracy for Realists*, Princeton, NJ: Princeton University Press.

Ackerman, B. & Fishkin, J. (2004) *Deliberation Day*, New Haven, CT: Yale University Press.

Adeleye, G. (1983) The purpose of the Dokimasia, *Greek, Roman and Byzantine Studies*, **24**, pp. 295–306.

Aldrin, P. & Hubé, N. (2011) Devenir les ambassadeurs de l'Europe. Une lecture politique de la première expérience de démocratie délibérative européenne, *Politique européenne*, **34**, pp. 95–134.

Aristotle (1986) The Athenian Constitution, in *Aristotle and Xenophon on Democracy and Oligarchy*, Berkeley, CA: University of California Press.

Aristotle, *Politics*, Book VI.

Arnold, T. (2014) Inside the Convention on the Constitution: A world first for constitutional change proposals, *The Irish Times*.

Aspinal, A. & Smith, E.A. (1959) *English Historical Documents 1783–1832*, London: Eyre and Spottiswood.

Bächtiger, A., Dryzek, J.S., Mansbridge, J. & Warren M.E. (2018) Deliberative democracy: An introduction, in Bächtiger, A., Dryzek, J.S., Mansbridge, J. & Warren, M.E. (eds.) *The Oxford Handbook of Deliberative Democracy*, pp. 1–32, Oxford: Oxford University Press.

Baïetto, T. (2020) 'Cela ne s'arrête pas lundi': des citoyens de la Convention pour le climat créent une association pour promouvoir leurs mesures, *France info*, 21 June.

Barbier, R., Bedu, C. & Buclet, N. (2009) Portée et limites du dispositif 'jury citoyen', *Politix*, **2**, pp. 189–207.

Barnett, A. & Carty, P. (2008) *The Athenian Option: Radical Reform for the House of Lords*, Exeter: Imprint Academic.

Barnett, Z. (2020) Why you should vote to change the outcome, *Philosophy and Public Affairs*, **48**, pp. 422–446.

Becker, M.B. (1967) *Florence in Transition. Vol. I*, Baltimore, MD: John Hopkins University Press.

Bedock, C., Bonin, L., Liochon, P. & Schnatterer, T. (2020) Une représentation sous contrôle: visions du système politique et réformes institutionnelles dans le mouvement des Gilets jaunes, *Participations*, **3** (28), pp. 221–246.

Beitz, C. (1989) *Political Equality*, Princeton, NJ: Princeton University Press.

Bell, D. (2015) *The China Model*, Princeton, NJ: Princeton University Press.

Bellantoni, A., Chwalisz, C. & Cesnulaityte, I. (2020) *Good Practice Principles for Deliberative Processes for Public Decision Making*, Paris: OECD.

Benhabib, S. (1992) *Situating the Self: Gender, Community and Postmodernism in Contemporary Ethics*, Cambridge: Polity Press.

Benkler, Y. (2002) Coase's Penguin, or, Linux and 'The Nature of the Firm', *Yale Law Journal*, **112** (3), pp. 369–446.

Blais, A. (2006) What affects voter turnout?, *Annual Review of Political Science*, **9** (1), pp. 111–125.

Blondiaux, L. (2008) *Le nouvel esprit de la démocratie. Actualité de la démocratie participative*, Paris: Seuil.

Blondiaux, L. & Manin, B. (2021) *Le tournant délibératif de la démocratie*, Paris: Presses de Sciences Po.

Bonin, H. (2017) Sur la 'nature' du tirage au sort en politique, *Politique et Sociétés*, **36** (1), pp. 3–23.

Bonott, M. (2017) *Partisanship and Political Liberalism in Diverse Societies*, Oxford: Oxford University Press.

Bouricius, T. (2013) Democracy through multi-body sortition: Athenian lessons for the modern day, *Journal of Deliberative Democracy*, **9** (1).

Bouricius, T. (2018) Why hybrid bicameralism is not right for sortition, in Gastil, J. & Wright E.O. (eds.) *Legislature by Lot: Transformative Designs for Deliberative Governance*, New York: Verso.

Bouricius, T. & Schecter, D. (2014) An idealized design for government. Part 2: Executive branch accountability, *Systems Thinking World Journal: Reflection in Action*, **3** (2).

Boussaguet, L. & Dehousse, R. (2007) L'Europe des profanes: l'expérience des conférences citoyennes, in Magnette, P. & Costa, O. (eds.) *Une Europe des élites? Réflexions sur la fracture démocratique de l'Union européenne*, pp. 242–258, Bruxelles: Editions de l'ULB.

Boussaguet, L. & Dehousse, R. (2008) Lay people's Europe: A critical assessment of the first EU Citizens' Conferences, *European Governance Papers*, EU´s 6th Framework Programme, Priority 7, C-08-02.

Bouvier, A. (2007) Démocratie délibérative, démocratie débattante, démocratie participative, *Revue européenne des sciences sociales*, **45** (1), pp. 5–34.

Brennan, J. (2011) The right to a competent electorate, *Philosophical Quarterly*, **61**, pp. 700–724.

Brennan, J. & Freiman, C. (2023) The bad news about the good news about voting: Why swing state voting is not effective altruism, *Journal of Political Philosophy*, **31**, pp. 60–79.

Brennan, J. & Hill, L. (2014) *Compulsory Voting: For and Against*, Cambridge: Cambridge University Press.

Brennan, J. & Landemore, H. (2022) *Debating Democracy: Do We Need More or Less?*, Oxford: Oxford University Press.

Bronner, L. (2023) L'addiction des politiques aux sondages confidentiels, *Le Monde*, 27 March.

Broome, J. (1990) Fairness, *Proceedings of the Aristotelian Society*, **91**, pp. 87–101.

Brown, M.B. (2006) Citizen panels and the concept of representation, *The Journal of Political Philosophy*, **14** (2), pp. 203–225.

Brown, W. (2015) *Undoing the Demos: Neoliberalism's Stealth Revolution*, New York: Zone Books.

Brucker, G.A. (1962) *Florentine Politics and Society: 1343–1378*, Princeton, NJ: Princeton University Press.

Bruter, M. (2005) *Citizens of Europe? The Emergence of a Mass European Identity*, Basingstoke: Palgrave Macmillan.

Buchstein, H. (2010) Reviving randomness for political rationality: Elements of a theory of aleatory democracy, *Constellations*, **17**, pp. 435–454.

Buchstein, H. (2015) Countering the 'democracy thesis' — sortition in ancient Greek political theory, *Redescriptions*, **18** (2), pp. 126–157.

Burland, A., Popelard, A. & Rzepskl, G. (dir.) (2021) *Le Nouveau monde. Tableau de la France néolibérale*, Paris : Éditions Amsterdam.

Burnheim, J. (1985) *Is Democracy Possible? The Alternative to Electoral Politics*, Cambridge: Polity Press.

Callenbach, E. & Phillips, M. (2008) *A Citizen Legislature*, Exeter: Imprint Academic.

Caluwaerts, D. & Reuchamps, M. (2012) The G1000: Facts, figures and some lessons from an experience of deliberative democracy in Belgium, *Re-Bel initiative conference*, **24**.

Caluwaerts, D. & Reuchamps, M. (2015) Strengthening democracy through bottom-up deliberation: An assessment of the internal legitimacy of the G1000 project, *Acta Politica*, **50** (2), pp. 151–170.

Caluwaerts, D. & Reuchamps, M. (2018) *The Legitimacy of Citizen-Led Deliberative Democracy: The G1000 in Belgium*, London: Routledge.

Canevaro, M. & Alberto, E. (2018) Extreme democracy and mixed constitution in theory and practice: *Nomophylakia* and fourth-century *nomothesia* in the Aristotelian *Athenaion Politeia*, in Bearzot, C., Canevaro, M., Gargiulo, T. & Poddighe, E. (eds.) *Athenaion Politeiai tra storia, politica e sociolgia, Aristotele, Pseudo-Senofonte*, pp. 104–145, Milan: LED.

Caplan, B. (2007) *The Myth of the Rational Voter*, Princeton, NJ: Princeton University Press.

CCC (2019) Official website of the Citizens' Climate Convention, [Online], https://www.conventioncitoyennepourleclimat.fr/.

CCC (2020) Official website of the Citizens' Climate Convention, final report, [Online], https://propositions.conventioncitoyennepourleclimat.fr/le-rapport-final/.

Cervera-Marzal, M. & Dubigeon, Y. (2013) Démocratie radicale et tirage au sort. Au-delà du libéralisme, *Raisons politiques*, **50**, pp. 157–176.

Chamayou, G. (2018) *La société ingouvernable. Une généalogie du libéralisme autoritaire*, Paris: La Fabrique éditions.

Chambers, S. (2009) Rhetoric and the public sphere: Has deliberative democracy abandoned mass democracy?, *Political Theory*, **37** (3), pp. 323–350.

Chambre des représentants (2019) *Proposition de modification du Règlement de la Chambre des représentants visant à permettre la création de commissions mixtes composées de parlementaires et de citoyens tirés au sort*, 0737/001, 12 November.

Chollet, A. & Manin, B. (2019) Les Postérités Inattendues de Principes Du Gouvernement Représentatif: Une Discussion Avec Bernard Manin, *Participations*, **23** (1), pp. 171–192.

Christiano, T. (1990) Freedom, consensus, and equality in collective decision-making, *Ethics*, **101**, pp. 151–181.

Christiano, T. (1996) *The Rule of the Many*, Nashville, TN: Westview Press.

Christiano, T. (2006) Democracy, in Zalta, E.N. (ed.), *Stanford Encyclopedia of Philosophy*, [Online], https://plato.stanford.edu/entries/democracy.

Chwalisz, C. (2021) Eight ways to institutionalise deliberative democracy, *OECD Public Governance Policy Paper*.

Chwalisz, C. (2022) A movement that's quietly reschaping democracy for the better, *Noéma*, 5 December.

Cobbett, W. (1811) *Parliamentary History of England. Vol. VIII 1722–1733*, London: Hansard.

Cohen, G. (2003) Facts and principles, *Philosophy & Public Affairs*, **31** (3), pp. 211–245.

Cohen, J. (2005) Deliberation and democratic legitimacy, in Maltravers, D. & Pike, J. (eds.) *Debates in Contemporary Political Philosophy: An Anthology*, pp. 352–370, London: Routledge.

Coleman, S. & Moss, G. (2012) Under construction: The field of online deliberation research, *Journal of Information, Technology & Politics*, **9** (1), pp. 1–15.

Conference of the Future of Europe (2021) *Rules of Procedure of the Conference on the Future of Europe*.

Conover, M., Ratkiewicz, J., Francisco, M., Gonçalves, B., Menczer, F. & Flammini, A. (2011) Political polarization on Twitter, *Proceedings of the International AAAI Conference on Web and Social Media*.

Courant, D. (2017) Thinking sortition, *IEPHI Working Papers*, **68**, 2017.

Courant, D. (2018) Penser le tirage au sort. Modes de sélection, cadres délibératifs et principes démocratiques, in Chollet, A. & Fontaine, A. (eds.) *Expériences du tirage au sort en Suisse et en Europe: un état des lieux*, pp. 257–282, Bern: Bibliothèque Am Guisanplatz.

Courant, D. (2019) Principles: A comparative analysis, in Gastil, J. & Wright, E.O. (eds.) *Legislature by Lot: Transformative Designs for Deliberative Govern-ance*, pp. 229–248, New York: Verso.

Courant, D. (2020) La Convention citoyenne pour le climat. Une représenta-tion délibérative, *Revue Projet*, **5** (378), pp. 60–64.

Courant, D. (2021) Les démocraties du tirage au sort. Légitimités et modèles institutionnels en conflit, *Raisons politiques*, **82**, pp. 13–31.

Cronin, T.E. (1989) *Direct Democracy: The Politics of Initiative, Referendum and Recall*, Cambridge, MA: Harvard University Press.

Crosby, N. & Nethercut, D. (2005) Citizen juries: Creating a trustworthy voice of the people, in Gastil, J. & Levine, P. (eds.) *The Deliberative Democracy Handbook*, pp. 111–119, San Francisco, CA: Jossey-Bass.

Cross, W.P. & Pilet, J.B. (eds.) (2015) *The Politics of Party Leadership: A Cross-National Perspective*, Oxford: Oxford University Press.

Crouch, C. (2004) *Post-democracy*, Cambridge: Polity Press.

Cuny-le callet, A. (2021) Vu de l'étranger. Référendum climat: Macron finit de dilapider son capital écolo, *Courrier International*, 7 July.

Curato, N., Dryzek, J.S., Ercan, S., Hendriks, C. & Niemeyer, S. (2017) Twelve key findings in deliberative democracy research, *Daedalus,* **146** (3), pp. 28–38.

Dahl, R. (1970) *After the Revolution? Authority in a Good Society*, New Haven, CT: Yale University Press.

Dahl, R. (1989) *Democracy and its Critics*, New Haven, CT: Yale University Press.

Dakowska, D. & Hubé, N. (2011) For or against the EU? Ambivalent attitudes and varied arguments towards europe, in Gaxie, D., Hubé, N. & Rowell, J. (eds.) *Perceptions of Europe: A Comparative Sociology of European Attitudes*, pp. 85–100: Colchester: ECPR Press.

D'Allens, G., Bœuf, N. & Dang, L. (2021) Convention pour le climat: seulement 10% des propositions ont été reprises par le gouvernement, *Reporterre*, 31 March (2 April).

Damay, L. & Delmotte, F. (2018) Les dialogues citoyens de la Commission européenne. Renforcer l'appartenance ou confirmer l'impuissance?, *Politique européenne*, **62**, pp. 120–150.

Daoulas, J.-B. (2020) Comment la Convention citoyenne sur le climat a échappé à Emmanuel Macron, *L'Express*, 23 October (14 December).

Davis, A. (1981) *Women, Race & Class*, New York: Vintage.

De Winter, L., Della Porta, D. & Deschouwer, K. (1996) Comparing similar countries: Italy and Belgium, *Res Publica*, **38** (2), pp. 215–235.

Delannoi, G. (2010) Reflections on two typologies for random selection, in Dowlen, O. & Delannoi, G. (eds.) *Sortition: Theory and Practice*, pp. 13–30, Exeter: Imprint Academic.

Delannoi, G. (2010) *Le retour du tirage au sort en politique*, Paris: Fondapol.

Delannoi, G. (2019) *Le tirage au sort. Comment l'utiliser?*, Paris: Presses de Sciences Po.

Delannoi, G., Dowlen, O. & Stone, P. (2013) *The Lottery as a Democratic Institution*, Dublin: Public Policy.

Destri, C. & Lever, A. (2023) Égalité démocratique et tirage au sort, *Raison publique*, **26**, pp. 63–79.

Devillers, S., Vrydagh, J., Caluwaerts, D. & Reuchamps, M. (2021) Looking in from the outside: How do invited but not selected citizens perceive the legitimacy of a minipublic?, *Journal of Deliberative Democracy*, **17** (1), pp. 149–159.

Díez Medrano, J. (2005) *Framing Europe*, Princeton, NJ: Princeton University Press.

Disch, L., van de Sande, M. & Urbinati, N. (eds.) (2019) *The Constructivist Turn in Political Representation*, Edinburgh: Edinburgh University Press.

Douglass, R. (2013) Rousseau's critique of representative sovereignty: Principled or pragmatic?, *American Journal of Political Science*, **57** (3), pp. 735–747.

Dowlen, O. (2008) *The Political Potential of Sortition: A Study of the Random Selection of Citizens for Public Office*, Exeter: Imprint Academic.

Dowlen, O. (2017) *Citizens' Parliamentary Groups, a proposal for democratic participation at constituency level*, Paris: NewDemocracy Foundation.

Dryzek, J.S. (2002) *Deliberative Democracy and Beyond: Liberals, Critics, Contestations*, Oxford: Oxford University Press.

Dryzek, J.S. (2007) Theory, evidence and the task of deliberation, in Rosenberg, S.W. (ed.) *Deliberation, Participation and Democracy: Can the People Govern?*, pp. 237–250, London: Palgrave Macmillan.

Dworkin, R. (2002) *Sovereign Virtue: The Theory and Practice of Equality*, Cambridge, MA: Harvard University Press.

Elster, J. (1986) The market and the forum: Three varieties of political theory, in Elster, J. & Hylland, A. (eds.) *The Foundations of Social Choice Theory*, pp. 103–132, Cambridge: Cambridge University Press.

Elster, J. (ed.) (1998) *Deliberative Democracy*, Cambridge: Cambridge University Press.

Elstub, S. & McLaverty, P. (2014) Introduction: Issues and cases in deliberative democracy, in Elstub, S. & McLaverty, P. (eds.) *Deliberative Democracy: Issues and Cases*, pp. 1–14, Edinburgh: Edinburgh University Press.

Élysée (2019) Conférence de presse à l'issue du Grand Débat national, 25 April.

Élysée (2020) Échanges avec les 150 membres de la Convention citoyenne pour le Climat, 10 January.

Engelen, B. (2009) Why liberals can favour compulsory attendance, *Politics*, **29**, pp. 218–222.

Engelen, B. (2013) Against the secret ballot: Toward a new proposal for open voting, *Acta Politica*, **48** (4), pp. 490–507.

Esterling, K., Fung, A. & Lee, T. (2015) How much disagreement is good for democratic deliberation?, *Political Communication*, **32** (4), pp. 529–555.

Estlund, D. (1997) Beyond fairness and deliberation: The epistemic dimension of democratic authority, in Bohman, J. & Rehg, W. (eds.) *Deliberative*

Democracy: Essays on Reason and Politics, pp. 173–204, Cambridge, MA: MIT Press.

Estlund, D. (2008) *Democratic Authority: A Philosophical Framework*, Princeton, NJ: Princeton University Press.

Estlund, D. & Landemore, H. (2018) The epistemic value of democratic deliberation", in Bächtiger, A., *et al.* (eds.) *The Oxford Handbook of Deliberative Democracy*, pp. 113–131, Oxford: Oxford University Press.

European Parliament, Council and European Commission (2021) *Joint declaration on the Conference of the Future of Europe. Engaging with citizens for democracy. Building a more resilient Europe*, March.

Extinction Rebellion (2021) Loi climat = mensonge de l'état, 31 March.

Feddersen, T., Gailmard, S. & Sandroni, A. (2009) A bias toward unselfishness in large elections: Theory and experimental evidence, *American Political Science Review*, **103**, pp. 175–192.

Finley, M. (1976) *Democracy Ancient and Modern*, London: Chatto & Windus.

Finlay, R. (1980) *Politics in Renaissance Venice*, London: Ernest Benn.

Fishkin, J. (1997) *The Voice of the People: Public Opinion and Democracy*, New Haven, CT: Yale University Press.

Fishkin, J. (2005) Experimenting with a democratic ideal: Deliberative polling and public opinion, *Acta Politica*, **40**, pp. 284–298.

Fishkin, J. (2009) *When the People Speak. Deliberative Democracy and Public Consultation*, Oxford: Oxford University Press.

Fishkin, J. (2018) *Democracy When the People Are Thinking*, Oxford: Oxford University Press.

Font, J., Pasadas Del Amo, S. & Smith, G. (2016) Tracing the impact of proposals from participatory processes: Methodological challenges and substantive lessons, *Journal of Public Deliberation*, **12** (1).

Fournier, P., van der Kolk, H. & Carty, R.K. (2011) *When Citizens Decide: Lessons from Citizen Assemblies on Electoral Reform*, Oxford: Oxford University Press.

France Info (2020a) Référendum, limitation à 110 km/h, écocide… Ce qu'il faut retenir du discours d'Emmanuel Macron devant la Convention citoyenne pour le climat, *France info*, 29 June.

France Info (2020b) Convention citoyenne pour le climat: comment le discours d'Emmanuel Macron sur les propositions a-t-il évolué?, *France Info*, 7 December.

France Info (2021) Convention citoyenne pour le climat: 'Une partie des citoyens sont dans une démarche politique', accuse Barbara Pompili, *France Info*, 2 March.

Fraser, N. & Honneth, A. (2003) *Redistribution or Recognition? A Political-Philosophical Exchange*, New York: Verso.

Funes, M., Talpin, J. & Rull, M. (2014) The cultural consequences of engagement in participatory processes, in Font, J., Della Porta, D. & Sintomer, Y. (eds.) *Participatory Democracy in Southern Europe: Causes, Characteristics and Consequences*, pp. 151–189, London: Rowman & Littlefield.

Gallo, N. (2022) Climat: 85% des mesures de la convention citoyenne reprises, selon Olivier Véran? Un chiffre surévalué, *AFP Factuel*, 16 September.

Garimella, V.R.K. & Weber, I. (2017) A long-term analysis of polarization on Twitter, *Proceedings of the International AAAI Conference on Web and Social Media*.

Garric, A., Gérard, M., Barroux, R., Mandard, S., Mouterde, P., Rey-Lefebvre, I., Valo, M., Lasjaunias, A. & Auffret, S. (2021) Que sont devenues les propositions de la convention pour le climat, qu'Emmanuel Macron s'était engagé à reprendre « sans filtre »?, *Le Monde*, 10 February.

Garsten, B. (2009), Representative government and popular sovereignty, in Shapiro, I., Stokes, S.C., Wood, E.J. & Kirshner, A.S. (eds.) *Political Representation*, pp. 90–110, Cambridge: Cambridge University Press.

Gastil, J. & Wright, E.O. (2018) Legislature by lot: Envisioning sortition within a bicameral system, *Politics & Society*, **46** (3), pp. 303–330.

Gastil, J. & Wright, E.O. (2019) *Legislature by Lot: Transformative Design for Collaborative Governance*, New York: Verso.

Geenens, R. (2007) The deliberative model of democracy: Two critical remarks, *Ratio Juris*, **20** (3), pp. 355–377.

Geenens, R. (2019) Political representation: The view from France, in Disch, L., van de Sande, M. & Urbinati, N. (eds.) *The Constructivist Turn in Political Representation*, pp. 89–103, Edinburgh: Edinburgh University Press.

Georgakakis, D. & Rowell, J. (eds.) (2014) *The Field of Eurocracy: Mapping EU Actors and Professionals*, Basingstoke: Palgrave Macmillan.

Geurtz, C. & Van de Wijdeven, T. (2010) Making citizen participation work: The challenging search for new forms of local democracy in the Netherlands, *Local Government Studies*, **36**, pp. 531–549.

Giles, J. (2005) Special report: Internet encyclopaedias go head to head, *Nature*, **438** (15), pp. 900–901.

Girard, C. (2021) La démocratie délibérative à grande échelle: des arènes locales à la délibération de tous, in Blondiaux, L. (ed.) *Le tournant délibératif de la démocratie*, pp. 67–96, Paris: Presses de Sciences Po.

Giraudet, L.-G., *et al.* (2022) 'Co-construction' in deliberative democracy: Lessons from the French Citizens' Convention for Climate, *Nature: Humanities and Social Sciences Commmunications*, **9**, 207, 22 June.

Goodin, R.E. (2003) Democratic deliberation within, in Fishkin, J. & Laslett, P. (eds.) *Debating Deliberative Democracy*, pp. 54–79, Oxford, Blackwell.

Goodin, R.E. (2007) Enfranchising all affected interests, and its alternatives, *Philosophy and Public Affairs*, **35** (1), pp. 40–68.

Goodin, R.E. (2008) *Innovating Democracy: Democratic Theory and Practice After the Deliberative Turn*, Oxford: Oxford University Press.

Goodin, R.E. & Niemeyer, S.J. (2003) When does deliberation begin? Internal reflection versus public discussion in deliberative democracy, *Political Studies*, **51** (4), pp. 627–649.

Goodwin, B. (2005) *Justice by Lottery*, Exeter: Imprint Academic.

Gourgues, G. (2013) *Les politiques de démocratie participative*, Grenoble: Presses universitaires de Grenoble.

Green, T.A. (1985) *Verdict According to Conscience*, Chicago, IL: University of Chicago Press.

Greenstein, S. & Zhu, F. (2018) Do experts or crowd-based models produce more bias? Evidence from Encyclopædia Britannica and Wikipedia, *MIS Quarterly*, **42** (3), pp. 945–959.

Greenstein, S., Gu, G. & Zhu, F. (2021) Ideology and composition among an online crowd: Evidence from Wikipedians, *Management Science*, **67** (5), pp. 3067–3086.

Gretton, R.H. (1910) Lot Meadow customs at Yarnton, Oxon, *Economic Journal*, **20** (77), pp. 38–45.

Griffiths, A. & Wollheim, R. (1960) Symposium: How can one person represent another?, *Proceedings of the Aristotelian Society*, Supplementary Volumes, **34**, pp. 187–224.

Grunberg, G. (2019) Les 'Gilets jaunes' et la crise de la démocratie représentative, *Le Débat*, **2** (204), pp. 95–103.

Guéniffey, P. (1993) *Le Nombre et la Raison. La Révolution française et les élections*, Paris: Editions de l'EHESS.

Guénon, R. (1953) *The Reign of Quantity and the Signs of the Times*, London: Luzac & Co.

Guérineau de Lamérie, N. (2020) Convention Citoyenne pour le Climat. Tirage au sort: mission accomplie?, *Socialter*, **42**, 5 August.

Guerrero, A. (2014) Against elections: The lottocratic alternative, *Philosophy and Public Affairs*, **42** (2), pp. 135–178.

Guerrero, A. (2021a) The epistemic case for non-electoral forms of democracy, in Hannon, M. & de Ridder, J. (eds.) *The Routledge Handbook of Political Epistemology*, pp. 419–429, New York: Routledge.

Guerrero, A. (2021b) The epistemic pathologies of elections and the epistemic promise of lottocracy, in Guerrero, A. (ed.) *Political Epistemology*, pp. 156–179, Oxford: Oxford University Press.

Guerrero, A. (2024) *Lottocracy*, Oxford: Oxford University Press.

Habermas, J. (1981) *Theorie des Kommunikativen Handelns*, Frankfurt: Suhrkamp.

Habermas, J. (1992) *The Structural Transformation of the Public Sphere: An Inquiry into a Category of Bourgeois Society*, Cambridge: Polity Press.

Habermas, J. (1996) *Between Facts and Norms: Contributions to a Discourse Theory of Law and Democracy*, Cambridge, MA: MIT Press.

Habermas, J. (2003) Rightness versus truth: On the sense of normative validity in moral judgments and norms, in *Truth and Justification*, pp. 237–275, Cambridge: Polity Press.

Hamilton, A., Madison, J. & Jay, J. (2008) *The Federalist*, Oxford: Oxford University Press.

Hansen, M.H. (1991) *The Athenian Democracy in the Age of Demosthenes*, Oxford: Blackwell.

Hansen, M.H. (1999) *Athenian Democracy in the Age of Demosthenes*, Bristol: Classical.

Hansen, M.H. (2014) Political parties in democratic Athens?, *Greek, Roman, and Byzantine Studies*, **54** (3), pp. 379–403.

Harivel, M. (2019) Le Tirage Au Sort Dans La République de Venise, *Mélanges de La Casa de Velázquez*, **49** (2), pp. 323–329.

Harrington, J. (1992) *The Constitution of Oceana*, Cambridge: Cambridge University Press.

Hayat, S. (2019) La carrière militante de la référence à Bernard Manin dans les mouvements français pour le tirage au sort, *Participations*, **HS**, pp. 437–451.

Headlam, J.W. (1933/1891) *Election by Lot at Athens*, Cambridge: Cambridge University Press.

Held, D. (2005) *Models of Democracy*, Cambridge: Polity Press.

Hennig, B. (2017) *The End of Politicians: Time for Real Democracy*, Unbound Digital.

Hergueux, J. (2023) Coopération en Ligne: 40 ans de Télétravail Volontaire, in Senik, C. (ed.) *Travail à Distance*, Paris: La Découverte.

Herodotus (1998) *The Histories*, Trans. Waterfield, Oxford: Oxford World's Classics.

Hong, L. & Scott, E.P. (2004) Groups of diverse problem solvers can outperform groups of high-ability problem solvers, *Proceedings of the National Academy of Sciences of the United States*, **101** (46), pp. 16385–16389.

Hong, L. & Scott, E.P. (2012) Some microfoundations of collective wisdom, in Landemore, H. & Elster, J. (eds.) *Collective Wisdom: Principles and Mechanisms*, pp. 56–71, Cambridge: Cambridge University Press.

Huesmann, C., Renkamp, A. & Petzol, W. (2022) *Europe Up Close: Local, Regional and Transnational Citizens' Dialogues on the Future of the European Union*, Gütersloh: Bertelsmann Stiftung.

Ignazi, P. (2017) *Party and Democracy: The Uneven Road to Party Legitimacy*, Oxford: Oxford University Press.

Ignazi, P. (2020) The four knights of intra-party democracy: A rescue for party delegitimation, *Party Politics*, **26** (1), pp. 9–20.

Isernia, P., Fischkin, J., Steiner, J. & Di Mauro, D. (2014) Vers une sphère publique européenne: le projet EuroPolis, in Kies, R. & Nanz, P. (eds.) *Les nouvelles voix de l'Europe: analyse des consultations citoyennes*, pp. 116–150, Windhof: Larcier Luxembourg.

Jacobs, L. (2003) *Pursuing Equal Opportunities: The Theory and Practice of Egalitarian Justice*, New York: Cambridge University Press.

Jacquet, V. (2017) Explaining non-participation in deliberative mini-publics, *European Journal of Political Research*, **56** (3), pp. 640–659.

Jacquet, V. (2020) *Comprendre la non-participation: Les citoyens face aux dispositifs délibératifs tirés au sort*, Brussels: Peter Lang.

Kent, D. (1978) *The Rise of the Medici Faction in Florence 1426–34*, Oxford: Oxford University Press.

Kostelka, F. & Blais, A. (2021) The generational and institutional sources of the global decline in voter turnout, *World Politics*, **73** (4), pp. 629–667.

Kovner, A. (2020) *Superminority*.

Kovner, A. & Sutherland, K. (2022) Turn down the noise on citizen assemblies, Paper delivered at *Contre le Tirage au Sort conference*, Université de Liège, 4 November.

Lafont, C. (2015) Deliberation, participation, and democratic legitimacy: Should deliberative mini-publics shape public policy?, *Journal of Political Philosophy*, **23** (1), pp. 40–63.

Lafont, C. (2019/2020) *Democracy Without Shortcuts: A Participatory Conception of Deliberative Democracy*, Oxford: Oxford University Press.

Lafont, C. (2023) Deliberative minipublics and the populist conception of representation as embodiment, in Landwehr, C., Saalfeld, T. & Schäfer, A.

(eds.) *Contested Representation: Challenges, Shortcomings, and Reforms*, pp. 32–45, Cambridge: Cambridge University Press.

Lafont, C. & Urbinati, N. (forthcoming) *The Lottocratic Mentality: Defending Democracy against Lottocracy*, Oxford: Oxford University Press.

Landemore, H. (2012) Why the many are smarter than the few and why it matters, *Journal of Public Deliberation*, **8** (1), pp. 1–12.

Landemore, H. (2013) Deliberation, cognitive diversity, and democratic inclusiveness: An epistemic argument for the random selection of representatives, *Synthese*, **190** (7), pp. 1209–1231.

Landemore, H. (2013) *Democratic Reason: Politics, Collective Intelligence, and the Rule of the Many*, Princeton, NJ: Princeton University Press.

Landemore, H. (2014) Yes, we can (make it up on volume): Answers to critics, *Critical Review: A Journal of Politics and Society*, **26**, pp. 184–237.

Landemore, H. (2020) *Open Democracy: Reinventing Popular Rule for the Twenty-First Century*, Princeton, NJ: Princeton University Press.

Lane, F.C. (1973) *Venice, a Maritime Republic,* Baltimore, MD: Johns Hopkins University Press.

Laws, J. (2014) *The Common Law Constitution*, Cambridge: Cambridge University Press.

Le Monde with AFP (2021) La convention citoyenne pour le climat juge sévèrement la prise en compte de ses propositions par le gouvernement, *Le Monde*, 28 February.

Lee, C. & Romano, Z. (2013) Democracy's new discipline: Public deliberation as organizational strategy, *Organization Studies*, **34** (5–6), pp. 733–753.

Lefort, C. (1988) *Democracy and Political Theory*, Cambridge: Polity Press.

Lefort, C. (2001) *Essais sur le politique, XIXᵉ–XXᵉ siècles*, Paris: Seuil.

Lemaire, J.-B. (2022) Whatever happened to the EU's 'citizens' panels'?, *EUObserver*, 8 October.

Lessig, L. (2009) *Code: And Other Laws of Cyberspace*, New York: Basic Books.

Lever, A. (2007) Mill and the secret ballot: Beyond coercion and corruption, *Utilitas*, pp. 354–378.

Lever, A. (2010) Compulsory voting: A critical perspective, *British Journal of Political Science*, **40** (4), pp. 897–915.

Lever, A. (2022) Citizen assemblies and the challenges of democratic equality, *The Conversation*, 5 December.

Lever, A. (2023) Random selection, democracy and citizen expertise, *Res Publica*, March.

Lever, A. & Volacu, A. (2018) Should voting be compulsory? Democracy and the ethics of voting, in Lever, A. & Poama, A. (eds.) *The Routledge Handbook of Ethics and Public Policy*, pp. 242–254, London: Routledge.

Levinson, S. (2014) A welcome defense of democracy, *Critical Review: A Journal of Politics and Society*, **26**, pp. 92–100.

Levitsky, S. & Ziblatt, D. (2018) *How Democracies Die*, London: Penguin Books.

Leydet, D. (2015) Partisan legislatures and democratic deliberation, *Journal of Political Philosophy*, **23** (3), pp. 235–260.

Leydet, D. (2019) Which conception of political equality do deliberative mini-publics promote?, *European Journal of Political Theory*, **18** (3), pp. 349–370.

Lezaun, J. & Soneryd, L. (2007) Consulting citizens: Technologies of elicitation and the mobility of publics, *Public Understanding of Science*, **16** (3), pp. 279–297.

Lieb, E. (2004) *Deliberative Democracy in America: A Proposal for a Popular Branch of Government*, University Park, PA: Pennsylvania State University Press.

Loevinger, L. (1961) The corporation as a power nexus, *The Antitrust Bulletin*, **6**.

López-Guerra, C. (2014) *Democracy and Disenfranchisement*, Oxford: Oxford University Press.

López-Rabatel, L. & Sintomer, Y. (2019) L'histoire du tirage au sort en politique: instruments, pratiques, theories, *Participations*, **HS**, pp. 20–27.

Lucardie, P. & Vandamme, P.É. (2022) Are political parties really indispensable? An overview of the alternatives, *ConstDelib Working Paper Series*, **18**, pp. 1–26.

Lui Président (coll.) (2022) Emmanuel Macron a-t-il tenu ses 400 promesses de campagne?, *Les Décodeurs*, Le Monde, 12 March.

Machiavelli, N. (1989) *Machiavelli – The Chief Works and Others*, Durham, NC: Duke University Press.

Macron, E. (2019) Déclaration de M. Emmanuel Macron, Président de la République, sur les défis et priorités de la politique gouvernementale à l'issue du Grand débat national, à Paris le 25 avril 2019, *vie publique.fr*, 25 April.

Magni-Berton, R. & Egger, C. (2019) *Le référendum d'initiative citoyenne expliqué à tous: Au coeur de la démocratie directe*, Limoges: FYP éditions.

Maia, R., Hauber, G., Choucair, T. & Crepalde, N. (2021) What kind of disagreement favors reason-giving? Analyzing online political discussions across the broader public sphere, *Political Studies*, **69** (1), pp. 108–128.

Mair, P. (2013) *Ruling the Void: The Hollowing of Western Democracy*, London: Verso.

Malkopoulou, A. (2015) The paradox of democratic selection: Is sortition better than voting?, in Palonen, K. & Rosales, J.-M. (eds.) *Parliamentarism and Democratic Theory: Historical and Contemporary Perspectives*, Leverkusen: Barbara Budrich Publishers.

Malleson, T. (2018) Should democracy work through elections or sortition?, *Politics & Society*, **46** (3), pp. 401–417.

Manin, B. (1985) Volonté générale ou délibération ? Esquisse d'une théorie de la délibération politique, *Le Débat,* **33**, pp. 72–94.

Manin, B. (1987) On legitimacy and political deliberation, *Political Theory*, **15** (3), pp. 338–368.

Manin, B. (1997) *The Principles of Representative Government*, Cambridge: Cambridge University Press.

Manin, B. (2005) Deliberation: Why we should focus on debate rather than discussion, Paper presented at the *Program in Ethics and Public Affairs seminar.*

Manin, B. (2012) *Principes du gouvernement représentatif*, Paris: Flammarion.

Manin, B. (2017) Political deliberation & the adversarial principle, *Daedalus*, **146** (3), pp. 39–50.

Manin, B. & Blondiaux, L. (2021) *Le tournant délibératif de la démocratie*, Paris: Les Presses de Sciences Po.

Mansbridge, J. (2003) Rethinking representation, *American Political Science Review*, **97** (4), pp. 515–528.

Mansbridge, J. (2019) Accountability in the constituent-representative relationship, in Gastil, J. & Wright, E.O. (eds.) *Legislature by Lot: Transformative Designs for Deliberative Governance*, pp. 189–203, New York: Verso.

Mansbridge, J. (2020) A citizen-centered theory, *Journal of Deliberative Democracy*, **16** (2), pp. 15–24.

Mansbridge, J., *et al.* (2010) La place de l'intérêt particulier et le rôle du pouvoir dans la démocratie délibérative, *Raisons politiques*, **42**, pp. 47–82.

Meehan, E. (2003) From government to governance, civic participation and 'new politics': The context of potential opportunities for the better representation of women, *Center for Advancement of Women in Politics*, School of Politics and International Studies, Belfast, Queen's University, occasional Paper, 5 October.

Mellina, M. & Dupuis, A. (2019) Tirage au sort et démocratie: l'évolution des usages du sort dans les républiques suisses (XVIIᵉ–XIXᵉ siècle), *Mélanges de la Casa de Velàzquez*, **49** (2), pp. 339–344.

Mellina, M., Dupuis, A. & Chollet, A. (2021) *Tirage au sort et politique: Une histoire suisse*, Lausanne: Presses universitaires polytechniques.

Mercier, H. & Sperber, D. (2017) *The Enigma of Reason: A New Theory of Human Understanding,* London: Allen Lane.

Michels, A. & De Graaf, L. (2017) Examining citizen participation: Local participatory policymaking and democracy revisited, *Local Government Studies,* **43**, pp. 875–881.

Michels, R. (2017/1911) *Political Parties: A Sociological Study of the Oligarchical Tendencies of Modern Democracy,* London: Routledge.

Mills, C. (2017) *Black Rights/White Wrongs,* Oxford: Oxford University Press.

Mineur, D. (2010) *Archéologie de la représentation politique. Structure et fondement d'une crise,* Paris : Presses de Sciences Po.

Mineur, D. (2015) La délibération préalable à la décision majoritaire: justification substantielle ou procédurale?, *Raisons politiques,* **60** (4), pp. 127–145.

Montanaro, L. (2012) The democratic legitimacy of self-appointed representatives, *The Journal of Politics,* **74** (4), pp. 1094–1107.

Montesquieu (1748/1973/1976/1979) *De l'esprit Des Lois,* Paris: Garnier.

Mouffe, C. (2000) *The Democratic Paradox,* London: Verso.

Mouffe, C. (2005) *The Return of the Political,* London: Verso Books.

Mouffe, C. (2016) *L'illusion du consensus,* Paris: Albin Michel.

Mráz, A. (2021) How to justify mandatory electoral quotas: A political egalitarian approach, *Legal Theory,* **27** (4), pp. 285–315.

Muirhead, R. (2014) The politics of getting it right, *Critical Review: A Journal of Politics and Society,* **26**, pp. 115–128.

Mulligan, T. (2018) Plural voting for the twenty-first century, *Philosophical Quarterly,* **68**, pp. 286–306.

Musil, R. (2011) *The Man Without Qualities,* London: Picador.

Najemy, J.M. (1982) *Corporatism and Consensus in Florentine Electoral Politics, 1280–1400,* Chapel Hill, NC: University of North Carolina Press.

Niessen, C. & Reuchamps, M. (2019) Le dialogue citoyen permanent en Communauté germanophone, *Courrier hebdomadaire du CRISP,* **21**, pp. 5–38.

O'Flynn, I. & Sood, G. (2014) What would Dahl say? An appraisal of the democratic credentials of deliberative polls and other mini-publics, in Grönlund, K., Bächtiger, A. & Setälä, M. (eds.) *Deliberative Mini-Publics: Involving Citizens in the Democratic Process,* pp. 41–58, Colchester, ECPR Press.

Ober, J. (1998) The Athenian Revolution of 508/7 BC, in Dougherty, C. & Kuuke, L. (eds.) *Cultural Poetics of Archaic Greece,* Oxford: Oxford University Press.

OECD (2020) *Innovative Citizen Participation and the New Democratic Institutions: Catching the Deliberative Wave*, Paris: OECD Publishing.

Offe, C. (1987) Democracy against the welfare state? Structural foundations of neoconservative political opportunities, *Political Theory*, **15** (4), pp. 501–537.

OIDP (2019) *The Ostbelgian Model: A Long-term Citizens' Council Combined with Short-Term Citizens' Assemblies.*

Okin, S. (1989) *Justice, Gender and the Family*, New York: Basic Books.

O'Leary, K. (2006) *Saving Democracy: A Plan for Real Representation in America*, Stanford, CA: Stanford University Press.

Ostrogorski, M.I. (1964) *Democracy and the Organization of Political Parties*, New York: Anchor Books.

Ostrom, E. (1990) *Governing the Commons: The Evolution of Institutions for Collective Action*, Cambridge: Cambridge University Press.

Owen, D. & Graham, S. (2018) Sortition, rotation, and mandate: Conditions for political equality and deliberative reasoning, *Politics & Society*, **46** (3), pp. 419–434.

Page, S.E. (2007) *The Difference: How the Power of Diversity Creates Better Groups, Firms, Schools, and Societies*, Princeton, NJ: Princeton University Press.

Paillou, S. & Revault d'Allonnes, D. (2021) Environnement: Macron enterre le référendum promis à la Convention citoyenne, *Le Journal du Dimanche*, 9 May.

Paine, T. (1945) *Complete Works*, New York: Citadel Press.

Papadopoulos, Y. (2013) *Democracy in Crisis? Politics, Governance and Policy*, London: Palgrave Macmillan.

Papadopoulos, Y. & Warin, P. (2007) Are innovative, participatory and deliberative procedures in policy making democratic and effective?, *European Journal of Political Research*, **46** (4), pp. 445–472.

Parkinson, J. (2006) *Deliberating in the Real World: Problems of Legitimacy in Deliberative Democracy*, Oxford: Oxford University Press.

Parlement de la Région de Bruxelles-Capitale (2018) *Proposition d'ordonnance spéciale visant à introduire la faculté de créer des commissions mixtes composées de citoyens tirés au sort et de députés bruxellois*, 660/1, 22 March.

Parlement de la Région de Bruxelles-Capitale and Assemblée réunie de la Commission communautaire commune (2019) *Proposition de modification du règlement visant à introduire la faculté de créer des commissions délibératives entre députés et citoyens composées de députés et invitant des citoyens tirés au sort à participer à leurs travaux*, n° 100/2 et 19/2, 4 December.

Parlement wallon (2017a) *Panel citoyen consacré aux enjeux du vieillissement. Déclaration consensus*, 12 May.

Parlement wallon (2017b) *Panel citoyen consacré aux enjeux du vieillissement. Compte rendu des travaux*, 12 May.

Parlement wallon (2020) Commission des affaires générales et des relations internationales, *Compte rendu intégral*, **5**, 14 September.

Parlement wallon (2021) *Proposition de décret institutionnalisant l'assemblée citoyenne et le conseil citoyen. Avis du Conseil d'État*, 221/2, 6 January.

Pedrini, S. & Bächtiger, A. (2010) Deliberative inclusion of minorities: Equality and reciprocity among linguistic groups in Switzerland, Paper to the *2010 Annual Meeting of the American Political Science Association*, Washington DC.

Penn, W. (1982) *The Papers of William Penn*, Philadelphia, PA: University of Pennsylvania Press.

Pettit, P. (2004) Depoliticizing democracy, *Ratio Juris*, 17 March, pp. 52–65.

Pettit, P. (2010) Representation, responsive and indicative, *Constellations*, **17** (3), pp. 426–434.

Phainikar, S. (2021) France's Citizen Climate Assembly: A failed experiment?, *Deutsche Welle*.

Phillips, A. (1995) *The Politics of Presence*, Oxford: Oxford University Press.

Phillips, A. (2004) Defending equality of outcome, *Journal of Political Philosophy*, **12** (1), pp. 1–19.

Pitkin, H.F. (1967) *The Concept of Representation*, Berkeley, CA: University of California Press.

Pitseys, J. (2017) Transparence et mutisme de la représentation politique: l'idéal de similarité, *Revue Philosophique de Louvain*, **115** (3), pp. 503–530.

Pope, M. (2023) *The Keys to Democracy: Sortition as a New Model for Citizen Power*, Exeter: Imprint Academic.

Pourtois, H. (2013) Mini-publics et démocratie deliberative, *Politique et Sociétés*, **32** (1), pp. 21–41.

Pourtois, H. (2016) Les élections sont-elles essentielles à la démocratie?, *Philosophiques*, **43** (2), pp. 411–439.

Prévost, A.F. (1728–1731) *Memoirs and Adventures of a Man of Quality* (from which *Manon Lescaut* is taken).

Przeworski, A. (2018) *Why Bother with Elections?*, Cambridge: Polity Press.

Queller, D.E. (1986) *The Venetian Patriciate*, Chicago, IL: University of Illinois Press.

Quicherat, L. & Daveluy, A. (1871) *Dictionnaire Latin-Français*, Paris: Hachette.

Ramond, C. (2019) *Rancière. L'égalité des intelligences*, Paris: Belin.

Ramond, C. (2023) *Introduction à Spinoza*, Paris: La Découverte.

Rancière, J. (1990) *Aux Bords du politique*, Paris: Osiris.

Rancière, J. (1992) *Les Mots de l'histoire. Essai de poétique du savoir*, Paris: Seuil.

Rancière, J. (1999) *Dis-agreement: Politics and philosophy*, Minneapolis, MN: University of Minnesota Press.

Rancière, J. (2005) *La haine de la démocratie*, Paris: La fabrique éditions.

Rancière, J. (2009a) *Et tant pis pour les gens fatigués*, Paris: Entretiens.

Rancière, J. (2009b) *Hatred of Democracy*, London: Verso.

Rancière, J. (2009c) *Moments politiques. Interventions 1977–2009*, Paris: La Fabrique.

Rawls, J. (1971) *A Theory of Justice*, Cambridge, MA: Harvard University Press.

Renkamp, A. & Vergne, A. (2020) *Citizens' Participation Using Sortition: A Practical Guide to Using Random Selection to Guarantee Diverse Democratic Participation*, Gütersloh: Berteslmann Stiftung.

Reuchamps, M. & Suiter, J. (2016) *Constitutional Deliberative Democracy in Europe*, Colchester: ECPR Press.

Reuchamps, M., Vrydagh, J. & Welp, Y. (eds.) (forthcoming) *The Handbook of Citizen's Assemblies*, Berlin: De Gruyter.

Rhenman, E. (1968) *Industrial Democracy and Industrial Management: A Critical Essay on the Possible Meanings and Implications of Industrial Democracy*, London: Tavistock.

Rhinehart, L. (1971) *The Dice Man*, New York: William Morrow.

Rhodes, R.A.W. (1997) *Understanding Governance: Policy Networks, Governance, Reflexivity and Accountability*, Buckingham: Buckingham University Press.

Ricoeur, P. (1997) *L'idéologie et l'utopie*, Paris: Seuil.

Rosanvallon, P. (2008) *La légitimité démocratique: Impartialité, réflexivité, proximité*, Paris: Seuil.

Rosanvallon, P. (2015) *Le bon gouvernement*, Paris: Seuil.

Rosanvallon, P. (2020) *The Populist Century*, Cambridge: Polity Press.

Rosenblum, N. (2008) *On the Side of Angels: An Appreciation of Parties and Partisanship*, Princeton, NJ: Princeton University Press.

Rousseau, J.-J. (2001) *Contrat social*, III, XV, Paris: G-F Flammarion.

Rubinstein, N. (1966) *The Government of Florence Under the Medici, 1434–1494*, Oxford: Clarendon Press.

Rummens, S. (2007) Democratic deliberation as the open-ended construction of justice, *Ratio Juris*, **20** (3), pp. 335–354.

Rummens, S. (2012) Staging deliberation: The role of representative institutions in the deliberative democratic process, *Journal of Political Philosophy*, **20** (1), pp. 23–44.

Rummens, S. (2016) Legitimacy without visibility? On the role of mini-publics in the democratic system, in Reuchamps, M. & Suiter, J. (eds.) *Constitu-*

tional Deliberative Democracy in Europe, pp. 129–146, Colchester: ECPR Press.

Rummens, S. (2018) Deliberation and justice, in Bächtiger, A., Dryzek, J.S., Mansbridge, J. & Warren, M. (eds.) *The Oxford Handbook of Deliberative Democracy*, pp. 132–143, Oxford: Oxford University Press.

Rummens, S. & Geenens, R. (2023) Lottocracy vs. democracy, *Res Publica*, forthcoming.

Rummens, S. & Geenens, R. (2023) *Lottocracy versus Democracy*, forthcoming.

Ryfman, P. (2007) Governance and policies in nongovernmental organizations, in Feher, M. (ed.) *Nongovernmental Politics*, New York: Zone Books.

Salamon, L. (2000) The new governance and the tools of public action: An introduction, *Fordham Urban Law Journal*, **28** (5), pp. 1611–1674.

Sartori, G. (1976) *Parties and Party Systems: A Framework for Analysis*, Cambridge: Cambridge University Press.

Saward, M. (ed.) (2000) *Democratic Innovation: Deliberation, Representation and Association*, London: Routledge.

Saward, M. (2010) *The Representative Claim*, Oxford: Oxford University Press.

Simonton, M. (2023) *'Ambition for Office' and the Nature of Election in Ancient Greek Democracy*, unpublished manuscript.

Sintomer, Y. (2007) *Le pouvoir au peuple*, Paris: La Découverte.

Sintomer, Y. (2011a) *Petite histoire de l'expérimentation démocratique. Tirage au sort et politique d'Athènes à nos jours*, Paris: La Découverte.

Sintomer, Y. (2011b) Tirage au sort et politique: de l'auto-gouvernement républicain à la démocratie deliberative, *Raisons politiques*, **42** (2), pp. 159–186.

Sintomer, Y. (2018) From deliberative to radical democracy? Sortition and politics in the twenty-first century, *Politics & Society*, **46** (3), pp. 337–357.

Sintomer, Y. & Talpin, J. (dir.) (2011) *La démocratie participative au-delà de la proximité: le Poitou-Charentes et l'échelle régionale*, Rennes: Presses Universitaires de Rennes.

Sirmans, M.E. (1966) *Colonial South Carolina – a Political History, 1663–1763*, Chapel Hill, NC: University of North Carolina Press.

Smith, D.A. & Tolbert, C.J. (2001) The initiative to party: Partisanship and ballot initiatives in California, *Party Politics*, **7** (6), pp. 739–757.

Smith, G. (2009) *Democratic Innovations: Designing Institutions for Citizen Participation*, New York: Cambridge University Press.

Smith, G. (2021) *Can Democracy Safeguard the Future?*, Cambridge: Polity Press.

Smith, G. & Setälä, M. (2019) Mini-publics and deliberative democracy, in Bächtiger, A., Dryzek, J.S., Mansbridge, J. & Warren, M. (eds.) *The Oxford*

Handbook of Deliberative Democracy, pp. 300–314, Oxford: Oxford University Press.

Sortition Foundation (2019) *Selection and Stratification: Bespoke Selection and Postal Services for Deliberative Processes.*

Spinoza, B. (2022) *Traité politique*, Paris: Flammarion.

Spinoza, B. (2023) *Éthique*, Paris: Flammarion.

Stewart, J.H. (1951) *A Documentary Survey of the French Revolution*, New York: Macmillan.

Stich, S. (2014) When democracy meets pluralism: Landemore's epistemic argument for democracy and the problem of value diversity, *Critical Review: A Journal of Politics and Society*, **26**, pp. 170–183.

Stone, P. (2009) The logic of random selection, *Political Theory*, **37** (3), pp. 375–397.

Stone, P. (2010) Lotteries and probability theory, in Dowlen, O. & Delannoi, G. (eds.) *Sortition: Theory and Practice*, pp. 157–172, Exeter: Imprint Academic.

Stone, P. (2011) *The Luck of the Draw: The Role of Lotteries in Decision Making*, Oxford: Oxford University Press.

Stone, P. (2016) Sortition, voting, and democratic equality, *Critical Review of International Social and Political Philosophy*, **19** (3), pp. 339–356.

Stone, P. & Malkopoulou, A. (2021) Allotted chambers as defenders of democracy, *Constellations*, online first.

Surowiecki, J. (2004) *The Wisdom of Crowds: Why the Many Are Smarter Than the Few*, London: Abacus.

Sutherland, K. (2008) *A People's Parliament*, Exeter: Imprint Academic.

Sutherland, K. (2017) *Election by Lot and the Democratic Diarchy*, PhD Thesis, University of Exeter.

Sutherland, K. & Kovner, A. (2020) Some problems of citizens' assemblies, *Academia Letters*, **23**.

Swain, C. (1993) *Faces, Black Interests: The Representation of African Americans in Congress*, Cambridge, MA: Harvard University Press.

Sydenman, M.J. (1974) *The First French Republic 1792–1804*, London: Batsford.

Talpin, J. (2007) *Schools of Democracy: How Ordinary Citizens Become Competent in Participatory Budgeting Institutions*, PhD dissertation in political science defended in the EUI (Italy).

Talpin, J. (2019) Le tirage au sort démocratise-t-il la démocratie? Ou comment la démocratie délibérative a dépolitisé une proposition radicale, *Participations*, **HS**, pp. 453–473.

Testart, J., Piasecki, F. & Morvan, C. (2013) Conventions de citoyens, *Sciences citoyennes.org*, 22nd May.

Tjalve, E. (1979) *Systematic Design for Industrial Products*, Technical University of Denmark Institute for Product Development.

Traill, J.S. (1975) The political organisation of Attica, *Hisperia Supplement*, **XIV**, 150.

Umbers, L.M. (2018) Against lottocracy, *European Journal of Political Theory*, Advance online publication.

Urbinati, N. (2006) *Representative Democracy: Principles and Genealogy*, Chicago, IL: University of Chicago Press.

Urbinati, N. (2019) Political theory of populism, *Annual Review of Political Science*, **22** (1), pp. 111–127.

Van Ingelgom, V. (2014) *Integrating Indifference: A Comparative, Qualitative and Quantitative Approach to the Legitimacy of European Integration*, Oxford: ECPR Press.

Van Parijs, P. (1987) A revolution in class theory, *Politics & Society*, **15** (4), pp. 453–482.

Van Reybrouck, D. (2013/2014) *Contre les élections*, Amsterdam: De Bezige Bij.

Van Reybrouck, D. (2015) La démocratie délibérative, in Reynaert, H., Reuchamps, M. & Verjans, P. (eds) *Démocratie représentative: vers la fin d'un modèle? Diagnostic et remèdes*, pp. 32–38, Bruxelles: Sénat de Belgique.

Van Reybrouck, D. (2016) *Against Elections: The Case for Democracy*, London: Vintage Digital.

Vandamme, P.É. (2017) Le vote justifié, *La Revue Nouvelle*, **7** (7), pp. 48–52.

Vandamme, P.É. (2018) Le tirage au sort est-il compatible avec l'élection?, *Revue française de science politique*, **68** (5), pp. 873–894.

Vandamme, P.É. (2018) Voting secrecy and the right to justification, *Constellations*, **25** (3), pp. 388–405.

Vandamme, P.É. (2019) Un sénat tiré au sort?, *Politique, revue belge d'analyse et de débats*.

Vandamme, P.É. (2021) Pluraliser les sources de légitimité? Trois défis, in Damay, L. & Jacquet, V. (eds.) *Les transformations de la légitimité démocratique. Idéaux, revendications et perceptions*, Louvain-la-Neuve: Academia-L'Harmattan.

Vandamme, P.É. (2021) Tirage au sort et conscience des injustices, *Raisons politiques*, **82**, pp. 107–124.

Vandamme, P.É. (2023) Citizens' assemblies and accountability, in Reuchamps, M., Vrydagh, J. & Welp, Y. (eds.) *De Gruyter Handbook of Citizens' Assemblies*, pp. 35–46, Berlin: De Gruyter.

Vandamme, P.É. & Verret-Hamelin, A. (2017) A randomly selected chamber: Promises and challenges, *Journal of Public Deliberation*, **13** (1).

Veysset, P. (2021) Convention citoyenne pour le climat: 'La note de 2,5 traduit un manque de cohérence du gouvernement', *TV5MONDE*, 24 December.

Vie publique (2021) De l'écotaxe à la taxe carbone, la difficile mise en œuvre du principe pollueur-payeur, *vie publique.fr*, 15 November.

Viktorovitch, C. (2021) Clément Viktorovitch x Bernard Manin: le grand entretien exclusif — Viens Voir Les Docteurs, *Clique TV*, 26 April.

Von der Leyen, U. (2022) *State of the Union Speech by EU President Ursula von der Leyen*.

Vrydagh, J., Devillers, S., Talukder, D., Jacquet, V. & Bottin, J. (2020) Les mini-publics en Belgique (2001–2018): expériences de panels citoyens délibératifs, *Courrier hebdomadaire du CRISP*, **2477–2478**, pp. 5–72.

Walzer, M. (1983) *Spheres of Justice: A Defence of Pluralism and Equality*, New York: Basic Books.

Warren, M.E. (2017) A problem-based approach to democratic theory, *American Political Science Review*, **111** (1), pp. 39–53.

Warren, M.E. & Pearse, H. (eds.) (2008) *Designing Deliberative Democracy: The British Columbia Citizens' Assembly*, Cambridge, Cambridge University Press.

Weber, M. (1965/1917) Essai sur le sens de la 'neutralité axiologique' dans les sciences sociologiques et économiques, in Weber, M., *Essais sur la théorie de la science*, pp. 475–526, Paris: Plon.

Weil, S. (2017/1950) *Note sur la suppression générale des partis politiques*, Paris: Climats.

White, J. & Ypi, L. (2016) *The Meaning of Partisanship*, Oxford: Oxford University Press.

Whitehead, D. (1986) *The Demes of Attica*, Princeton, NJ: Princeton University Press.

Williams, B. (2005) *In the Beginning Was the Deed: Realism and Moralism in Political Argument*, Princeton, NJ: Princeton University Press.

Williams, M.S. (1998) *Voice, Trust and Memory: Marginalised Groups and the Failure of Liberal Representation*, Princeton, NJ: Princeton University Press.

Wojcik, S. (2011) Participer… et après? L'expérience des Consultations européennes des citoyens 2009, *Politique européenne*, **34**, pp. 135–166.

Wolfson, A.M. (1899) Forms of voting in the Italian communes, *American Historical Review*, **V** (1), pp. 1–22.

Wright, E.O. (2010) *Envisioning Real Utopias*, London: Verso.

Xenophon (1940) *Memorabilia, in Plato and Xenophon Socratic Discourses*, London: Dent and Sons.

XR (2022) *Citizens' Assembly*.

Yardi, S. & Boyd, D. (2010) Dynamic debates: An analysis of group polarization over time on Twitter, *Bulletin of Science, Technology & Society*, **30** (5),
pp. 316–327.

Young, I.M. (2000) *Inclusion and Democracy*, Oxford: Oxford University Press.

Young, I.M. (2011) *Justice and the Politics of Difference*, Princeton, NJ: Princeton
University Press.

Youngs, R. (2022) EU democracy after the Conference on the Future of
Europe, *Carnegie Europe*.

Zakaras, A. (2010) Lot and democratic representation: A modest proposal,
Constellations, **17** (3), pp. 455–471.

Biographical Notes

Vincent Aerts is assistant at the Institute for Public Decision-Making at the University of Liège and is currently working on his doctoral thesis. His research focuses on democracy, political representation, political parties, democratic innovation and the resignation of elected representatives.

Jessy Bailly has a PhD in Political Science. He initially specialised in bottom-up forms of citizen involvement, leading to a doctoral dissertation on citizen debt audits in France, Spain and Belgium. He has published articles in peer-reviewed journals such as *Participations, Revue internationale de politique comparée, Droit et société* and *Social Movement Studies*. At present, Bailly's scholarly pursuits have led him to delve into the intricate dynamics of top-down participation citizen procedures, as manifested within the framework of European institutions. An area of particular interest is his examination of the Conference on the Future of Europe, a focal point through which he draws insightful comparisons with other European Union citizen procedures that involve processes such as sortition.

Jason Brennan is the Robert J. and Elizabeth Flanagan Family Professor of Strategy, Economics, Ethics and Public Policy at Georgetown University's McDonough School of Business. He is the author of sixteen books, including *Democracy: A Guided Tour* (Oxford UP 2023), *Debating Democracy* (Oxford UP 2021), with Helene Landemore, *Against Democracy* (Princeton UP 2016) and *Compulsory Voting: For and Against* (Cambridge UP 2014), with Lisa Hill. His books have been translated thirty times into fifteen languages.

Gil Delannoi is a Senior Researcher (CEVIPOF) and Professor of Political Theory at Sciences Po. He created and co-organised the research programme of workshop series on sortition at Sciences Po and other universities from 2008 to 2013. Among his publications on democracy and sortition: *Le Tirage au sort, comment l'utiliser?* (Presses de la Fondation nationale des Sciences Politiques 2019); *Sortition: Theory and Practice* (with Oliver Dowlen) (Imprint Academic 2010); "Le tirage au sort comme opération et comme procédure" in *Expériences du tirage au sort en Suisse et en Europe (XVIe-XXIe siècles)* (Bibliothèque Am Guisanplatz 2018). "Sortition in Current Democratic Regimes: So you want to make a draw?" in *Complementary Democracy* (De Gruyter 2022).

Chiara Destri is Postdoctoral Researcher at Goethe University Frankfurt. She has been Marie Curie Fellow at Sciences Po, Postdoctoral Fellow at Justitia Amplificata and Max Weber Fellow at the European University Institute. Her work has been published in international journals such as *Political Studies* and *Ethical Theory and Moral Practice*.

Born in 1953, **Oliver Dowlen** initially trained and worked as a visual artist. In the 1980s he was active in the UK anti-nuclear movement and was involved with a number of single issues. In the 1990s, he completed a part-time MPhil dissertation at the University of Hertfordshire on the subject of Marx's concept of alienation; in 2002–07 he undertook a DPhil in Politics at New College, Oxford. The subject of the doctorate was the political potential of sortition and the thesis was the joint winner of the PSA Ernest Barker prize for the best doctoral thesis of 2007. The thesis was published by Imprint Academic in 2008. He has continued to explore this theme in shorter publications, conference papers and chapters in academic volumes for the last 16 years. He currently lives and works in the UK and is affiliated to CEVIPOF Sciences Po as an associated researcher.

Raf Geenens is Professor of Ethics and Legal Philosophy at KU Leuven's Institute of Philosophy. His research is situated at the intersection of ethics, political philosophy and legal theory. In the past years he was the principal investigator of several large research projects in the field of constitutional theory, focusing on such notions as sovereignty and constitutional identity, especially in the context of the Belgian Constitution. He is currently completing a monograph on French philosopher Claude Lefort. In addition, Raf Geenens has a vivid interest in the history and philosophy of dance.

Geoffrey Grandjean is Professor in the Faculty of Law, Political Science and Criminology at the University of Liege, Belgium. He has been the Head of the Department of Political Science since 2022. His research and teaching focus is on Belgian and European political history and political institutions. He is the Publishing Director of the journal *Cahiers Mémoire et Politique* and is a member of the editorial board of the journal *Politics of the Low Countries*. From 2021 to 2024, he has been the Chairman of the French-speaking Belgian Political Science Association. In 2022, he was appointed Associate Researcher in the Law School of Sciences Po Paris. He is currently a member of the Scientific Support Committee for the Citizens' Assemblies in the Parliament of Wallonia, Belgium.

Archibald Gustin is a PhD student at the University of Liège (Institut de la décision publique) and at the Vrije Universiteit Brussel (ECHO). His PhD regards the gender politics of far right parties in Western Europe. More specifically, Archibald studies the way the Rassemblement national and Vlaams Belang articulate femonationalist and homonationalist discourses to anti-gender politics from a discursive-theoretical perspective. Archibald is also interested in the mainstreaming of far right politics and by theories of democracy.

Jerome Hergueux is an Assistant Research Professor at the French National Center for Scientific Research (CNRS), a Research Affiliate at the Center for Law and Economics at ETH Zurich and a Faculty Associate at the Berkman Klein Center for Internet & Society at Harvard University. Professor Hergueux is a social scientist operating at the boundaries between psychology, economics, data science and the law. His interest lies in uncovering how psychological and cognitive traits shape our behaviour, with a particular focus on cooperation and decision-making.

Alex Kovner is a retired data scientist with a Master's degree in math from UC San Diego. He blogs about sortition at alexkovner.com and equalitybylot.com, and is currently writing a book on the superminority method.

Cristina Lafont is Harold H. and Virginia Anderson Professor of Philosophy at Northwestern University. She is the author of *Democracy without Shortcuts: A Participatory Conception of Deliberative Democracy* (Oxford UP 2020); *Global Governance and Human Rights* (Spinoza Lecture Series, van Gorcum 2012); *Heidegger, Language, and World-disclosure* (Cambridge UP

2000); *The Linguistic Turn in Hermeneutic Philosophy* (MIT Press 1999). Some of her recent articles include "Deliberative Minipublics and the Populist Conception of Representation as Embodiment" in *Contested Representation: Challenges, Shortcomings, and Reforms* (Cambridge UP 2023); "Democracy without Shortcuts: An Institutional Approach to Democratic Legitimacy" in *In Search of Another Universalism: Seyla Benhabib and the Future of Critical Theory* (Columbia UP forthcoming).

Annabelle Lever is Professor of Political Philosophy at Sciences Po, Paris (IEP, Paris) and Permanent Researcher at CEVIPOF. She is the author of *On Privacy* (translated as *De La Vie Privée*); *A Democratic Conception of Privacy*; editor of *New Frontiers in the Philosophy of Intellectual Property*; and co-editor of the *Routledge Handbook of Ethics and Public Policy*, of *Ideas that Matter: Democracy, Justice, Rights* and of *The Critical Review of International Social and Political Philosophy* (CRISPP). She has published widely on privacy, equality, security, bioethics, democracy and on the ethics of voting. She is the coordinator of the Horizon 2020 project, Reconstructing Democracy in Times of Crisis: A Voter-Centred Perspective (REDEM) (https://www.redem-h2020.eu/) and holds an honorary doctorate from the University of Aalborg.

Didier Mineur, PhD Hab., is a Franco-Belgian researcher. He is a former fellow of Sciences Po Paris and of Sorbonne University and is currently Full Professor in Political Philosophy in Sciences Po Rennes (Brittany, France). He has published many articles and studies in the history of modern philosophy and in political theory. He is the author of three books: on the concept of political representation (*Archéologie de la représentation politique. Structure et fondement d'une crise*, Presses de Sciences Po 2010), on the french jurist Carré de Malberg (*Carré de Malberg. Le positivisme impossible*, Michalon 2010) and on the majority rule (*Le pouvoir de la majorité. Fondements et limites*, Classiques Garnier 2017).

Charles Ramond is a University Professor (Paris 8, Department of philosophy/Research Unit 4008 LLCP). His work focuses on modern (mainly Spinoza) and contemporary philosophy. Latest books include: *Jacques Rancière: The Equality of Intelligences* (Belin 2019); *Twenty-Four Studies in the Philosophy of Ordinary Language* (Lambert Lucas 2022); *Introduction to Spinoza* (La Découverte 2023).

Stefan Rummens is Full Professor of Political Philosophy at the Institute of Philosophy of KU Leuven (Belgium). His research focuses on topics within democratic theory such as deliberation, representation, populism, militant democracy and the rise of technocracy. He has a side interest in the work of Wittgenstein and the problem of free will. His work has been published in journals such as *Constellations*, *The Journal of Political Philosophy*, *Political Studies*, *European Law Journal* and *Erkenntnis*.

Keith Sutherland is an Honorary Research Fellow in the Department of Politics, University of Exeter. He was awarded a PhD in 2017 with the thesis *Election by Lot and the Democratic Diarchy*. He is currently preparing a book manuscript (with Alex Kovner) entitled *Superminority: On Sortition and Democracy* and is co-editor (with Gil Delannoi and Oliver Dowlen) of the *Journal of Sortition*, which is due to be launched in 2024.

Nadia Urbinati is Kyriakos Tsakopoulos Professor of Political Theory at Columbia University. She is the author of *Me the People: How Populism Transforms Democracy* (Harvard UP 2019); *The Tyranny of the Moderns* (Yale UP 2015); *Democracy Disfigured: Opinion, Truth and the People* (Harvard UP 2014); *Representative Democracy: Principles and Genealogy* (University of Chicago Press 2006); and *Mill on Democracy: From the Athenian Polis to Representative Government* (University of Chicago Press 2002). With Cristina Lafont she is completing a book manuscript titled *The Lottocratic Mentality: Defending Democracy against Lottocracy* (forthcoming for Oxford UP).

Clarisse Van Belleghem holds a Master's degree in Philosophy and a Master's degree in Political Science from the Université catholique de Louvain (UCLouvain). She is currently a PhD student at UCLouvain. Her research in public policy analysis focuses on the use of knowledge by policy makers during COVID-19 crisis. Her area of interests are theories of democracy (political representation, direct democracy, drawing of lots), and the "fabrication" of public policy (knowledge utilisation, role of experts, legitimisation processes and so on).

Pierre-Étienne Vandamme is an FWO Senior Postdoctoral Researcher in political philosophy at KU Leuven (RIPPLE). He has been doing research on sortition for several years, published in journals such as *The Journal of Deliberative Democracy*, *Politics & Society*, *Swiss Political Science Review* and *Representation*. He is the author of *Démocratie et justice sociale* (Vrin 2021).

Index